JOHN DALTON

BLOOMSBURY STUDIES IN MODERN ARCHITECTURE

Series Editors: Tom Avermaete and Janina Gosseye

The Modern Movement was a broad and multifaceted phenomenon which revolutionized the field of architecture. During the twentieth century, modern architects across political, cultural and geographic divides radically changed the everyday lives of millions of people. However, our knowledge of the Modern Movement remains largely limited to the names of a few famed designers.

Bloomsbury Studies in Modern Architecture sheds light on those modern architects who have languished in the shadows of their canonical peers. Placing particular emphasis on the way in which these architects defined the relationship between architecture and modernity in their respective political, cultural, and geographic contexts, this series seeks to construct a more nuanced and fine-grained understanding of the Modern Movement, and the global networks that underwrote it.

Previous titles in the series:
Ernesto Nathan Rogers, by Maurizio Sabini
Sibyl Moholy-Nagy, by Hilde Heynen
Kay Fisker, by Martin Søberg
Karl Langer, edited by Deborah van der Plaat and John MacArthur

Forthcoming titles in the series:
Ludwig Hilberseimer, by Scott Colman
Esguerra Sáenz Urdaneta Samper, edited by Maarten Goossens, Hernando Vargas Caicedo and Catalina Parra
PAGON, by Espen Johnsen

JOHN DALTON

Subtropical Modernism and the Turn to Environment in Australian Architecture

Elizabeth Musgrave

BLOOMSBURY VISUAL ARTS
LONDON • NEW YORK • OXFORD • NEW DELHI • SYDNEY

BLOOMSBURY VISUAL ARTS
Bloomsbury Publishing Plc
50 Bedford Square, London, WC1B 3DP, UK
1385 Broadway, New York, NY 10018, USA
29 Earlsfort Terrace, Dublin 2, Ireland

BLOOMSBURY, BLOOMSBURY VISUAL ARTS and the Diana logo are
trademarks of Bloomsbury Publishing Plc

First published in Great Britain 2023
Paperback edition published by Bloomsbury Visual Arts 2025

Copyright © Elizabeth Musgrave, 2023

Elizabeth Musgrave has asserted her right under the Copyright,
Designs and Patents Act, 1988, to be identified as Author of this work.

For legal purposes the Acknowledgements on pp. xvi–xviii constitute
an extension of this copyright page.

Cover design by Eleanor Rose
Cover image: Dalton House, photograph by Harry Sowden © Sue Dalton

All rights reserved. No part of this publication may be reproduced or transmitted
in any form or by any means, electronic or mechanical, including photocopying,
recording, or any information storage or retrieval system, without prior
permission in writing from the publishers.

Bloomsbury Publishing Plc does not have any control over, or responsibility for,
any third-party websites referred to or in this book. All internet addresses given
in this book were correct at the time of going to press. The author and publisher
regret any inconvenience caused if addresses have changed or sites have
ceased to exist, but can accept no responsibility for any such changes.

A catalogue record for this book is available from the British Library.

Library of Congress Cataloging-in-Publication Data
Names: Musgrave, Elizabeth, author.
Title: John Dalton : subtropical modernism and the turn to environment in
Australian architecture / Elizabeth Musgrave.
Description: London : Bloomsbury Visual Arts, 2023. | Series: Bloomsbury studies
in modern architecture | Includes bibliographical references and index.
Identifiers: LCCN 2023000353 (print) | LCCN 2023000354 (ebook) | ISBN 9781350291515
(hardback) | ISBN 9781350291553 (paperback) | ISBN 9781350291522 (pdf) |
ISBN 9781350291539 (epub) | ISBN 9781350291546
Subjects: LCSH: Dalton, John 1927–2007–Criticism and interpretation. | Midcentury
modern (Architecture)–Australia. | Architecture and climate–Australia. |
Architecture–Environmental aspects–Australia.
Classification: LCC NA1605.D35 M87 2023 (print) | LCC NA1605.D35 (ebook) |
DDC 720.92–dc23/eng/20230215
LC record available at https://lccn.loc.gov/2023000353
LC ebook record available at https://lccn.loc.gov/2023000354

ISBN:	HB:	978-1-3502-9151-5
	PB:	978-1-3502-9155-3
	ePDF:	978-1-3502-9152-2
	eBook:	978-1-3502-9153-9

Series: Bloomsbury Studies in Modern Architecture

Typeset by Integra Software Services Pvt. Ltd.

To find out more about our authors and books visit www.bloomsbury.com
and sign up for our newsletters.

CONTENTS

List of Illustrations vii
Foreword xiii
Acknowledgements xvi
List of Abbreviations xix

INTRODUCTION 1

1 INTRODUCING JOHN DALTON AND THE LANDSCAPE OF POST-WAR AUSTRALIA 11

John Dalton: Early life in précis 12
Becoming an Architect in Queensland 18
Professional practice 21
Queensland is different: Climate conditioning local practice 27
The 'Environmental Era' begins: Architecture's re-turn to environment 32
Myth and identity: Australia's 'fictional landscapes' 34

2 DISCOVERING THE IDIOMATIC: DETAIL IN ART AND ARCHITECTURE 37

Dalton & Heathwood Architects: The Plywood Exhibition House 38
'Four Houses' by Dalton & Heathwood, Architects 41
The Contemporary Art Society Queensland Chapter 46
The 'verandah series' 50
'sun + life + useful form' 53

3 FORM AND ITS EXPERIENCE: DESIGNS FOR 'SUNLIGHT, SHADE AND SHADOW' 63

Brisbane's climate 'stated in detail' 63
Evolution of the Dalton House 1: The linear house 66
Experiencing the 'Hot Humid Zones' 76

Evolution of the Dalton House 2: Crippled + split skillion roof forms 78
The 'Dalton Section' refined 85

4 ENVIRONMENT AS PROVOCATION AND NARRATIVE: DALTON THE ACTIVIST 90

Action and reaction: *Broadside* and *diametrix* 95
Advocacy: The buzzword was ecology 99
Proto-environmentalism in practice 104
Courtyard houses: Additive processes 106
Courtyard houses: Erosion of a volume 113

5 ECOLOGIES IN PRACTICE: STRUCTURING THE INTERACTIONS OF INDIVIDUAL AND COMMUNITY 116

Structuring interdisciplinarity: Art and Music Building 118
Structuring non-hierarchical relations: University House 123
Planning for the incidental: The Bardon Professional Development Centre 127
Individual and community: Hall of Residence, Kelvin Grove 130
Environmental paradigms at work in the institutional project 134

6 SYNTHESIZING ENVIRONMENTAL AND ARCHITECTURAL PERSPECTIVES 137

The postmodern/modern divide and the pleasures of architecture 139
Brisbane comes of age 141
Last houses 144

CONCLUSION: LEGACIES OF 'SUNLIGHT SHADE AND SHADOW' 150

A style for the Australian subtropics 151
Praxis: Architecture engaging sunlight, shade and shadow 154
Dalton in the twenty-first century 157
The environmental response 160

Notes 163
General Bibliography 188
Index 205

ILLUSTRATIONS

1.1 John and Helen Dalton c. 1936 13
1.2 John Dalton in uniform c. 1948 14
1.3 Young bushwalkers, John Dalton and Sheila Harvey c. 1951 17
1.4 Student Project work. Diploma IV. Proposal for a New Parliament House 19
1.5 Shield design for standards to line the processional route at the Brisbane International Airport, for Queen Elizabeth II 1954 Royal tour 20
1.6 Perspective drawn by John Dalton, of the Burnie Board Administrative Building, 1955, by Theo Thynne and Associates 21
1.7 Photograph of Sue Stirling and John Dalton c. 1962 24
1.8 Generic Queensland house, possibly Ipswich 29
1.9 The Speare House (1958) and Jacobi House (1957) illustrated together in the RAIA Queensland Chapter publication *Buildings in Queensland* (1959) 30
1.10 Schubert House, Yandina, 1972. Architect: Gabriel Poole 31
2.1 Plywood Exhibition House, 1957, designed by Peter Heathwood. Sections drawn by John Dalton. Courtesy of Sue Dalton 39
2.2 'Four Houses by John Dalton and Peter Heathwood Architects', *Architecture and Arts*, September 1959 42

2.3	Speare House, 1958, Dalton and Heathwood Architects, 'Four Houses', *Architecture and Arts*, September 1959 44
2.4	Perspective by Dalton of Spinks House, 1956, Dalton and Heathwood Architects 45
2.5	John Dalton, 'County Stanley, Parish of Indooroopilly' c.1956. Mixed media on hardboard 48
2.6	John Dalton's entry in the 1960 Warana-Caltex Prize, 'South Queensland Landscape – Gympie' c. 1960 49
2.7	John Dalton, 'sea-nymph and a sailor', 1952. Ink and gouache on card 50
2.8	John Dalton, 'Immediacy at Fingal', 1959. Acrylic on board. Entered in the Queensland Centenary Eisteddfod Art Competition, 1959 52
2.9	Design Development. Dalton House, Fig Tree Pocket, 1960. John Dalton Architect and Associates 55
2.10	View from kitchen north to bushland. Dalton House, Fig Tree Pocket, 1960 56
2.11	View through sun-patio to living room. Dalton House, Fig Tree Pocket, 1960 56
2.12	North Elevation, Dalton House, Fig Tree Pocket, 1960 57
2.13	Plan, Tremont Flats, Dean Street, Toowong, 1960 58
2.14	Street view, Tremont Flats, Dean Street, Toowong, 1960 58
2.15	'the verandah' as it appeared in *Architecture in Australia* in March 1964 60
2.16	Atrium, Wilson House, Mt Coot-tha Road, Toowong, 1964 (demolished) 61
3.1	Plan, Brick Manufacturers of Queensland Competition, 1962. First Prize design, John Dalton Architect and Associates 68
3.2	Breezeway, Leverington House, Kenmore Road, Kenmore, 1961 68

3.3 Plan, Neale House, Rosebery Street, Chelmer, 1962 (demolished) 69

3.4 Plan, Magee House, Woodfield Road, Moggill, 1963 70

3.5 Magee House, Woodfield Road, Moggill, 1963. View from the street of the south elevation 70

3.6 Perspective drawn by John Dalton of the Neale House, 1962, viewed from the north 71

3.7 East elevation of the Wilson House for Patrick and Pam Wilson, Mt Coot-tha Road, Toowong, 1964 (demolished), demonstrating how the end elevation is arrived at by 'filling in the section' 72

3.8 View of the living room interior, Wilson House. Photographed *c.* 1965 by John Dalton 73

3.9 Pam Wilson and her son in her bush garden designed by Landscape Architect, Arne Fink. Photographed *c.* 1965 74

3.10 'Morocco' Homestead for Stan and Noela Wippell St George, 1963. Original timber homestead is visible in the background 75

3.11 Two pages from 'Houses in the Hot-Humid Zone', *Architecture in Australia*, March 1963 77

3.12 Section of the Wilson House, Mt Coot-tha Road, Toowong, 1964 (demolished) 80

3.13 Section of the Graham House, Gower Street, Taringa, 1966 80

3.14 East elevation of the Graham House, Gower Street, Taringa, 1966 81

3.15 Plan of the Hughes House, Brookfield Road, Brookfield, 1966 82

3.16 View to Hughes House, Brookfield Road, Brookfield, 1966 82

3.17 Section of the Dunlop House, Jesmond Road, Fig Tree Pocket, 1970 83

3.18 View to north elevation of Dunlop House, Jesmond Road, Fig Tree Pocket, 1970 84

3.19 Bucknell Residence, Sutton Street, Chelmer, 1968 85

3.20 Interior, Strugnell House, Grandview Road, Pullenvale, 1971 85

3.21 Rabaa House, Kimba Street, Chapel Hill, 1967 88

4.1 A selection of issues of *Broadside* 1966–9 97

4.2 A selection of issues of *diametrix* 1969–72 98

4.3 View to Smith House, Brookfield Road, Brookfield, 1966 105

4.4 Interior of Hughes House, Brookfield Road, Brookfield, 1966 106

4.5 Design Development drawings for Vice-Chancellor's Residence, University of Queensland, St Lucia, 1972 108

4.6 View to entry, Vice-Chancellor's Residence, University of Queensland, St Lucia, 1972 109

4.7 'Atrium', Vice-Chancellor's Residence with stair climbing to bridge, University of Queensland, St Lucia, 1972 109

4.8 View from entry to reception rooms, Vice-Chancellor's Residence, University of Queensland, St Lucia, 1972 110

4.9 View to Peden Residence, 'Merindah', Glenhurst Street, Pinjarra Hills, 1975 111

4.10 Courtyard, Peden Residence, Pinjarra Hills 112

4.11 Design development plan drawn by John Dalton, Chick House, Roedean Street, Fig Tree Pocket, 1977 114

4.12 View to garden from 'lanai', Chick House, Roedean Street, Fig Tree Pocket, 1977 115

4.13 View of the Chick House with garden terraces, Chick House, Roedean Street, Fig Tree Pocket, 1977 115

5.1	Plan of the Art and Music Building, Darling Downs Institute of Advanced Education, Toowoomba, 1974	119
5.2	View from central quadrangle across Art and Music Building roofscape to Darling Downs landscape taken on completion of project in 1974	121
5.3	University House and Community Services Building, Griffith University, Nathan, 1974	125
5.4	View to University House taken on approach from the north	125
5.5	Robin Gibson, Humanities Library and Administration Building, Griffith University, Nathan, 1973	126
5.6	View to Bardon Professional Development Centre, Simpsons Road, Bardon, 1976 (demolished 2014)	128
5.7	Part plan of the Bardon Professional Development Centre, Simpsons Road, Bardon	129
5.8	Dining terrace overlooking Ithaca Creek, Bardon Professional Development Centre, Bardon, 1976	129
5.9	Courtyard, Bardon Professional Development Centre, Bardon, 1976	130
5.10	Site Model, Hall of Residence, Kelvin Grove, constructed by John Dalton Architect and Associates	132
5.11	Section of four-person Maisonette, Hall of Residence, Kelvin Grove, with annotations overlay by Dalton	133
5.12	View of Hall of Residence taken from north-east. The chimney to a fireplace in the Community Centre is in the centre of this view	133
6.1	'Lambtail Cottage', Herbert Street, Allora, 1975–81	145
6.2	Working Drawings, Extensions to existing O'Dwyer Homestead, 'Mt Manning', Condamine, 1981	146
6.3	Working Drawings, Coughlan House, Allora, 1981	147
6.4	View to the Coughlan House, Allora	147

6.5 North elevation, Hendry House, 'Burrandool', Carwoola Street, Bardon, 1986 148

7.1 'Los Nidos' Resort, Hastings Street, Noosa, 1972 (demolished *c.* 1985) 152

7.2 Four houses in Ironside Street, St Lucia, 1979, designed by Fergus Johnston Architect 153

7.3 Interior, Ironside Street houses, St Lucia, 1979, designed by Fergus Johnston Architect 153

7.4 Indooroopilly House by Vokes and Peters, 2007 159

FOREWORD

The Modern Movement was a broad and multifaceted phenomenon that revolutionized the field of architecture. Throughout the twentieth century, and across political, cultural and climatic divides, modern architecture radically changed the everyday lives of millions of people. Yet, to this day, our knowledge of this sweeping and omnipresent occurrence remains largely limited to the names of a few famed designers.

In spite of growing research into the Modern Movement and its various actors, most published works focus on a select list of grandmasters. This narrow view restrains our understanding of what the Modern Movement in architecture was, as it limits our insight into the breadth and complexity of the networks that underwrote it and undercuts the possibility of a more holistic and fine-grained understanding of its impact on architectural culture and the built environment.

The Bloomsbury Studies in Modern Architecture book series seeks to address this dearth. It sheds light on those who played pivotal roles in propelling the Modern Movement in architecture but who have, nonetheless, languished in the shadows of their better-known (and extensively published) canonical peers. Examining the works and ideas of this 'shadow canon', this book series does not aspire to canonize those to whom it offers a platform, but rather to construct a more detailed understanding of the different actors that propelled the Modern Movement across the globe, as well as the relationships that existed between these different actors, and the ways in which they contributed to the proliferation, recalibration, acculturation and transculturation of modern architecture.

Like many of those included in this series, John Dalton (1927–2007) is someone who seems to have been hiding in broad daylight. At the time that he was practising, his work – both built and written – was published widely, not only locally (in Brisbane or Queensland), but also nationally and even internationally. His Musgrave House of 1973, for instance, which he designed for the parents of Elizabeth Musgrave, the author of this book, was featured in the first edition of Bannister Fletcher's *A History of Architecture* to include Australian examples. Throughout the 1960s and 1970s, Dalton contributed to architectural discourse in Australia through his contributions to the Melbourne-based journal *Cross-Section* and as contributing editor to *Architecture in Australia*, which is still today the country's most widely read and highly respected architectural magazine. In Brisbane, where Dalton was based, he was highly regarded for his domestic designs that adopted a modern architecture idiom, cleverly adapted to Queensland's subtropical climate and vernacular (colonial) architecture.

Yet today, there are few architects and architectural historians outside Brisbane who know of John Dalton and his work. One can only speculate as to the reason(s) why Dalton has not received the same attention (or acclaim) as some of his contemporaries, such as Robin Boyd (1919–71), Harry Seidler (1923–2006) or even Glenn Murcutt (b.1936), who is only nine years his junior. A first reason often cited by those familiar with the socio-political geography of Australia (including Musgrave) is the fact that unlike Boyd, who practised in Melbourne, and unlike Seidler and Murcutt, who practise(d) from and (mostly) in and around Sydney, Dalton settled in Brisbane and worked mostly in the state of Queensland. Although an early settlement of the British in Australia, Queensland developed more slowly than other Australian states. Throughout the twentieth century, progressive and then conservative governments practised a statist agrarian socialism that did not favour education or culture. If by the mid-twentieth century, Sydney and Melbourne had become cosmopolitan cities with an interest in modern art and architecture, the image of Brisbane remained that of a large country town living in the shadow of its attempts to become a city in the late nineteenth century. From the 1960s, tourism, mining and then a sunbelt migration pattern began to propel the state towards its present prosperity. However, this rapid modernization of the economy, with its demand for natural resources and rapacious and largely unplanned or corrupt development of city buildings and beach resorts, reinforced the state's image as a place in which culture, including modern art and architecture, was not valued.

The comparison with Boyd and Seidler brings to light another likely reason for Dalton's elision from Australia's contemporary architectural historiography, which has to do with provenance. Unlike Boyd who was a scion of the Boyd artistic dynasty in Australia, Dalton, like Seidler, migrated to Australia from Europe. If Dalton arrived from Britain in 1950 with a National Diploma in Building from Leeds Technical College, Seidler was born in Vienna and fled to Australia in 1946, via Britain, Canada and the United States, where he studied at Harvard under Walter Gropius, Marcel Breuer and Josef Albers. This connection with these revered grandmasters of the Modern Movement is often cited by historiographers who credit Seidler for promoting and advancing the Bauhaus aesthetic down under.

The comparison with Murcutt, who is today arguably *the* most famous Australian architect, is somewhat more puzzling, as Dalton and Murcutt seem to have more in common. Both men were born in Britain – Murcutt to Australian parents – both specialized predominantly in domestic designs, and both share a clear dedication to working with the nuances of the local climate and natural conditions in their architecture. Dalton's 'sunlight, shade and shadow' mantra, which Musgrave carefully unpacks in this book, shares clear affinities with Murcutt's 'touching the earth lightly' approach. Yet if this approach shot the latter to Pritzker-prize-winning fame, it did not do the same for Dalton. Here, the (slight) difference in age is likely an important factor. If Dalton's designs heralded the development of an environmentally tuned architecture in Australia in the early 1960s, Murcutt established his practice when such a 'critical regionalist' approach had become widely accepted, if not mainstream. Furthermore, by 2002, when Murcutt won the Pritzker prize, many of his famed domestic designs of the 1970s, 1980s and 1990s were (still) in good nick, whereas many of Dalton's houses have since been (partially) demolished or insensitively altered. So, in addition to having the right pedigree and being in the right place, being there at 'the right time' is important too. Those who remember Dalton, such as Musgrave, describe him as 'stylish, charming and outspoken'. Some even go as far as to suggest that he was – in the context of Brisbane – the George Clooney of his day: In short, a person well placed to overcome the stigma of 'poor' provenance – of being a Ten Pound Pom – and the restrictions that come with practising in (a perceived) cultural backwater. If in the 1960s, Dalton's 'environmental' designs were ahead of their time, by the 1990s and early 2000s, their modernist aesthetic was likely perceived as old hat by a new generation of architects and architectural critics singing the praises of critical regionalism and postmodernism in Australia.

Whatever the reason(s) why Dalton has thus far been largely overlooked, Elizabeth Musgrave's book on the architect and his work is a very welcome contribution to the Bloomsbury Studies in Modern Architecture series. In addition to shedding light on the divergent paths and approaches adopted by modern architects in the twentieth century, it also draws attention to ecologies in practice, understood not only as the development of low-tech solutions for climate-responsive design, but also as an architecture of social sustainability acknowledging the relationship between the individual and the collective.

Finally, a critical reflection. Although Dalton is indeed a shadowy figure in the historiography of twentieth-century modern architecture whose work deserves greater attention, it remains awkward to claim that a white British man who relocated to Australia in 1950 through an assisted migration scheme has been 'overlooked'. The progression of the Modern Movement in architecture often came at the expense of indigenous populations who were colonized; their culture either denied or (mis)appropriated. This dark shadow of the Modern Movement – the flip side of this sweeping and omnipresent occurrence – also deserves greater critical scrutiny in our contemporary architectural historiography.

Tom Avermaete and Janina Gosseye
Series editors

ACKNOWLEDGEMENTS

At the height of his professional career John Dalton was commissioned by my parents John (1936–98) and Judith Musgrave (1937–2020) to design a home for a site on the banks of the Brisbane River, 'Maiwar', in the language of the Turrbal people. The Musgrave House (1973) featured in the local press was referred to by architectural historian Professor Jennifer Taylor in her publication *Australian Architecture Since 1960* (1985)[1] and listed in the nineteenth edition of *Sir Bannister Fletcher's A History of Architecture* (1987),[2] the only example of domestic work from Queensland in the first edition of that tome to include Australian architecture. Yet as I progressed through my formal architecture studies very few academics spoke about Dalton. Having observed how the waxing and waning of theoretical positions and architectural styles plays out over time, it became apparent to me that my studies in the 1980s coincided with significant generational shifts in disciplinary culture. Dalton's architecture was published widely and recognized locally through awards and exhibited nationally and internationally at the time it was built, but then moved into obscurity. Dalton did not typically socialize with his clients, and I met him only after writing to him when my mother was moving out of the family home in 2003. It would be remiss of me now not to remember my now-deceased parents who in commissioning a 'Dalton House' fifty years ago unwittingly fixed the trajectory of my life.

I acknowledge the Turrbal and Jagera people, the Traditional Custodians of country on which the events in this narrative occurred. I pay respect to their Elders past and present and extend that respect to all Aboriginal and Torres Strait Islander people today. I am very aware that this narrative belongs to a time when Aboriginal and Torres Strait Islander people were marginalized in a dishonourable and shameful way, and their special connection to land and sea was not recognized or valued.

This book greatly extends research undertaken for a doctoral thesis, not at the beginning of an academic career, but after thirty years of practice as an architect and academic focused on studio teaching. At the time of its writing, only one other detailed study of Dalton's work existed – an undergraduate thesis (1975) by Noel J Robinson supervised by Bill Greig, which sought to establish whether Dalton's houses were ideal for Brisbane.³ My mother had permitted her house to be one of two houses tested by Robinson for the efficacy of climate-responsive design measures; the findings were inconclusive. Interestingly, a second thesis completed by Stephen Sims and supervised by Max Horner on the more general topic of Environmentalism (2000) retested the climate responsiveness of the Musgrave House with positive findings.⁴

A number of impediments meant research was not straightforward. Many significant works by Dalton's practice have been demolished, partially demolished or significantly altered. Dalton was not a good archivist of material. From 1979, he maintained two offices: one at Sylvan Road Toowong, which he shared with Dan Callaghan, and another in a restored Methodist Church in Herbert Street, Allora, which he shared with his wife Sue. Material that was at Toowong is now in the Fryer Library at The University of Queensland. Material at Allora remains with Sue Dalton but will in time also be offered to the Fryer Library. Original design and contract drawings for many projects were missing. Drawings for some houses were discovered in the possession of owners, whilst drawings for the larger educational projects were accessed through the Queensland Public Works Archive. Dalton commissioned photographs from eminent photographers, including Richard Stringer, Geoff Dauth and the Keen brothers. Others like Harry Sowden approached Dalton. Many negatives and prints still exist undamaged, but some were cropped to create a series of A4 pages showcasing select projects which were scanned to a CD-ROM or were incorporated into a series of collages, a post-rationalization of his own career. There were many surprises amongst Dalton's papers too, letters, transcripts of his polemical texts and contributions to journals and magazines, and his own slides, photographs, drawings and paintings.

As part of the research for my thesis, I met with and interviewed clients and employees of John Dalton Architect and Associates, and colleagues and former students. I remain grateful to Ian and June Cameron, John and Maureen Strugnell, Ken and Barbara Leverington, Noela and Jill Whippel, Mary-Lou O'Dwyer, Kent Farbach, Pam and Jeffrey Chick and Andrew and Jenny Byth for welcoming me in their homes and to Haig Beck, Jackie Cooper, Ray Hughes, Patrick Moroney, Gabriel Poole and Lindsay Clare, Peter Lambert, Gordon Holden, Spence Jamison, Dan Callaghan, Charles Ham and Jennifer Taylor for their time and generosity in this initial phase of work. To this list I can add others, and also my thanks for consenting to interview, including Pam Wilson, Haig Beck and Jackie Cooper (again), Paul Memmott, Fergus Johnston, Peter Brown, Mark Thompson, Mark Roehrs and Michael Leo. Students of architecture and interior architecture courses, now practising in their respective fields, who provided me with material assistance, include Gordon Macindoe, Sarah Manderson, Nikki Hammond, Nick Russell, Keith Starr and Erin Dawson.

I am indebted to research undertaken by Peta Dennis for her undergraduate thesis on 1960s houses in Brisbane (1999) supervised by Professor Jennifer Taylor,⁵ and to Janina Gosseye, Deborah van der Plaat, John Macarthur, Andrew Wilson and Robert Riddel for the archive of interviews at *Digital Archive of Queensland Architecture* (qldarch.net). Unfortunately, John Dalton's death from cancer in 2007 meant he did not contribute to this project.

I am grateful to editors Tom Avermaete and Janina Gosseye for envisaging this important series and for their sound advice together with that of the manuscript's anonymous reviewers. I am indebted to Professor Philip Goad for his kind and generous support during and after my PhD candidature and to colleagues and friends Robert Riddel, Haig Beck and Jackie Cooper, Pedro Guedes, Brit Andresen and Douglas Neale for their encouragement. I remember Peter O'Gorman and Max Horner, both now deceased, who were important teachers and mentors. It was Max Horner who first impressed on me Dalton's significance to Brisbane architecture.

Sue Dalton provided unfettered access to records, letters, the library and drawings of John Dalton Architect and Associates. I spent many days looking at material, which was set out for me in the church at Allora, and shared lunches prepared by Sue in her delightful garden at 'Lambtail Cottage'. I could not have achieved this book without her assistance. Jane Shrapnel and Amanda Turner, John and Sheila Dalton's daughters, have been open and gracious in sharing their memories, as was their mother, Dalton's first wife Sheila, who passed away shortly after my meeting with her.

Finally, I acknowledge the support family, especially that of my husband and partner in architecture John Price, who in 2004 guided to completion a downsized home for Judith Musgrave that reimagined the qualities of her 'Dalton House'.

ABBREVIATIONS

AA	Architectural Association, London
AASA	Australian Architecture Students Association
ACT	Australian Capital Territory
AD	*Architectural Design*
AILA	Australian Institute of Landscape Architects
BAT	Brisbane Arts Theatre
BCC	Brisbane City Council
CAE	College of Advanced Education
CAS	Contemporary Art Society
CEBS	Commonwealth Experimental Building Station
CHI	Consolidated Homes Industries
CM	*Courier Mail*
C-S	*Cross-Section*
CTC	Central Technical College
DDIAE	Darling Downs Institute of Advanced Education
Diss.	Dissertation
HRKG	Hall of Residence Kelvin Grove
HVAC	Heating Ventilation Air Conditioning
NSW	New South Wales
QASA	Queensland Architecture Students Association
QIF	Queensland Industries Fair

QIT	Queensland Institute of Technology
QLD	Queensland
QUT	Queensland University of Technology
RAF	Royal Air Force
RAIA	Royal Australian Institute of Architects, now Australian Institute of Architects
RIBA	Royal Institute of British Architects
SAHANZ	Society of Architectural Historians of Australia & New Zealand
TAFE	Technical and Further Education
UIA	International Union of Architects
UNSW	University of New South Wales
UQ	The University of Queensland
USQ	University of Southern Queensland
VIC	Victoria

Notes

1. Jennifer Taylor, *Australian Architecture since 1960* (Sydney: Law Book Co., 1986), 121.
2. John Musgrove ed., *Sir Bannister Fletcher's A History of Architecture* 19th ed. (London: Butterworth, 1987), 1518.
3. Noel J. Robinson, 'Dalton Houses 1956–1975: An Exemplar for Brisbane's Domestic Architects?' (B.Arch Thesis, The University of Queensland, 1976), 53–111.
4. Stephen Sims, 'Writing the Landscape: Architectural Invention and the Synthesis of Environmental and Architectural Design' (B.Arch. Thesis, The University of Queensland, 2000).
5. Interviews conducted by Peta Dennis, 'Architectural Practice in Postwar Queensland (1945–1975): Building and Interpreting an Oral History Archive', Fryer Library, UQ:372416.

INTRODUCTION

John Dalton (1927–2007) was a controversial figure within the architecture community of 1960s Queensland; stylish, charming, outspoken, he was admired by many but an irritant to members of Brisbane's architectural establishment. His reputation as the best domestic architect in Brisbane was formed early in the decade and sprang from a succession of rigorously detailed houses for a subtropical climate. Within the wider Australian profession, Dalton's name was associated with modernism in the subtropics: one of very few Queensland architects alongside Hayes and Scott, whose work was identified at the beginning of the 1960s as both interesting and not derivative of imported styles.[1] This reputation, carefully curated at the outset of his career, does not fully encapsulate the wide range of interests and activities that engaged John Dalton across his career as architect, artist and advocate, nor does it fully describe his contribution to the development of an environmentally tuned architecture in Queensland.

John Dalton was born in Leeds and immigrated to Australia through an assisted migration scheme, arriving in Brisbane in 1949 aged twenty-one, with a National Diploma in Building from Leeds Technical College, a keen eye and a desire to escape the bleak industrial landscape of northern England. Sundrenched, subtropical Brisbane, capital city of Queensland, could not have provided a greater contrast to Leeds. In Brisbane Dalton realized an opportunity that might not otherwise have been available to him by enrolling to study architecture at Brisbane's Central Technical College (CTC) and graduating in 1956 to embark on a productive and influential career.

'Sunlight, shade and shadow' became Dalton's self-professed motto, and his modus operandi, established early and sustained throughout his career, was 'Sun + Life + Useful Form = Magic'.[2] Through his painting, writing and practice, he drew local architects' attention to the uniqueness of Queensland's environment and the potential of its regional vernacular, the 'Queensland house' for abstraction. He also drew national attention to Queensland's own distinctive modernism. Although his work was published, exhibited nationally and internationally in its day, and recognized by his peers with a swathe of awards and citations, little has been written about Dalton and his practice, John Dalton Architect and Associates. There are reasons for this oversight. As an immigrant in 1950s Brisbane – then an overgrown country town – he was considered an outsider from the start. Handsome, enigmatic, with a polite but formal manner that concealed shyness, he was often perceived as aloof. Intense, forthright and unafraid to be critical of his peers he earned the displeasure of many of them. But more significantly Dalton's insights into a local architecture – clearly expressed in a series of polemical texts and presentations – were recognized as a truth absorbed into the practices of Queensland architects. It has been said that Dalton's insights were self-evident or that other Queensland architects had similar thoughts. It is true he was in complete accord with the zeitgeist of the times. Yet Dalton was alone in Queensland in articulating his architectural preoccupations clearly. No other Queensland architect from that era expressed themselves or their architectural position and intentions as consistently and in such quintessentially architectural ways as Dalton did. In doing so he operated as a conduit by which the local profession engaged with architectural discourse in Australia. He also reflected back to a local profession he considered too complacent, the potential of a located design process. His insights provided a foundation for what is now accepted as a defining characteristic of Queensland architecture, the tuning of architecture to its environment. But instead of being identified as a significant figure in the development of this culture, the lessons articulated more clearly by Dalton than by anyone else are buried in the equivalencies of generalist histories focused on climate responsiveness and architectural form. This narrative draws out Dalton's lessons to examine them in some detail.

Through writing and painting Dalton celebrated the subtropical natural environment that he, an Englishman, had unexpectedly found himself immersed in. He highlighted the experiential qualities of the traditional Queensland house – the antipodean version of the bungalow favoured by the British for colonies in tropical climates – specifically how its verandah spaces amplified a way of life animated by patterns of light and shadow.[3] In doing so he validated the humble local Queenslander as a precedent in design from first principles. But he also sought to situate Queensland architecture in the national consciousness as a regionally derived modernist architecture, following a template used by Robin Boyd (1919–71) – Australia's eminent critic and the architect and the critic Dalton most admired – who in 1948 had identified a 'school or idiom of domestic architecture' in Melbourne, Victoria, the 'Port Phillip Idiom'.[4] By promoting the work of his practice and that of his peers in journals and magazines and engaging this work in contemporaneous debates at the national level, Dalton helped to dispel Queensland's cultural cringe.

The 1960s and 1970s were a time of transition, across society, as well as within the discipline. Dalton's roles as a contributing editor and commentator and as an architect engaged in painting and practice placed him pivotally within the architecture, art and design communities of Brisbane across this period. He was clearly fascinated by architecture as a discipline as well as the profession he practised. A voracious reader concerned to 'stay abreast of the times', he subscribed to numerous international magazines and journals, and ordered books, often air-freighting them to Australia to avoid the delay of a lengthy sea voyage. Publications by John Dewey, Herbert Read, Lewis Mumford and Richard Neutra on environment, art and human psychology found space on his shelves alongside books by Sibyl Moholy-Nagy, G E Kidder Smith, Peter Collins and Bernard Rudofsky on the changing nature of modernism and Lawrence Halprin on urban landscapes. This reading is reflected in Dalton's many activities. His architectural preoccupations are self-disclosed, evident in letters, journal articles, pamphlets and lectures; even his art practice is revelatory of a personal position on architecture. By probing this material, it is possible to establish how Dalton's views are interwoven with the cultural and architectural setting in which he worked in the formation of a position on architecture, and how he interacted with, borrowed from and contributed to disciplinary debates and discourse.[5] Ultimately it provides a lens onto how Dalton's developing position on architecture informed his process of architectural design.

There are two points in Dalton's practice where subtle but observable changes in his built work are shown to correspond with an evolution in his thinking. Both changes disclose an increase in awareness around how architecture might engage environment. Yet enhanced engagement is not arrived at through a conscious or ideologically driven environmentalism but through incremental shifts in perception flowing from Dalton's relentless concern to remain abreast of emerging themes, and which, accrued across time effected a gradual turn to environment. The first of these changes is a revision of the dominant architectural paradigm operating in Queensland in the 1950s and 1960s – the notion that Queensland architecture needed to respond practically to the problems presented by climate. Dalton supplemented this paradigm by drawing attention to a mostly benevolent sun as the source of delight. In doing so he entertained the possibility of a modernism with local inflection whilst foregrounding the veracity of architectural experience. Delight results from idiomatic form in sunlight responding to the demands of living, casting patterns of shade and shadow in summer and preserving pools of warmth in winter. Delight results when inside and outside spaces are open to each other, admitting breezes which are not only cooling but variable and laden with the smells and sounds of the bush. He perceived the edge of building form not only as an envelope conditioning interior space but as an element framing relationships between the occupant and their immediate environment. And he presented the verandah spaces of the Queensland vernacular as the reference point in the development of a local idiom. Dalton's opinions, effectively a critique of functionalist modernism, already differed in one important regard from Boyd's much earlier descriptions of the Port Phillip Idiom as an instance of regionalism in Melbourne. The distinction rests in the extent to which Dalton emphasized the experiential dimensions of space. He recognized the twofold nature of idiomatic form to be both pragmatic and poetic, and to be familiar whilst also being new. The formulation of such ideas and their absorption into his position on architecture are the result of discoveries in art as much as his reading in architecture. Their impact on his practice is not immediate, but he clearly sought ways – within the constraints of his client's limited budgets – to test new ideas and thinking. Over time and through reflective practice, the characteristic language of the 'Dalton House' became confirmed – white masonry walls supporting dark stained timber-framed boxes and pergolas, pitched roofs of trimdeck or tiles with deep overhangs and the use of horizontal datum lines. The correlation between Dalton's growing appreciation of the architecture-environment relationship and the incremental changes wrought in his architecture are traced in this narrative.

The second shift in Dalton's practice from the mid-1960s coincides with press of a more widespread cultural nature. On the one hand, a growing awareness around the rate of observable change in the environment resulted in a proliferation of environmental movements. Dalton's response to these global movements was more radical than that of his peers. On the other hand, the challenge to existing power structures and institutions from the post-war, baby-boomer generation, then coming-of-age, seeded an anti-establishment counterculture. Many elected to follow Timothy Leary's advice to 'turn on, tune in, drop out'. As was his habit, Dalton immersed himself in reading around these new developments broadly but also specifically in relation to architecture's intersections with science, philosophy, computations. He remained open to new theories and the impacts they had on the discipline of architecture. Of interest to him were ideas emerging into planning and architecture from ecology involving systems thinking and networks.

From the late 1960s, environments were increasingly framed in discourse as ecosystems,[6] interconnected webs of organisms and their environments in a constant state of flux to which humans, considered simply as another organism, respond and contribute. Such a conception when applied to architecture presupposes an operational architecture – one that orients occupants in relation to each other and to their environment. From the mid-1960s, the societal consequences of architects' actions were drawn into focus; there was a broadening in the discipline's understanding of the many interdisciplinary dimensions to the human-environment dynamic. It became clear that through the ordering of elements of building form, the architect creates environments that establish the social and political relations between individuals, communities and institutions.[7] In work from the late 1960s we observe Dalton experimenting with these new ideas about architecture in a series of buildings characterized by their fragmented forms. These buildings are not air-conditioned. The relationship between inside and outside space remained unhindered by the need to achieve airtightness. Dalton resisted the use of air-conditioning to achieve comfort and was not impressed by research underway at the University of Queensland testing solar air conditioning for domestic situations in a '"Solair" House'. Passive cooling strategies were associated in his mind with a humanist architecture and desirable for even the largest projects.[8] Dalton's larger projects frequently deployed the same language of idiomatic form associated with the 'Dalton House' with the consequence that their environmentalist ambitions have been largely overlooked. In large and small projects alike, formal expression followed on from the ordering of environmental systems and the relationship of territory through the dispositions of walls and volumes of space. Environmental consequences became the primary consideration in Dalton's design process. Unlike Dalton's earlier shift in thinking to address the idiomatic, which was heralded by a series of polemics published in journals, the activities contributing to this shift in thinking – his teaching, involvement with Queensland Architecture Students Association (QASA) and their conventions, and with the Contemporary Art Society (CAS) Queensland Chapter – were kept discrete and are most evident in a series of handbills circulated amongst students, *Broadside* and *diametrix*.

Despite widespread concern amongst the general population about the health of planet earth, environment was not, at the time that Dalton was beginning his practice, part of the general architectural purview. In his own writings and correspondence Dalton called for an 'indigenous response' or an 'authentic' architecture. Tellingly the use of 'indigenous' did not imply a greater engagement with First Nations knowledge about environment, rather Dalton was calling for an architecture responding to the contingencies of a particular location, time and way of life. For Dalton, location determined the position of the sun, its diurnal and seasonal rhythms and hours of sunlight. Location also determined the weather that generated air movements and conditioned local ecology. Dalton's design responses to environment were not just pragmatic and functional but harnessed physical conditions and social structures in ways intended to enhance the enjoyment of life.

This narrative traces how Dalton arrived at his concern for an ethical and sensible architecture that worked with site, micro-climate and material fabric in the making of settings that were spatially and formally choreographed to their environment. It examines the relationship between environmentalist movements and the formation of environmental perspectives in architecture and asks: what was environmental architecture in the 1960s and 1970s and how did environmental perspectives extend the essentialist view of climate as the primary preoccupation of architects and driver of modernism and innovation in (sub) tropical Queensland? It is not, nor is intended to be, a survey. Rather it uses select works to articulate more explicitly the case for linking Dalton's work to a nascent environmentalism. John Dalton Architect and Associates completed more than 130 projects dating from 1960, and unfortunately many interesting works are under-described or mentioned here only in passing, including the Los Nidos Resort at Noosa (1972 demolished 1985), the Arts Theatre, Brisbane (1962), and a series of budget houses, amongst them the Strugnell (1971) and Salter (1970)

Houses and project homes for Consolidated Housing Industries (CHI) from 1968. Unfortunately, many of Dalton's significant buildings have disappeared, including the Bardon Professional Development Centre (1976 demolished 2014), the Wilson House (1964 demolished) and Vice-Chancellor's Residence (1972 demolished 2000), or been partially demolished as in the case of the Halls of Residence, Kelvin Grove (1974). In Queensland's humid conditions, frequent downpours and active white ant and termite infestations, timber-framed structures deteriorate without maintenance. Unfortunately, in a city that is rapidly densifying it is too easy to argue the case for demolition of white ant damaged structures resulting in the rapid disappearance of mid-century modern houses in Brisbane.

Environment presents certain methodological challenges to a study in architecture. The term is used to reference both a knowledge base with interdisciplinary reach and a particular set of specific circumstances to be addressed through design. Whilst it is now well understood that humans and their environments are 'co-productive', environment has not figured greatly in historical accounts of architecture as a cultural endeavour, except in those moments across time when the nature-human connection has emerged as a particular preoccupation of architecture and therefore productive of culture. The rustic or classical landscapes of the picturesque are framed in architectural discourse as a reaction to industrialization manifest in a desire to replicate an earlier imagined world in which humans were in harmony with nature. Similarly, nineteenth-century national romantic movements in architecture are framed as a reaction to the universalizing tendency of classicism drawing on the relationship between built form and the landscape of a particular place to recapture local character. In comparison to these earlier fascinations with nature, the architecture discipline has been challenged by the emergence of environment in the 20th century as an issue underpinned by science but with an interdisciplinary reach and many dimensions.

The methodological challenge presented by environment has been the focus of some recent debate by architectural historians. Much commentary has focused on how to mediate the vaguely defined and shifting field of environment with architecture's established discourses and methodologies which have traditionally relied on art historical methodologies and focused on matters of architectural form.[9] The contemporary conception of environment asks us to consider architecture not as form alone or a 'thing in itself' but as 'a relational product' and the outcome of a process that is alert to the potential of intentional relationships for architecture.[10] As a perspective or a framework for action, it has been usefully described as 'a *rubric* through which the world is comprehended'.[11] Comparisons have been made with feminism, Marxism or postcolonial studies, which are also perspectives with the capacity to shed light on a range of disciplines.[12] Environmentalist perspectives differ from architectural movements underpinned by theory; consequently, environmental thinking in built work must be uncovered by different means.

Most recently Daniel Barber has recommended a *longue-durée* engagement with work, in which 'media' is both 'method and evidence' for identifying new insights.[13] His technique is demonstrated in an analysis of climate responsiveness in work by Le Corbusier, Lúcio Costa and others, essentially an unpicking of design intentions through the analysis of the images and diagrams produced by those architects.[14] In *Uncommon Ground: Architecture, Technology, and Topography* (2002) David Leatherbarrow analysed work by Richard Neutra, Antonin and Noémi Raymond and Aris Konstantinidis to uncover their intentions for tuning buildings to site and to dispute the view that modern architecture is disconnected with landscape.[15] British academic and architect Royston Landau's close analysis of select architects' work in *New Directions in British Architecture* (1968) enabled him to draw conclusions about Postmodernism in British architecture. Landau argues that transitions within a culture of architecture are best teased out through analysis of the work of key individuals; it is the individual architect who absorbs social and cultural shifts in perspective and translates new disciplinary theories and practices into action.[16] In each instance, analysis of an individual's practice is used to provide a finer grain of information to balance more generalist or dominant historical accounts.[17] A careful probing of work by John Dalton Architect and Associates makes it possible to see how different environmental perspectives were negotiated and accommodated within the framework of disciplinary discourse and absorbed into Dalton's personal position on architecture.

Chapter 1 begins by introducing John Dalton and setting out the facts of his life, his migration to Australia, education and early practice, and situating his work locally and nationally and in relation to the themes that resonated in accounts of Queensland architecture in the second half of the twentieth century. This chapter then moves into a discussion around the emergence of environmentalism from the 1960s, when perceptions of an imminent environmental crisis impacted the political, cultural and social landscape, leading to a focus within the architecture discipline on human-environment interactions. This chapter establishes a context for understanding Dalton's contribution to the discipline over the years of his practice.

Chapter 2 describes Dalton's early practice experiences, his interest in art, the circumstances surrounding his first short-lived partnership with Peter Heathwood and the establishment of John Dalton Architect and Associates, the name under which he practised for the next twenty-seven years. It provides a lens onto the development of Dalton's personal preoccupations at a time when they were just coming into view, and how by reading widely, painting and questioning Dalton felt his way towards an understanding of architecture as a source of delight, and as overlaid with associations. It discusses the insights that underpin the first phase of change in his work – the role of idiomatic detail in linking the pragmatic and the poetic in architecture, the sun as a constant and the source of magic, the existing

Queensland house as a precedent for architectural experience and the edge of building form as the site where issues intrinsic to architecture intersect.

Chapter 3 analyses houses built between 1960 and 1970 and describes the changes in formal expression that reflect a shift in Dalton's practice to a regionally derived modernism. It traces the evolution of a distinct language of architectural form that has come to be associated with the 'Dalton House'. It also describes the testing and adaptation of specific strategies and ideas in plan and section that led to the solution known locally as the 'Dalton section'. Whilst promoting the value of 'sunlight shade and shadow' to the creation of sensory environments, Dalton was also engaging in correspondence regarding an authentic Australian architecture, using the work of his and other practices to demonstrate what form it might take in Queensland.

Chapter 4 shifts from a discussion around purely domestic environments to focus on Dalton's activism in relation to the city, landscape and architectural education. From 1967 Dalton self-published a series of handbills – *Broadside* from 1967 to 1969 and *diametrix* from 1969 to 1972 – and circulated them to students of architecture in Queensland. In publishing his own 'zine' he was aligning himself with students against an establishment profession and conservative education system, but he also sought to improve debate by introducing key social, political and environmental issues. The insights made during this period underpin a second phase of change in Dalton's work. How issues intersected with Dalton's architectural practice is evident in commissions for houses and larger institutional projects between 1967 and 1979. These works reveal the use of narrative to link building form to site, resulting in compositionally and spatially richer work that intentionally engages immediate environment.

Chapter 5 describes John Dalton Architect and Associates responding to new thinking and practices in commissions for four campus buildings that explore architecture's new social orientation and its intersection with new pedagogical approaches. These projects deployed borrowed strategies such as 'mat' and 'cluster' to the specific circumstances of a particular location and programmatic brief, and provide the clearest indication of Dalton's understanding of how architecture constructs and embodies relationships between individuals, communities and institutions.

Chapter 6 sheds light on a second wind in Dalton's professional life that came after the closure of his Queen Street office. Analysis of a group of later houses by Dalton including the Coughlan House, Allora (workings drawing completed for a bottle of wine), the O'Dwyer Homestead, Mt Manning (1981), Lambtail (1981) and the Methodist Church Studio, Allora, show how Dalton sought to reconcile postmodernist practices within his own environmentalist framework in a series of works that are whimsical and poetic – nothing like the subtropical modernist houses that he is renowned for. Finally, a conclusion reflects on Dalton's legacy as a teacher and a practitioner. It places Dalton's practice in relation to that of architects who followed him in the 1980s and 1990s in order to reflect on his legacy for Queensland architecture. It reveals Dalton as precursor to a group of ethical and environmentally aware modernist architects who worked conscientiously with a design process directed at enabling occupants to 'adjust their senses' in relation to their world.

The events described within these chapters took place on the lands of the Turrbal and Jagera people. The Turrbal called their country 'Meanjin'. They inhabited a place of great beauty before the establishment of the Moreton Bay Penal Settlement and later arrival of free settlers. When Dalton arrived as an immigrant from post-war UK, Aboriginal and Torres Strait Islander people were subject to the Queensland government's racist policies of protection and assimilation and the 1967 Australian Referendum had not yet been envisaged. Under the Queensland *Aboriginals Protection and Restriction of the Sale of Opium Act* 1897, 'protection' was effected through the creation of Aboriginal reserves. Aboriginal and Torres Strait Islander people were corralled onto reserves and their movement and working arrangements controlled. The children of Aboriginal and Torres Strait Islander descent, the Stolen Generation, were removed from their families by government agencies and church missions to be 'integrated' into 'white' society under a policy of assimilation. Protection and assimilation policies effectively rendered Aboriginal and Torres Strait Islander people and their culture invisible in the post-war era. The success of the 1967 Referendum triggered changes to the Constitution and the dismantling of discriminatory state government legislation practices but whilst the Referendum carried great symbolic meaning, material change was very slow. It was the High Court ruling in the Mabo Case handed down in 1992 that finally extinguished the policy of *terra nullius* – 'land belonging to no one' – thereby recognizing the legitimate prior occupation of Australia by Aboriginal and Torres Strait Islander people. But in the 1950s the people of the Turrbal and Jagera clans were relegated to missions and reserves some distance from their own country; removed from public life, they are also missing in this narrative.

Similarly, at the time of Dalton's arrival, Brisbane society was extremely conservative, and the professions were dominated by men. Women's employment rights and their access to clubs and bars were restricted. The second wave of feminism was unleashed in Brisbane as late as 1965, when two women chained themselves to the footrail of the public bar of the Regatta Hotel, Toowong in protest at Queensland's restriction of public bars to men only. Dalton's attitude to women was typical of his era – old-fashioned, chivalrous or chauvinist. His writings in the 1960s are smattered with gendered language whilst the transcript of a speech delivered to students at a girls' school reveals deeply embedded views on women's role and influence in the home.[18] Yet Dalton continued to move with his times and when I met him in later life, he was full of admiration for the women architects he knew. Changes in attitude to race and gender form part of the social and political context for this narrative.

Environmental concerns are once more the focus of research in many different fields including architectural history. This account takes the reader back to the point in time when environment was emerging as a disciplinary concern in Australia in relation to modernist architecture. It traces over a period of architectural history, most usually framed through reference to climate responsive and regionalist modernism, and which has focused overwhelmingly on matters of architectural form. It looks more closely and inclusively at the material to hand to identify how relational thinking which might now be identified as environmental emerged to become embedded in Dalton's practice of architecture. It offers a new perspective, one in which architecture is considered, not as an isolated artefact but as the outcome of processes concerned to generate intentional relationships.[19] Examining buildings through such a lens reveals the role that architecture plays in structuring our physical and social worlds and is a salient reminder that such a view continues to offer new possibilities for architecture.

1 INTRODUCING JOHN DALTON AND THE LANDSCAPE OF POST-WAR AUSTRALIA

The circumstances by which John Harold Dalton arrived in Australia from post-war Europe are not unusual in Australian history. A policy of 'Populate or Perish' meant that between 1945 and 1960 1.6 million 'New Australians' arrived from Europe, with many going on to make important contributions to the nation's culture and economy. John Dalton arrived in Australia under the Assisted Passage Migration Scheme, a preferential migration scheme directed at encouraging Britons to Australia. Under this scheme, an adult passage cost ten pounds sterling, essentially the fee for processing documents. Migrants travelling under the scheme became known as Ten Pound Poms. They were promised employment prospects, housing and a better lifestyle but were required to stay in Australia for two years or repay the cost of their passage. There was no skills requirement; applicants were to be under forty-five years of age and in sound health. Most Ten Pound Poms found work in manufacturing, mining or large infrastructure projects. It was not anticipated that a Ten Pound Pom would attend an Australian university and become a leading architect.

Consequently, Dalton is unlike Harry Seidler (1923–2006), Australia's most acclaimed modern architect, who arrived in Sydney Australia in 1948 with an impressive resume, having studied with Walter Gropius at Harvard Graduate School and Josef Albers at Black Mountain College, and worked briefly with Marcel Breuer in New York and Oscar Neimeyer in Rio de Janeiro, Brazil. Seidler had only intended to stay in Sydney long enough to complete a house commission for his parents. Nor is Dalton like Karl Langer (1903–69), the Austrian émigré architect and town planner who studied at the Viennese Academy under Peter Behrens before completing his doctor of philosophy at the Vienna University, or his wife Gertrude (1908–84), who completed her doctor of philosophy in Art History at the Sorbonne. Karl and Gertrude Langer fled Vienna to escape the

Third Reich and arrived in Brisbane in 1939, a cultural backwater, as political refugees. Dalton is also unlike Constantino A. Doxiadis, the pioneer of 'ekistics', who as an established architect and town planner attempted to settle in Brisbane in 1951, establishing a firm, Tecton Constructors. Unsuccessful in securing work Doxiadis returned to Greece to resume his successful career.[1] Dalton arrived in Australia as an adventurer, a structural draftsperson with a building certificate, lured by slick advertising to the promise of a better life. But he had a good eye, and the sensibilities characteristic of a sound English education. Despite Australia re-focusing its attention on the United States in the post-war era, Britain was still the motherland and in 1950s Brisbane polite society deferred to all things British. Dalton's essential Englishness was to his benefit in professional circumstances early in his career; it was often assumed erroneously that he achieved his qualifications before arriving in Australia.

Brisbane in 1949 was a strange mixture of rigid social habits, a sparsely settled landscape, bright sunlight and vibrant colours. A big country town famed for the lethargy of its citizens, it was reputed to be a place where nothing ever happened, 'where poetry could never occur'.[2] However, Brisbane's conservative skin concealed a vibrant counter-cultural arts scene, tolerated by its establishment class as one of the aberrations of subtropical heat and geographical remoteness. Brisbane may have felt uncanny to Dalton on his arrival, but it says much that after two years he did not travel back to Leeds, as he had promised his father he would.

John Dalton: Early life in précis

John Harold Dalton was born in Richmond Mount, Leeds in 1927, to Laura [nee Skitt] (1889–1935) and Arthur Harold Dalton (1886–1956) and was the fourth of five children. A boy, Arthur, born a few years before Dalton did not survive infanthood and Dalton grew up with two older sisters, Bettie (1919–??) and Sallie (1922–2022) and one younger, Helen (1929–2008).[3] After their mother died allegedly of asthma when Dalton was seven years old and Helen five, Bettie and Sallie assumed much of the responsibility for raising their younger siblings, despite their own youth.[4] Dalton was in hospital himself, when his mother had her attack and recounted that on discharge his family initially led him to believe that she would be coming home soon, leaving it to him to work out the truth.[5] Sallie first learnt of her mother's death when she overheard her father telling the neighbours the following morning.[6]

Laura Skitt was the daughter of a Leeds merchant family. Her grandfather, John Skitt, was a colourful figure who established an army disposal store, although how he acquired the capital to open his business is surrounded by mystery. Family lore recounts his disappearance for a number of years, and it was rumoured that he travelled to Australia or South Africa and made his fortune in gold or diamonds.[7] Dalton's father, Arthur Harold Dalton, known as Harold, was the son of a Deputy

Chief Constable in the Leeds police force. Harold Dalton was a popular man, with a varied working life; after working in the fish markets as a youngster, he was employed as a solicitor's clerk, before joining the Civil Service and finally enlisting in the British Army. On leaving the army he was persuaded by Laura Skitt to work for her father as manager of Charles Skitt Limited Government Contractors and Army Stores in Kirkstall Road, Leeds, a decision he claimed later to have regretted.[8] Working for his father-in-law provided Harold Dalton with security and after the death of his wife, was a way of keeping the family together, but was not fulfilling for him.

The family moved from Richmond Mount to Headingly then on the outskirts of Leeds when Sallie was nine, Dalton four, and Helen two years old (Figure 1.1). Dalton caught trout in the Meanwood Beck, played cricket and kept rabbits.[9] In conversation with a colleague many years later, Dalton recalled attending an Ashes Test match between England and Australia at nearby Yorkshire County Cricket Club, during which records were broken by the Australian batsmen.[10] Although he was very young, he was captivated by the tanned Australians in their cream silk 'whites'. The idea of a sun-burnt country struck him as very romantic.

Dalton was twelve years old when the Second World War erupted. The arrival of the war in Leeds caused much excitement. Leeds, a manufacturing and rail hub, was subjected to nine separate bombing raids by the German Luftwaffe but was spared the intensity of raids visited on larger centres such as Liverpool, Glasgow, Sheffield or Hull. Many children were evacuated from Leeds in anticipation of bombing raids, but Dalton and his sisters were not. Due to censorship laws that limited reporting, the extent of damage from bombing raids on cities in the north of England was not reported. A children's newsletter listing John Dalton as editor, ran with the banner 'RAID ON LEEDS'. It describes in detail a raid on the night of 8 March 1941 that impacted Cardigan Road, Headingly, destroying a number of houses.[11] On this night the Luftwaffe dropped their cargo short of their target, gasometers,

FIGURE 1.1 John and Helen Dalton c. 1936. Photograph reproduced courtesy of Sue Dalton.

heavy machinery and munitions works along Kirkstall Road. Instead, incendiaries and bombs landed in and around Cardigan Road, very close to where Dalton and his family lived. The newsletter noted many unexploded devices including one outside the home of Dalton's aunt and uncle. The worst raid on Leeds occurred on the 14/15 March which severely damaged the City Hall, Leeds City Museum and many other parts of the city.

After attending St Chad's Church of England School,[12] Dalton trained at the Leeds Technical School between 1944 and 1946, where he completed the National Diploma in Building (London). This was a rigorous programme focused entirely on the technical and Dalton satisfied his assessors in Building Construction, Building Drawing, Building Science and Mechanics, Business Economics and Accounts, Steel and Reinforced Concrete, Builders' Quantities, and Engineering Equipment of Buildings.[13] On completing his Building Diploma, Dalton was conscripted into the Royal Air Force and between 1947 and 1948 was posted to Austria and Bad Eilsen, a former spa town in Germany, as an Architectural Draftsman working on reconstruction projects in Hamburg and Hanover (Figure 1.2). He was given command of the Print Shop at RAF HQ and charged with managing 'a dozen sullen German print operatives' who had been attached to the administrative wing of Focke-Wulf Flugzeugbau, the manufacturer of military aircraft during the Second World War. His German charges had been evacuated to Bad Eilsen during the war along with portfolios of detailed aerial photographs of every town and city in the UK. One of his charges, a former aircraft plant foreman, produced a souvenir for Dalton: a photograph of a map of Old Leeds 'ready for the bombers' with a quote from the German poet Johann Christoph Friedrich von Schiller on its reverse side.[14] Years later, Dalton would reflect that Leeds was very lucky to have

FIGURE 1.2 John Dalton in uniform c. 1948. Photograph reproduced courtesy of Sue Dalton.

survived the war relatively intact. He was profoundly shocked by the devastation of war-ravaged Europe and surprised to find the average 'dreaded Hun' was a decent person. He did not lead a social life in Germany, but appears to have used the time productively, attending Bückeburg Technische Hochschule in 1948.[15] Dalton remained on the RAF reserve list after completing service in Germany and was not formally discharged until 6 September 1949.[16]

After returning to the UK in 1948 Dalton was engaged as a draftsperson working on prefabricated, permanent housing in the structural drawing office of Riley Constructional Systems, a department of Leeds company Charwood Wharton and Co Ltd., contractors and exporters of coal and coke, steel and concrete building products.[17] He also worked as a supervisor for building contractors Protheroe and McNab Ltd.[18] At about this time Dalton and his childhood friend Robin Machell conceived a plan to travel together to Australia on the Assisted Passage Migration Scheme sponsored by the Australian Government. Despite the prospect of employment, housing and a better lifestyle, Dalton promised his father that he would return to Leeds to study for the Anglican priesthood. He also promised Kari Svendsen, the Norwegian girl he met in Europe, that he would return.[19] When Robin Machell withdrew from their migration plan, Dalton decided to continue alone and was interviewed by an Australian Government official in Leeds on Tuesday 26 April 1949.[20] On his application form Dalton listed Structural Engineer as the occupation he proposed to follow in Australia and included alongside his National Diploma in Building, trade training at Leeds College of Technology specifically in bricklaying and plumbing. Young, skilled and in sound health he was exactly the type of applicant the migration scheme hoped to attract. On 28 July 1949 he boarded the RMS *Ormonde* at the Port of Tilbury bound for Australia.[21] Dalton's ship docked briefly in Melbourne, Victoria, which although cosmopolitan was bleak and grey and reminded him of Leeds. Although he had indicated Victoria as his preferred place of residence on his Overseas Settlement application form, he travelled onto Brisbane, the capital city of Queensland[22] where he disembarked on 8 September 1949. That Dalton did not return to Leeds as promised was a matter of much regret to him, as his father died on 12 November 1956 at the age of seventy-one. Dalton would not return to the UK until 1972.

Sponsorship was not a requirement for migrants to gain employment in Queensland and Dalton quickly found work as a draftsman in the office of the Brisbane City Council (BCC) under the direction of City Architect, Frank Gibson Costello (1903–89).[23] Sleepy subtropical Brisbane had been a major military base for Allied Forces during the Pacific War and was re-establishing its civic infrastructure post-war. Much of the work that was completed by Dalton during his employ at the BCC was directed towards this end. Dalton's supervisor Costello had trained in architecture at the Sydney Technical College and as the recipient of a travelling scholarship from the Board of Architects of NSW, had travelled extensively in Europe in 1928 and studied Town Planning Studies and Civic Design at London University.[24] Amongst Australians travelling in Europe in the interwar period there was a fascination with the civic work of Dutch architect, Willem Marinus Dudok. Even relatively small projects completed under Costello's direction demonstrated a similarly strong civic sense in the manipulation of scale and proportion[25] and a restrained modernism in terms of expression.[26] Dalton appears to have worked closely with Costello, who credits him with the design of the BCC displays at the Queensland Industries Fair (QIF) in 1952,[27] which was awarded the Gold Medal by The Royal National Agricultural and Industrial Association of Queensland. When in 1952 the Office of the City Architect was downgraded by a new administration to 'Brisbane City Council Building Works' and the City Architect, Deputy City Architect, and Deputy City Planner were dismissed, Costello provided Dalton with a glowing reference describing him as 'a neat painstaking and accurate draftsman' with 'a real interest in his work' and 'a fine sense of initiative and appreciation of the overall design'.[28] A search through BCC archives reveals drawings signed JHD for Sub Stations, the Mount Crosby Water Filtration Plant, and a number of park structures including the Mt Coot-tha Lookout and additions to its historic Kiosk.[29] For Dalton, working in the Office of the City Architect brought into sharp focus the distinction between building as a technical problem and architecture. The BCC is where Dalton was first introduced to European Modernism and where he shifted his focus from structural engineering to architecture. His friendship with Eric Buchanan, originally from Melbourne, was an important catalyst in this shift. Dalton and Buchanan lived in the same lodgings in Kangaroo Point.[30] At the BCC, Dalton also made the acquaintance of Carl Hammerschmidt, a Danish émigré who, after the disbanding of the BCC Planning and Building Department, worked with Karl Langer before moving to Melbourne[31] and Heinz Jacobsohn, a Polish-born German-educated émigré architect who departed Brisbane to join C.A. Doxiadis in his practice in Greece.[32]

Dalton met his first wife, Sheila Harvey (1926–2015), through a bushwalking club he was encouraged to join by a work colleague, and Sheila's friend Betty Kelly (Figure 1.3).[33] The group included Ian and June Cameron and Don and Barbara Leverington, who along with Brian and Betty Kelly would later commission Dalton to design their homes.[34] Sheila's mother Eldorene Joyce Nussey (1896–1993), known as Rene, belonged to an established Darling Downs grazing family and had grown up at the historic Goomburra Homestead. Her father, Richard Stoddard Harvey (1886–1936), had served in the Australian Imperial Forces in the First World War and saw action in France, before returning home to Allora, a regional town on the Darling Downs and becoming a farm manager.[35] His death through suicide forced Rene, Sheila and her two brothers to move to Warwick, the nearest major regional town, where Rene took employment as boarding house mistress at Slade School, the Anglican boys' school and Sheila attended St Catharine's Church of England Grammar School for girls. After completing her teacher-training Sheila's first appointment was to Nunkulla, a one-teacher school west of Toowoomba.[36] At the time she met Dalton, Sheila was a primary school teacher and boarding house mistress at St Margaret's Anglican Girls' School, in Ascot, Brisbane. A strong personality, Sheila and Dalton became close and married on 18 August 1951 at St Mark's Anglican Church, Warwick.

The popularity of bushwalking during the 1950s reflected the changing perceptions of white Australians towards native flora and indigenous landscapes in

FIGURE 1.3 Young bushwalkers, John Dalton and Sheila Harvey c. 1951. Courtesy of Jane Shrapnel and Amanda Turner.

general.[37] To Dalton's European sensibilities however, the dense tropical rainforests of the Lamington Plateau south of Brisbane and the scruffy dry eucalypt forests of the D'Aguilar Ranges west of Brisbane would have appeared alien and exotic. Through bushwalking Dalton made connections with other young professionals and university academics, many of whom were, like him, new arrivals in Brisbane. He also joined the Johnsonian Society and became involved with art societies, jazz, and Brisbane's repertory theatre company, the Arts Theatre. Through these connections Dalton developed an appreciation for modernism as an attitude of mind and as an approach integrating art, architecture and design. In 1951 Sheila and John Dalton joined the Queensland Art Gallery Society 'Friends of the Gallery'[38] and in 1961 they became foundation members of the Contemporary Art Society Queensland Chapter (CAS), a group of progressive artists, writers, academics and philosophers credited with shaping the alternative cultural and social life of Brisbane.[39] Dalton regularly attended Brisbane's jazz clubs and visited El Rocco jazz bar in Kings Cross when in Sydney.[40] It was at a gathering of jazz musicians – members of the 'Varsity Five' – in 1961 at the home of Bryan and Betty Kelly (the Kelly House was designed by Dalton in 1960) that Dalton first met Sue Stirling (nee Crozier, 1941–).

For the first few years of their married life, John and Sheila Dalton lived in a flat in the Old Town Hall, South Brisbane. Their neighbours were English expatriate architect John Hitch and his Danish wife, Lilly. Lilly encouraged the couple's interest in design, especially European design whilst John Hitch (1915–2010), would eventually be Dalton's fourth year studio teacher.[41] When in 1952, South Brisbane Town Hall was converted from flats for use by the Queensland Conservatorium of Music, the Daltons' bought a block of land at Moordale Street, Indooroopilly, then on Brisbane's western fringe, where Dalton designed and built his first house. Ultimately John Dalton and Sheila's relationship was not a happy one, despite the arrival of their two daughters, Penelope (1954–), who as a young girl changed her name by deed poll to Jane, and Amanda (1958–). Amanda reflects that her parents were not well suited, noting astutely that both had childhoods marred by the traumatic loss of a parent.[42] Although Sheila had been an anchor for Dalton during his early years in Brisbane, they divorced in 1972.

Becoming an Architect in Queensland

Encouraged by Sheila and his colleagues, Dalton enrolled to study architecture at Brisbane's Central Technical College (CTC) in 1952. His enrolment was delayed whilst the standing of his qualifications from Leeds College of Technology was confirmed.[43] He was also required to complete a scholarship paper in the subject of Art by the Queensland Department of Public Instruction. He passed this prerequisite subject in December 1952 and was given an advanced standing entry to the Diploma course.[44] Sheila continued working as a primary school teacher to support the couple whilst Dalton undertook his studies in the evening and worked in architecture practices during the day. The first years of Dalton's Diploma were completed at CTC and the final three years, alongside bachelor's degree students, at The University of Queensland (UQ). At CTC Dalton was taught by Bruce Lucas (1898–1973) and Charles Fulton (1906–88), both of whom he regarded highly, whilst at UQ, in addition to Hitch, he encountered Professor Robert Cummings (1900–89), Athol Bretnall (1909–2004), Campbell Scott (1921–2007) and Dr Karl Langer who lectured in planning and landscape. Dalton considered the architects who taught him to be 'honourable men'.[45]

Dalton's peers remember him as a serious and more worldly student, possibly because he was slightly older and distanced from them by his experiences in post-war Germany.[46] Renowned Brisbane architect Robin Gibson (1930–2014) became aware of Dalton's arrival into the University cohort at an exhibition of student work. Completed and graded student work was customarily pinned to the walls of the exhibition space where it was able to be viewed by all in the academe. Comparisons could be made between schemes and yardsticks for standards established. Typically, students would be more interested in work by students a few years ahead, whereas Gibson remembers being drawn to the work of a student one or two years behind him. He recalled a Gordon Cullen style presentation, recognizing it as the work of a mature designer and discovered its author to be a good-looking Englishman with a deep sonorous voice.[47] Gibson and Dalton became friends and eventually colleagues at Theo Thynne and Associates.

Few of Dalton's student projects have survived. Two designs completed in his final year – schemes for a hospital and a replacement State Parliament House complex – are almost identical in their plan arrangements. With their programmes accommodated into wings and organized around a centrally located foyer and sequence of courtyards, they demonstrate symmetry, balance and functional planning. Only the room names are different. Perspectives of these student projects reveal strategies borrowed from the Burnie Board Administration Building (Figure 1.4). Dalton passed his final project in 1956 and was awarded a Diploma in Architecture in absentia by the University of Queensland in 1957; he was already busy with private practice at the end of 1956.

Whilst studying part-time, Dalton was employed in the Commonwealth Department of Works (1953), where, amongst other things, he designed

FIGURE 1.4 Student Project work. Diploma IV. Proposal for a New Parliament House. Courtesy of Sue Dalton.

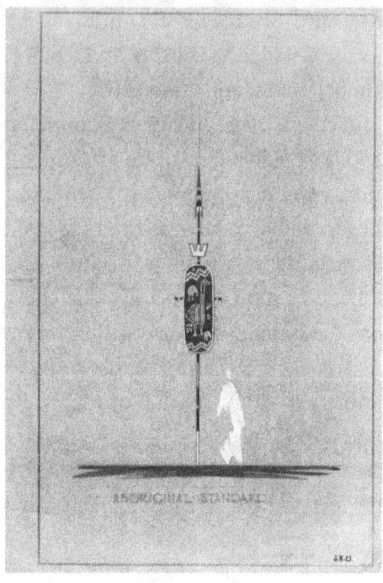

FIGURE 1.5 Shield design for standards to line the processional route at the Brisbane International Airport, for Queen Elizabeth II 1954 Royal tour. Source John Dalton's slide collection.

banners and decorations for Commonwealth Buildings, including Brisbane's Custom House and the Brisbane Airport, a group of sheds left by the American air force after demobilization, to celebrate the 1954 visit of Queen Elizabeth II to Brisbane (Figure 1.5).[48] The adoption of aboriginal motifs on some of these banners may have been considered *avant-garde* in 1953 but would be judged today as an act of cultural appropriation. He was employed briefly at Cook & Kerrison, where, by his own admission, as a second-year student he found himself out of his depth,[49] before taking a position in 1954 in the office of Hayes and Scott. The partnership between Campbell Scott and Edwin Hayes (1918–97) was considered one of Brisbane's leading practices designing climate-responsive dwellings. Believing he had arrived at the 'pinnacle' of the profession, he was disappointed to be let go after only twelve months when the office ran out of work.[50] He was immediately hired by Don Winsen (1927–2014), an associate at Theo Thynne & Associates where Robin Gibson also worked. Dalton found the collaborative, design studio culture at Theo Thynne & Associates to his liking and very different from the strict office rule of Campbell Scott. The drawing office staff at Theo Thynne and Associates would drink together on Friday evenings at the Queens Hotel in Creek Street or Breakfast Creek Hotel, Newstead. It was on one of these outings that John Dalton, Robin Gibson and Don Winsen met Gabriel Poole (1934–2020), a jackeroo recently returned to Brisbane and enrolled to study medicine. By the end of the evening, Dalton and Gibson had convinced the young man to enrol in architecture.[51] Dalton remained at Theo Thynne & Associates until graduation in 1956, working on several significant projects including the Day Residence (1955), the Burnie Board House (1955) and the Burnie Board Administration Building (1955) (Figure 1.6).

FIGURE 1.6 Perspective drawn by John Dalton, of the Burnie Board Administrative Building, 1955, by Theo Thynne and Associates. Courtesy of Sue Dalton.

After graduation it was not uncommon for young Australian architects to travel to Europe to work, study and travel. Initially the most popular destination for Australian architects abroad was London, but after the Second World War, as Australia looked less to Europe for cultural direction, North America became a more desirable destination for young graduates. Dalton's friend Robin Gibson travelled overseas and worked in the offices of James Cubit & Partners and Casson and Condor in London. Another, Graham Bligh, studied briefly at the AA in London before working in the office of Maxwell Fry and Jane Drew. Some years later, Steven Trotter, awarded an RAIA Sisalkraft Research Scholarship, circumnavigated the globe visiting cities in the torrid zones and publishing his research as *Cities in the Sun* (1963).[52] Dalton did not have the financial means to travel to Europe or America immediately after completing his studies although he would later travel to Japan, the UK and Southeast Asia in the 1970s. Instead, he and fellow student, Peter Heathwood (1933–2022) devised a plan, which would enable them to open a practice together after graduation. Both submitted entries to a competition for the design of a plywood demonstration house agreeing that if either won, they would use the prize money to open a practice. Heathwood's entry to the Plywood Exhibition House Competition was awarded first prize. Dalton completed construction drawings whilst Heathwood was away on his honeymoon.[53] The Plywood Exhibition House, built to Dalton's construction drawings at the Brisbane Exhibition Grounds, attracted enormous public interest.

Professional practice

Dalton and Heathwood Architects was established in late 1956 with offices in the City Mutual Building, Queen Street, a prestigious address in the Brisbane CBD. The practice was successful from a professional point of view, and completed – in addition to domestic commissions – work on the Belvedere Hotel in the bayside suburb of Woody Point, retail fit-outs and service stations for Neptune and Shell Oil companies. Even though they tended to work on separate projects the two men did not have a good working relationship and parted ways after only three years. In later years Heathwood reflected that he and Dalton did not design the same way and 'firmed their convictions by arguing all bloody day'.[54] It is probable that Dalton would have described these same encounters as robust debate. Their attitude to practice also differed. Dalton was relentless, working seven days a week, night and day, as Heathwood describes it 'lots of energy but not much fun'.[55] They formally dissolved their partnership and Heathwood vacated their Queen Street office sometime between 25 December 1960 and 16 January 1961.[56] Dalton continued practising as John Dalton Architect & Associates and before long his work was achieving recognition nationally. His practice was diverse and included work on schools for the Queensland Department of Public Works, showrooms and office fit-outs for industry and as consultant to engineers Cameron and McNamara on infrastructure projects including Kangaroo Point Pedestrian Footbridge and Overpass and the Barron Falls Bridge in Far North Queensland.[57]

In 1963 Dalton engaged his first 'associate', Haig Beck (1944–) a student at CTC, who would eventually complete his architecture education at the AA in London. In London Beck would become Assistant Editor of *The Architect's Journal* (1970–1), Joint-Editor with Martin Spring and Editor of *Architectural Design* (1976–9) before launching *International Architect* with Jackie Cooper in 1979.[58] Until the late 1960s Dalton continued to engage one assistant, usually the best student in the Diploma programme. Beck was followed in 1964 by John Kupfer and on his departure in 1968 by Charles Ham (1948–), who remained with Dalton for ten years, becoming his longest-serving associate.[59] Whilst Dalton was away for two weeks, the newly employed Ham, then a second year student, completed a design for a house for which Dalton had been commissioned and built a model. The house was built to Ham's design and thereafter models became standard office practice.[60]

John Dalton Architect and Associates comprised John Dalton and Charles Ham until 1970 when commissions for the Vice-Chancellor's Residence and Darling Downs Institute of Advanced Education projects arrived in quick succession. Even at its busiest the office generally comprised a core of four employees with others brought in as required to assist with the production of drawings. Those who worked in John Dalton Architect and Associates include Hedley Kidd, Michael Fanning, Tim Macrossan, Chris Gibbs, Peter Chilton, Stanley Witchell, and Peter Brown. 'Mateship' was a defining characteristic of Australian society and public life at this time.[61] Dalton's office reflected the very gendered, 'blokey' character of the profession in Brisbane in the 1960s and 1970s and the only woman employee, Morag Papi (then Morag Leslie) joined the practice in 1978.[62]

Dalton by his own admission was not interested in being 'very modern'. The Miesian approach to domestic projects adopted by Robin Gibson did not interest him.[63] He preferred a more humanist modernism aligning with his interest in Scandinavian architecture and design. Ham recalls that Dalton's practice was collaborative. Ideas would be thrashed out in debate, but Dalton gave his employees the opportunity to develop their design ideas and room to manoeuvre with those designs.[64] Ham notes this was unlike the experience of his peers at Robin Gibson's practice. In 1977, Dalton permitted Ham to work on a project outside the office, a very rare concession. The Church of the Holy Trinity, Banyo, to replace a timber church destroyed by fire was a project that was unlikely to have much fee attached to it. Ham worked on this project with his friend Peter McDougall, who in order to participate was required to take leave from his position in the Public Works Department. Their efforts were awarded in 1978 with a RAIA Citation, the same year that the Bardon Professional Development Centre by John Dalton Architect and Associates won the RAIA Bronze Medal.[65]

Dalton's employees were required to maintain and reference a 'gen' book, which provided 'general rules of thumb' information on dimensions, ratios and details for design and documentation. Dalton relied on his old Leeds textbooks *Building Construction* Volumes 1–3 (1943) by W.B. McKay, which Ham noted were more advanced than Australian codes on a range of issues including percentage of light required for rooms, insulation, tie-downs and bracing and weather conditioning. He notes that Dalton's recipe for stairs $2R + G = 24$ inches (610 mm) sits in the middle of the current code dimensional requirement for stairs. Dalton was most concerned with human scale and brought light switching and doorknobs down in height – to enable 'things to come to hand'.[66] He recognized a dimensional difference between British and Australian designs on the one hand, and Danish and Swedish designs on the other. The 900 mm height preferred by British for sills became the 720–50 mm preferred by the Scandinavians and handrails were at 865 mm [2 feet 8 inches], which Dalton called the 'feel height'.[67] Within the office projects were known by their client's names and only Government commissions were given a job number. The office managed projects on-site using a Job Book with double carbon copy. The Job Book would be taken to site, where instructions were written directly into the book and signed off by the builder on-site. One copy would be left with the builder.[68]

Both Chares Ham and Haig Beck recall intense conversations with Dalton on all manner of subjects – the lessons gleaned from early Australian buildings, climate determinism, energy consciousness, social responsibility, the ugliness creeping into Australia's cities.[69] No topic was out of bounds. Conversations on architecture were fuelled by articles from the many journals the office subscribed to over the years including *Abitare, Casabella, RIBA Journal, Progressive Architecture, The Architectural Review, The Japan Architect, Architecture and Urbanism, Domus, Schoner-Wohen* and *Architectural Design*. Ham recalls discussing the work of Corbusier and Aalto and key Australian figures including Bruce Rickardt, Pettit and Sevitt, but strangely not Glenn Murcutt. Murcutt had not yet achieved the critical acclaim he would in the 1990s and flew under the Dalton office radar. Time would be set aside for the whole office to explore tricky design problems such as master planning of units on a difficult site. Dalton would often cite Athol Bretnall, reminding his office 'we're only as good as the last magazine', which Ham interpreted to mean 'don't give up the hunt; keep looking'.[70]

Beck and Ham also recall that Dalton struggled with feelings of guilt over his deteriorating relationship with Sheila and his deepening entanglement with Sue Stirling (nee Crozier) whom he met in 1961. Suzanne (Sue) Elizabeth Crozier had grown up in Hunters Hill, a north shore suburb of Sydney, where she attended the prestigious Presbyterian Ladies College. When her father was appointed initially to oversee the establishment and later the management of Queensland Oil Refineries at Lytton, the Crozier family relocated to Brisbane in 1957, purchasing a house in Seventh Ave, St Lucia. Sue was enrolled at Somerville House but did not finish her schooling, because at the age of sixteen, she married Christopher (Kit) Stirling, the 21-year-old son of her St Lucia neighbours. Their daughter Fiona was born in 1958. Kit, who managed a family business with his brother Peter, was often away and Sue, left alone with a toddler, had limited opportunities to socialize. It was on a rare outing, accompanying a girlfriend to a party at the home of Bryan and Betty Kelly for members of the jazz band 'Varsity Five', that she met Dalton. Dalton's reputation was already established through rumour, good looking and charming but dangerous, and Sue was already acquainted with stories about his stormy relationship with Sheila.[71]

Dalton and Sue's relationship was not clandestine and Sheila tolerated the situation with stoicism. Whilst an extramarital relationship did not raise eyebrows within the community of artists and musicians that Sheila and Dalton frequented and Brisbane society ignored philandering behaviour when it was not on display, the more conservative members of the architecture profession were affronted by the open way Dalton and Sue conducted their relationship (Figure 1.7).[72] Their status as a couple appeared to be less of a concern to those close to Sue, as both her parents and her husband separately commissioned houses from Dalton. The Crozier (1961) and Stirling (1963) Houses are both located in Moggill.

FIGURE 1.7 Photograph of Sue Stirling and John Dalton c. 1962. Courtesy of Sue Dalton.

In 1964 Sue left her husband Kit Stirling to commence nursing, living in the nurses' quarters at St Andrew's War Memorial Hospital. After graduating at the top of her cohort she considered post-graduate study in Melbourne, but Dalton finally resolved his personal dilemma by leaving Sheila. In February 1968, Sue and Dalton moved into their new unit at 'Burrawood' (1965–6 demolished 2021) designed by Graham de Gruchy Architect (1924–). They married on 20 October 1972 after Dalton's divorce was finalized. Sheila returned to work as a teacher after her divorce but remained in the Dalton House at Fig Tree Pocket, living there until shortly before her death in 2015. She and Dalton remained on good terms.[73]

Until the mid-1970s, Dalton's work was published in professional journals more frequently than any other Queensland architect.[74] His early high profile owes much to the alignment of his practice with Melbourne-based *Architecture and Arts*, a journal that, like *Arts & Architecture*, the US journal it sought to emulate, had a particular focus on the modern house.[75] In the ten-year anniversary edition of *Architecture and Arts* in 1962 editor Kenneth McDonald addressed Dalton's work directly: 'In Queensland, by the time *Architecture and Arts* was getting on its feet by virtue of the amount of quality work being produced, suitable for inclusion in its pages, John Dalton had developed a strong personal approach to building which was primarily concerned with simplicity, sunlight and shadow.'[76] In the accompanying photographic survey Dalton's work was presented alongside work by Harry Seidler, Peter Muller, Arthur Baldwinson, and Robertson and Hindmarsh who practised in Sydney; David Chancellor, Grounds, Romberg and Boyd, John Mockridge and Peter McIntyre in Melbourne; and Cameron, Chisholm and Nichol in Western Australia – arguably Australia's most celebrated modernist architects at that time.

Between 1956 and 1987 work by Dalton and Heathwood and John Dalton Architect and Associates was recognized with local Institute awards and exhibited internationally, including in an exhibition of Australian architecture at the Lausanne Fair, Switzerland (1959); the Qantas Exhibition of Australian Architecture, London (1962); exhibitions at Expo 67 in Montreal, Canada (1967) and Expo 70 in Osaka, Japan (1970); in Vienna Austria (1970) and with the Australia Council's 'Old Continent New Buildings' Exhibition (1983). Dalton was also active in art and architecture in numerous other ways.

Between 1963 and 1971 he augmented his practice with part-time studio teaching in the Faculty of Architecture at the University of Queensland and was appointed to the Faculty Board in 1969. For many students Dalton personified stylish urbanity. Cohorts of young people would regularly gather in the apartment in 'Burrawood' to drink wine and talk, amongst them future UQ academics Peter O'Gorman and Paul Memmott. Dalton and Sue also made their thirty-eight-acre property at Brookfield, 'Capra' available to students for building experiments, an activity that was eventually banned by the then Chair of Architecture, Professor Gareth Roberts after complaints from neighbours about behaviour.[77] From

1967 Dalton wrote, published and circulated a series of handbills, *Broadside* and *diametrix* to students of architecture in Queensland. The demands of small practice and expense meant that he did not travel often but in 1969 he travelled with Landscape Architect, Arne Fink in South-East Asia and in 1970 a trip to Japan coincided with the Japan Expo in Osaka. In 1972, he and Sue, newly married, travelled together to the UK.

Dalton was elected to the Royal Australian Institute of Architects (RAIA) Queensland Chapter Council in 1966 serving until 1970, was elevated to Fellow of the RIBA in 1968 and of the RAIA in 1969, and to Life Fellow of the RAIA in 1982. In his roles as the anonymous Queensland contributor to *Cross-Section* (1960–73) and contributing editor to *Architecture in Australia* (1963–71) Dalton actively promoted Queensland architecture to a national audience. He also edited the CAS newsletter and the RAIA Queensland Chapter newsletter *Centreline* for several years, using these as a platform to promote contemporary art by his CAS friends to the local profession. He was an Executive Member of the Council for the Queensland Art Gallery Society (1960–74) and of the CAS Queensland Branch (1965–70). Whenever he could, Dalton promoted emerging issues, advocating for the role of art in architecture, principles of climate design and eventually environmental perspectives in architecture. He remained an inveterate letter writer and activist for architecture and design his entire life.

Dalton closed his city office in Queen Street in 1979. He was disenchanted with the profession, its development driven direction and its new fascination with Postmodernism. The economic downturn triggered by the 1973 Oil Crisis was particularly severe in Queensland, resulting in fewer commissions. Dalton's longest employee, Charles Ham had left to set up his own practice in 1978. Before winding up, Dalton found his most recent appointment, Peter Brown a position in the office of his friend Robin Gibson. Brown stayed in the strictly regimented 'Gibbo' office for three weeks before joining Hedley Kidd in Charles Ham's practice.[78]

For some years Dalton and Sue had spent an increasing proportion of their time at 'Lambtail', Allora with Dalton often leaving his Queen Street office on Thursday afternoon.[79] In 1979 the couple moved their primary residence to Allora in Dalton's words 'in search of the authentic Australian experience'.[80] Allora, a rural hamlet 160 kilometres south-west of Brisbane is located on the fertile Darling Downs at an elevation 600 metres above sea level. Its climate is characterized by a cool winter. This tree-change was confusing to Dalton's professional colleagues who interpreted it as retirement, rather than a retreat from the demands of full-scale practice. He continued to maintain a residence and office at 'Burrawood' and travelled back and forth between Brisbane and Allora. Although he completed several interesting projects, maintained his correspondence and began teaching again, this time at the Queensland Institute of Technology, he never regained the professional standing he had previously enjoyed. He died of cancer at Canossa Private Hospital, Oxley in 2007 aged seventy-nine.

Dalton is remembered as a complex character; his dark moods were challenging for family and employees. But he was also charming, interested and interesting, good company and never boring. His employees remember him as intense but personable, never a bully or rude – a very good mentor.[81] His humour was often self-deprecating, 'having a dig ….tongue in cheek'.[82]

Dalton's contribution to architecture was cemented in national and local histories of architecture very early in his career, framed in relation to climate-responsive modernist architecture.[83] In later narratives it was associated with regionalism. This narrative looks past the categories of style that are conventionally used to describe work to argue that Dalton's most important legacy is a socially responsible, materially efficient and precisely detailed architecture concerned with bringing occupants into proximity with their environment, an approach now understood to be an environmental approach.

Queensland is different: Climate conditioning local practice

At the time of Dalton's arrival, Queensland was both geographically and culturally remote from the major population centres of Sydney and Melbourne. Early accounts of Australian architecture, mostly by southern-base historians presented Queensland architecture as uninteresting,[84] or treated it separately on the basis of its (sub)tropical climate.[85] The view of Queensland architecture as a straightforward solution to the problems posed by subtropical or tropical climate has a long history.

The state of Queensland covers a vast area and varies in climate from hot humid tropical and savannah in the north, to arid in the west and temperate in the southeast. It is prone to regular natural disasters including droughts, floods and the impact of tropical cyclones along its coastline. Due to coastal ranges and wide river estuaries, it developed a decentralized settlement and infrastructure pattern. The issues impacting European settlement in Queensland differed from those in southern colonies setting its social and cultural trajectory on a slightly divergent course and leading to its reputation for being laid-back and easy-going. A consequence of decentralization was that a large proportion of the population lived in towns along the coastline and not in the capital city of Brisbane located in the southeast corner of the state. The obstacles confronting European settlers in Queensland meant scholarly forums were more engaged with colonial debates around issues of acclimatization to tropical conditions.[86] The view that tropical climates were degenerative and unhealthy for European settlement underpinned much of this debate, persisting to inform research in tropical medicine and impacting matters of health and housing for the tropics.[87] Research escalated during and after the Second World War, conducted by the Queensland Tropical

House Committee (QTHC) established by the State Government in 1942 and the Commonwealth Experimental Building Station (CEBS) established in 1944 at Ryde, Sydney.[88] Initially the interests of the CEBS and the QTHC were aligned in defining conditions for comfort in relation to the tropical house, thereby ensuring the dominance of climate science in Queensland's architectural discourse.[89] Research confirmed principles for climate-responsive design in the tropics: the need to orientate north-south; to shade elevations to reduce solar heat gain and glare through overhangs and screens in summer; to maximize cross-ventilation including through manipulation of building cross-section to achieve pressure gradients capable of generating air movements.

Two publications by architects connected with these government initiatives became particularly influential in promoting climate-responsive modernism in architecture. Walter Ralston Bunning (1912–77), an executive officer of the Commonwealth Housing Commission and founding member of the short-lived Modern Architectural Research Society, published *Homes in the Sun* in 1945,[90] whilst Karl Langer, a non-executive member of the QTHC, published *Subtropical Housing* in 1944. Langer used *Subtropical Housing* to promote modernist architecture and modern town planning principles from the perspective of physiological need – 'the avoidance of fatigue', 'the provision of light and avoidance of glare' and 'economy'.[91] It was illustrated with plans made by Campbell Scott of airy, slab-on-ground pavilions oriented for sun penetration and breezes and with living spaces opening into patios and garden settings. In the minds of young Queensland practitioners these designs resonated with images of West Coast American architecture, which they saw illustrated in journals such as *Arts & Architecture*. As Australian culture and politics pivoted away from British influence towards the United States in the post-war years, open, airy pavilions were seen as the appropriate architecture to support the lifestyle that they and their clients now aspired to. In this way, climate became strongly implicated in the reception of modernism in Queensland.

Langer's promotion of modernism was realized through a thinly veiled critique of the vernacular domestic building type, widely referred to as the Queensland house. Referred to here as 'vernacular' to distinguish it from other more permanent and architect designed colonial buildings, this house is a timber bungalow, typical of bungalows found in other British colonies, elevated on stumps above the ground with verandahs and a pyramid roof (Figure 1.8). The experience of growing up in one is deeply embedded in the psyche of generations of Queensland citizens and the distinctive character of suburban Brisbane is derived from its repetition across an undulating topography. It is intrinsic to Queensland's cultural identity, its qualities and affinity with the rampant vegetation of its garden setting celebrated in art, poetry and poetic prose.[92] Yet references to the Queensland house in architectural writing from the 1950s reveal its paradoxical position in relation to modernist architecture: members of the QTHC including Langer argued that its interior rooms were dark and airless and the source of physiological discomfort – an unsatisfactory model for climate-responsive housing in the subtropics – whereas

FIGURE 1.8 Generic Queensland house, possibly Ipswich. Photo taken by John Dalton. Courtesy of Sue Dalton.

its form was championed by Australia's foremost architectural critic Robin Boyd (1919–71) and his Brisbane-based colleague Peter Newell (1916–2010) as holding the potential for a 'Corbu style transformation' in domestic architecture.[93] In 'St Lucia: A housing revolution is taking place' (1950) Boyd and Newell identified in the work of young architects in the suburb of St Lucia, the seeds of an 'architect instigated revolution', which they hoped would eventually deliver the much-anticipated modernist transformation of the 'Brisbane style'.[94] Boyd defined 'Brisbane style' in the *Australia's Home: Its Origins, Builders, and Occupiers* (1952) as a timber version of southern models of domestic architecture but raised on 'stilts',[95] and the result of Brisbane architects' penchant for following southern 'styles' rather than innovative thought.

Dalton's arrival in Brisbane, his architectural education and his early artistic pursuits occurred against the backdrop of this debate about climate and the efficacy of Queensland's popular vernacular house. As the 'other' to a modern architecture, this house cannot be ignored for it will be seen that Dalton along with his colleagues selectively borrowed elements of its form and abstracted its characteristics. Appropriation and translation increased the points of resonance between the traditional house and the mid-century climate-responsive house.

The scale of this resonance is aptly demonstrated in *Buildings of Queensland* (1959), one of the earliest histories of Queensland architecture published by the Royal Australian Institute of Architects Queensland Chapter to commemorate the Centenary of Queensland's separation from New South Wales. In *Buildings of Queensland*, instances of climate-responsive mid-century modern architecture are described through reference to the characteristics they shared with the vernacular house.[96] The Jacobi House (1957) by Hayes & Scott is described as 'a small house embodying the traditional stumps and verandah on three sides'.[97] The Speare House

FIGURE 1.9 The Speare House (1958) and Jacobi House (1957) were illustrated together in the RAIA Queensland Chapter publication *Buildings in Queensland* (1959). EJA Weller, *Buildings of Queensland*, page 27. Copyright Institute of Architects Queensland Chapter.

(1958) by Dalton and Heathwood 'uses traditional trellis and perforated underbuilding in a fresh form' (Figure 1.9).[98] The Head House (1956) also by Dalton and Heathwood is described as 'a simple shaped home showing the continued use of the verandah.'[99] Through their persistent iteration as exemplars of Queensland architecture in publications, journals and popular magazines the Jacobi, Speare and Dalton (John Dalton Architect & Associates, 1960) houses became the enduring images of Queensland's modernist architecture throughout Australia.[100] This narrative was only replaced from the mid-1970s when the vernacular tradition, its historical references and constructional systems became the source of inspiration for a new generation of young practitioners. In the latter half of the twentieth century, historical accounts of Queensland architecture were more typically framed through reference to Critical Regionalism; the Jacobi, Speare and Dalton Houses were superseded by images of work that more explicitly referenced a vernacular tectonic such as Gabriel Poole's Schubert House (1972) (Figure 1.10) and Rex Addison's Taringa House (1975).

Explicit references to an environmental approach in Australian architecture did not occur until historical accounts written in the 1990s. In these accounts, an environmental approach is linked by commentators and historians to the activities of certain architects working in the 1970s; Dalton is included on this list of 'protoenvironmentalist' architects. Amongst the first to identify Dalton's contribution to an environmental approach was architect and historian Jennifer Taylor (1935–2015), who in *Australian Architecture Since 1960* (1985) identified Dalton as 'the principal voice for the neglected merits of the Queensland environment'.[101]

FIGURE 1.10 Schubert House, Yandina, 1972. Gabriel Poole. Photo Gabriel Poole. Copyright Elizabeth Poole.

In *Australian Architects: Rex Addison, Lindsay Clare and Russell Hall* (1990) Queensland academic Michael Keniger (1947–) noted that 'John Dalton came to specialise in extracting the most quality possible from a site and its environment through a considered placement of the building and through a studied control of its elements in plan and section.'[102] Sydney architect and author Graham Jahn (1958–) is possibly the first to identify Dalton with an explicitly environmental architecture, one focusing not only on physical and contextual circumstances but also on an awareness of the consequences of design decisions for material efficiency, energy and budget. In *Contemporary Australian Architecture* (1994) Jahn argued that considerations such as the need to address site and climate with very limited budgets are intrinsic to a socially and ethically aware practice of architecture. He linked characteristics observed in the work of certain architects in the 1970s to an emergent environmental practice in the 1990s and included John Dalton alongside Ken Woolley and members of the Sydney School in New South Wales, Graeme Gunn and David Glashen in Melbourne and Gabriel Poole and Patrick Moroney in Queensland as architects who 'produced case study designs which harnessed environmental factors in a modest "low style" fashion of bagged brickwork and split skillion roofs and highly resolved detailing'.[103] Jahn describes these architects as:

> regionally inspired, modernist-sympathisers who relied on detail and invention and were essentially confined to residential design. They shared an approach that was largely anti-art, anti-style and anti-establishment; squarely aimed at issues of life-quality, justifiable use of land, materials and energy resources. It was a quiet, low maintenance ideology of social responsibility.[104]

Jahn notes that although proto-environmental architects practising in the 1970s influenced a subsequent generation of environmentally aware architects, they received little recognition for this aspect of their practice either at the time or in subsequent years. Some, like Dalton and Poole received belated recognition when their work was noted in exhibitions and publications arising from the Queensland Government sponsored initiative HEAT: *Queensland's new wave of environmental architects*.[105] Intended to promote Queensland architecture within Queensland and to facilitate the export of architectural and related design services to South-East Asia and China, HEAT acknowledges a tradition of environmentalist thinking in Queensland – a lightweight and permeable architecture tuned to site, climate and way of life – which it argued is continuing. John Dalton is cited as influential but his role in effecting a turn to environmental thinking is not elaborated upon.

The 'Environmental Era' begins: Architecture's re-turn to environment

As Dalton's practice flourished during the 1960s, matters of environmental degradation erupted into public consciousness globally. Whilst environmental historians concede it is difficult to date the onset of modern environmental consciousness with any precision,[106] its geneses is often associated with the 1962 publication of Rachel Carson's *Silent Spring*, which linked the disappearance of native habitat to intensive agricultural practices.[107] A raft of scientific publications drew attention to the sudden escalation of environmental alteration brought about by increased consumerism and cheap energy prices during the 1950s and 1960s.[108] Sometimes referred to as the Environmental Era, the period between 1960 and the new millennium marks a time when humans realized they were not the centre of their world, that they were responsible for the degradation of their own planet and that they needed to act immediately to address the problems created by science and industry.[109] Predictions of imminent ecological collapse galvanized the environmental movement globally; in reality not a single movement but an assortment of often single-issue focused campaigns deploying approaches from the scientific and rational, to the mystical, the awareness raising and political.[110] In Queensland, the developmental ethos characteristic of a colonial mindset persisted, meaning that environmental degradation continued unchecked.[111] Even in sleepy Brisbane, the pollution of land, the river and its tributaries arising from the poor siting of industry, unrestricted suburban development, a lack of basic infrastructure and traffic congestion was becoming increasingly problematic.

Younger Australian architects encountered environmentalism through activism in relation to specific issues such as the proposed destruction of historic inner-city suburbs to make way for infrastructure or urban renewal projects. Others encountered environmentalism through one of the other correlated political, social and cultural changes confronting society during the 1960s. Activism and protests – against the escalation of the Vietnam War, ballot conscription, unsympathetic development in cities, or in support of feminist campaigns such as equal pay for equal work and recognition and reparation for Australia's First Nations people – galvanized the younger generation. The Cold War, brought closer by Australia's military alliance with USA added to anxiety by raising the spectre of nuclear annihilation. Modern environmentalism was just one more front in a significant generational and counter-cultural divide. In Queensland, any challenge to authority was thwarted by the increasingly authoritarian regime of Johannes Bjelke-Petersen (1911–2005), Premier of Queensland from 1968 to 1987 whose term is remembered today for its restriction of liberties, extension of police power and institutional corruption. The impact of Bjelke-Petersen's conservativism on the intellectual and artistic life of Queensland was substantial. Radical thought, previously tolerated, was suppressed, marches were violently repressed and ultimately banned and an exodus of artists and young intellectuals to southern states ensued.

Within the discipline of architecture, the 1960s environmental turn correlated with critiques of modernist design processes, their focus on functionalism and centralized planning and lack of regard for local circumstances. It correlated with the emergence of radical new postmodern theories, the recovery of history, and challenges to architecture from the new fields of landscape and urbanism. The notion of environment as a dynamic, open-ended web of interactions – an ecology – prompted interest in network and systems thinking. Although a global trend and embraced by a younger generation of architects, the significance of environmentalism, and the opportunities it presented, was overlooked by much of the Brisbane profession.

Yet amongst many academics the transdisciplinary character of environment was welcomed for its capacity to link the humanities and the sciences, to challenge boundaries and provide insights into the complex questions confronting a modern world. This awareness was reflected in the establishment of programs of environment studies and environmental science in new universities built to accommodate a generation of young adults, born during the post-war baby boom. New programmes of architecture adopted names incorporating environment and established programmes contemplated name changes. In 1957, landscape architect Ian McHarg introduced a seminar course titled 'Man and Environment' at the University of Pennsylvania.[112] Ian Bentley delivered a series of lectures titled 'Responsive Environments' at the Department of Architecture and the Joint Centre for Urban Design at Oxford Polytechnic and in 1970 Richard Llewellyn-Davies established a programme in environmental design at The Bartlett School of Architecture, University College London.[113] Closer to home, the Queensland Institute of Technology (QIT), the former CTC, introduced an interdisciplinary

School of the Built Environment in 1975[114] whilst the Faculty of Architecture at the University of Queensland began investigating the introduction of a Faculty of Environmental Design in 1969.[115] Many architecture programmes introduced 'man [sic] environment studies' into their curriculums, thereby bringing into focus the social and political consequences of architecture in the design of environments. Such courses contributed to critiques of modern planning and design processes as insensitive and alienating.

These more radical changes to the discipline of architecture induced by the social and political press of the 1960s intersected with discourses already underway and evident in the earlier writings of key figures in architecture such as Lewis Mumford, Richard Neutra and Richard Buckminster Fuller, and in other fields such as philosopher and educationalist John Dewey. Mumford and Neutra both drew from empirical research in fields such as bioscience and psycho-physiology to form their conceptions of human-environment interactions. They already understood that the planet was in a state of crisis of human making but believed it capable of rescue through planning and design. Mumford who was concerned with the relationship between technology and liveability in the recovery of the earth's equilibrium warned of the consequences to environment of unfettered growth and the unchecked use of technology in *Technics and Civilization* (1934) and the *Culture of Cities* (1938). Neutra, leaning on his experience of working with Frank Lloyd Wright, believed that liveability – individual and community happiness and emotional equilibrium – could only be achieved through organically oriented design.[116] In *Survival Through Design* (1954) Neutra set out principles for the practice of an environmental architecture directed at bringing humans into harmony with their natural world, which he saw as essential to 'organic evolution'. Tellingly, Neutra's principles focused on the experience of the occupant in an environmental setting and not on the expression of an architectural form. His writings project a modern view of environment – derived from his reading in science – as dynamic and open-ended with humans integrated in a symbiotic, rather than hierarchical relationship with nature. Such proto-environmentalist conceptions fascinated Dalton, and colour his writing from the 1960s and the gearing of his practice towards an environmental approach over time.

Myth and identity: Australia's 'fictional landscapes'[117]

The spread of environmentalism in the 1960s also intersected with European Australians growing appreciation for Australian landscapes. Landscape had long been implicated in the construction of a distinctive national identity.[118] Amongst the culturally constructed tropes for this identity were images embodying myths of a (white) settler culture, a convenient trope that excluded the vanquished and dispossessed Aboriginal and Torres Strait Islander people. At the time of Dalton's practice, and despite the range of topographies and climates across the continent, one particular landscape image attached to this myth became ingrained in the Australian psyche – the image of a settler's homestead in a vast interior landscape. The image embodies the fiction of (white) settlers pushing into the continent's interior and along its coastline, thwarted by and overcoming the forces of nature and the resistance of First Nations people. Such myths emphasize individual personal freedom and self-determination in a supposedly class-free society and ignore the motivation for settlement; to profit from the supply of raw materials and produce to Europe.[119] Settler myths rely on the concept of *terra nullius*, which in a sense licenced the Frontier Wars, and was not overturned until the 1992 Mabo judgement in the High Court of Australia established the existence of Native Title in Australian Common Law.

The settler myth is evoked in an editorial essay in the June 1961 edition of *Architecture and Arts* titled 'Post War Domestic Architecture' that focuses on identifying the shared characteristics of form that might underpin a national style.[120] It was projected to a global audience in exhibitions of Australian art and in official exhibits at international expos in Montreal (1967) and Osaka (1970) curated by Robin Boyd.[121] Some twenty years later the myth is evident in the images selected by Haig Beck and Jackie Cooper for the front matter of the 1984 edition of *International Architect,* titled *Detailing, National Identity, and a Sense of Place in Australian Architecture*. The cover of *International Architect* features a delicate pencil illustration by Noela Hills of the Birdsville Hall (1983) designed by Richard Allom Architect and documented by Robert Riddel, its sheltering roof etched against the arc of a desert horizon confirming the fragility of human habitation in a vast and relentless landscape. In his foreword for this edition of *International Architect*, Daryl Jackson acknowledges that by the 1980s the majority of Australian people lived on the edge of the Australian continent, not in its arid heart, and in suburban settings, not the bush. Despite the settler myth having lost its relationship to truth, Jackson expresses his view of architecture as a 'cultural mediator that entails mythmaking as an exploratory survival technique'.[122] The Australian Council Design Arts Board kept the settler myth alive in the 1980s through their selection of architecture to exhibit internationally. The Board's preference for a touch-this-earth-lightly, lightweight idiom of exposed steel frames and corrugated iron taps into what Melbourne academics Paul Walker and Karen Burns describe as the 'fictional landscapes' of bush mythology.[123]

The darker side of settler myths was first revealed by artists such as Arthur Boyd whose poignant depictions of half-caste child brides reveal the artist's distress on visiting Central Australia in 1953 and witnessing the plight of First Nations people. Today, 'settlement' myths have been thoroughly unpacked by scholars, including Henry Reynolds, Bill Gammage, Tom Griffiths and Libby Robin and most recently by film and television screenwriter and director,

Arrernte and Kalkadoon woman, Rachel Perkins, and reframed as the violent dispossession and occupation of Aboriginal and Torres Strait Islander people's country.[124] But when John Dalton completed banners for the 1954 visit of Queen Elizabeth II which incorporated Aboriginal imagery in a decorative way and when he commenced his practice in 1956, settler myths were a dominant trope. As an Englishman they were not his myths; he was introduced to them as an outsider but embraced them nevertheless as intrinsic to the physical and cultural landscapes he was responding to.

White Australians awakening to the beauty of native landscapes is evident from the beginning of the twentieth century, most particularly in a preoccupation within the arts with Australian landscapes and flora and fauna.[125] This awakening is also documented in the activities of local historical and arts societies, bushwalking groups, the demise of Acclimatization Societies, and even the biographies of pioneering families.[126] Yet the historiography of landscape design in Australia has been developed only recently and is already being overtaken by another imperative – the desire to understand country, its flora and fauna from First Nations people's perspectives. This desire became an urgent need in the twenty-first century after a series of catastrophic fires and floods, drew into focus and seeded a new respect for Aboriginal and Torres Strait Islander people's deep knowledge of country. However, this narrative returns to an earlier point in time when environment was just emerging into view as a concern with political, social and ecological dimensions and when destruction of the fragile beauty of the Australian environment was becoming evident to all. It is interested in how new insights into environment impacted the making of architecture.

Today an environmental approach to architecture is understood as a deliberate approach underpinned by thinking that posits humans as living beings, inseparable from and shaped by the environments in which they live. Environmental thinking manifests in an architecture informed by intentions concerned to bring humans into a closer association with their world and necessarily privileges the experience of humans, understood as social, emotional and physiological beings. Such a view, which was beginning to emerge into focus in Australia during the 1960s, intersected in Queensland, with an existing disciplinary preoccupation with climate responsive design. This narrative focuses on unpacking the circumstances of this intersection as it impacted the thinking and practice of one Brisbane architect, John Dalton.

2 DISCOVERING THE IDIOMATIC: DETAIL IN ART AND ARCHITECTURE

In September 1959, an article titled 'Four houses' in *Architecture and Arts* showcased materially efficient, climate-responsive modernist houses by the young practice Dalton & Heathwood, Architects. In accompanying text, the two recently graduated architects claimed they 'hoped to live long enough to see the end of craft building methods and the advent of industrialised building technique'. They also expressed commitment to architecture's 'social responsibility to the future'.[1] Shortly afterwards, between 1960 and 1964 Dalton published a series of polemical texts in *Architecture and Arts* and *Architecture in Australia* arguing for the interdependence of the technical and the artistic and promoting the sun as the source of phenomenon to be manipulated for sensory delight. Architecture's real purpose, Dalton now claimed, was to dispense 'joy' and 'happiness,' and not merely the physiological 'comfort' expected of climate-responsive design.[2] Texts reveal another new conviction – Dalton's belief that the technical and aesthetic dimensions of architecture intersect in the detail. Although his views at this stage have been criticized by some as inchoate or even as a posturing, it is clear Dalton believed that the poetic dimensions of architecture relied on attention to detail and that the poetic was spatial and experiential, not merely formal. In intimating possibilities for resonance with prior experiences, Dalton revealed the extent to which he recognized affinities between modern architecture and the traditional Queensland house.

By 1964 Dalton had adopted 'sunlight, shade and shadow' as a personal manifesto, one that he promoted widely in both the architectural and popular press, including in 'women's' magazines such as *Australian Home Beautiful* which were much maligned by his colleagues. By 1964 a shift is also discernible from a focus on form and its precise detailing to the capacity of detail for architectural expression and spatial experience. What discoveries prompted this shift? Tracing the development of Dalton's thinking through his painting and polemical writing provides a lens onto the development of his architectural preoccupations at a time when they were just coming into view.

Dalton & Heathwood Architects: The Plywood Exhibition House

Much has been written about the importance of climate and comparatively little about the role of the construction detail in mid-century modernist architecture in Queensland. The resources-reliant boom-bust economy of Queensland was, and always had been, less secure than that of other states. A low manufacturing base meant that materials were difficult to obtain and more expensive than in southern states, especially during the housing sector boom that occurred after the lifting of post-Second World War building restrictions in 1952. The conservative culture, a benign climate and out-door lifestyle induced a disinterest in architecture: in his *Australia's Home* (1952), Robin Boyd noted a lack of 'house-proudness' and a greater interest in yachts and cars.[3] But for young architects, expensive materials and shortages in supply ensured a greater commitment to design innovation in the pursuit of a rational structure and material efficiency. A culture of invention and ingenious solutions developed within a very narrow frame of reference. Early houses by Dalton & Heathwood Architects were achieved on very small budgets and were notable for their functional planning, attention to principles of climate design and the clarity of their formal composition. Every element necessary for construction also contributed to a compositional integrity. Dalton's experience in Leeds designing pre-fabricated houses for a global market would have instilled a comprehensive knowledge of and facility with the technical aspects of building and construction. Both Dalton and Heathwood had worked with Campbell Scott who drilled his student employees in planning to accommodate material standardization, fastidious detailing and an understanding of the consequences of detail resolution for formal expression. From Scott, Dalton learnt the importance of a datum for integrating diverse elements and establishing a unified expression; the belt rail under a bank of windows would become a characteristic Dalton detail. He also examined the work of international architects, including work by Alvar Aalto, Arne Jacobson and the architects of the Case Study program in Los Angeles.[4]

John Dalton and Peter Heathwood established their practice after graduating in 1956, using prize money from a Queensland Plywood Board Corporation-sponsored competition calling for the design of a house demonstrating the contemporary use of plywood products. As part-time students, they had both worked for six years in other architects' practices whilst studying and recognized in the competition an opportunity to launch their careers as independent

practitioners. They both submitted entries to the competition and formed a pact that if one or other of them won the £3000 prize on offer they would use it to establish a partnership.[5] Heathwood's entry was successful and in late 1956 Dalton & Heathwood Architects opened their office in Queen Street, Brisbane City.[6] The winning scheme was announced in Brisbane's *Courier Mail* newspaper as the 'House of Tomorrow', a by-line appropriated from media coverage of Robin Boyd's 1949 'House of Tomorrow'. It was illustrated with a perspective drawn by Dalton complete with his characteristic *l'homme architecturale*. Dalton documented the winning design for construction whilst Heathwood was on his honeymoon (Figure 2.1) and it was built at the Exhibition Showgrounds, Newstead, in time for the Royal National Show in August 1957.

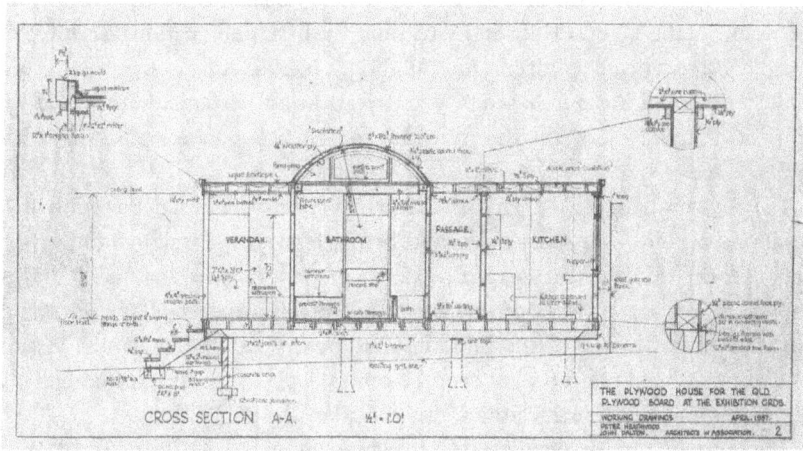

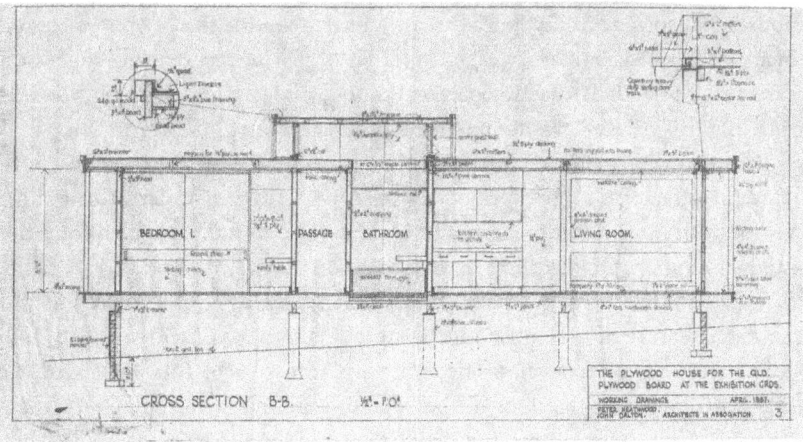

FIGURE 2.1 Plywood Exhibition House, 1957, designed by Peter Heathwood. Sections drawn by John Dalton. Courtesy of Sue Dalton.

By the 1950s plywood had been rehabilitated globally as a material for architecture; its potential for economy and standardization was already well established by Richard Neutra's 1936 'Plywood Model Demonstration House' in Los Angeles,[7] Marcel Breuer's 1949 'House in the Garden' for the Museum of Modern Art, New York, and the Case Study Houses in Los Angeles from 1945. Together with numerous local exemplars including Boyd's 'House of Tomorrow' constructed at the Melbourne Show Grounds, these exhibition houses had already confirmed plywood as intrinsic to a modern aesthetic and modern design[8]. Yet, Brisbane citizens still associated ply with holiday beach shacks and industrial sheds. The Queensland Plywood Board Corporation design competition sought to change the perception of a largely sceptical local housing market. By March 1958 over 100,000 people – one fifth of Brisbane's population – are recorded as having visited the Plywood Exhibition House at the RNA Showgrounds.[9] It also attracted interest from the profession and in 1958 was named by *Architecture and Arts* as one of the '10 Best Houses in Australia', the first time a national architecture award had recognized a Queensland building.[10] In 1963 it was offered for sale by public tender and was purchased by Peter Heathwood's sister and brother-in-law, Don and Patricia Marshall who moved it to The Gap where it remains to this day.[11]

The Plywood Exhibition House comprised a raised framed box with three elevations to view – the fourth elevation being set against a wall to a railway line embankment. Arrival and departure were by sets of wide 'floating' stairs. An emphatically flat roof was considered an acceptable experiment in subtropical Brisbane, only because of the building's temporary exhibition nature. A non-ventilating skylight pop-up vault over the centrally placed bathroom was hailed as 'a dramatic and functional feature well received by the public'.[12]

The house adopts an efficient square plan form, organized as a circuit for the purposes of display and based on a three-foot module – the size of a plywood sheet. It incorporates a variety of styles and profiles of ply internally including striated and textured plywoods, plastic-coated plywoods and marine-grade plywoods for wet areas. Ply is painted, stained or left natural. There is a nod to Alvar Aalto in the detailed treatment of a single internal column.

Careful attention to the principles of climate design orders the building envelope with each elevation responding differently to the particular conditions contingent upon it. On the north, a deep terrace and entry deck excluded summer sun and admitted winter sun. The east and west edges contained the most remarkable feature of the house, the 'fernery' – a narrow three-foot-deep slot of space between the glazed wall of the house and three sets of Thurlow blinds fixed between the roof and the floor at the edge of building form. Thurlow blinds, a proprietary timber venetian blind, were the traditional treatment for verandah edges in Queensland houses and had previously been used by Dalton working with Robin Gibson in the Day House (1955) for Theo Thynne and Associates.[13]

In a traditional Queensland house, the 'fernery' is an extension of the verandah space used for propagating exotic orchids and ferns.¹⁴ It is a space that Heathwood would have been familiar with through childhood experiences, not Dalton. The Plywood Exhibition House 'fernery' addressed multiple design issues. It addressed the problem of low sun angles in morning and afternoon. It provided the equivalent of large roof overhangs and deep shadow without the loss of formal qualities, and enabled air movement and cross ventilation without the loss of privacy. Its formal expression enabled comparisons to be made with the traditional Queensland house, whilst delivering a modern pavilion with a tri-partite expression; like the Queensland house it was a timber framed and braced box but braced with ply rather than vertical-jointed boards and with an horizontal expression. It was also a solution that addressed the major criticism levied by proponents of modernism at the spaces of the Queensland house; that the interior rooms of the Queensland house were dark and airless. The question of how to reconcile a layered edge and the need for light and ventilation was an ongoing debate for young Queensland architects. It was a question that Gabriel Poole recalls perplexed Dalton when they worked together at Theo Thynne and Associates and that Poole would solve in a different way some years later in his celebrated Schubert House, Yandina, (1972).¹⁵ In the Plywood Exhibition House through a conflation of verandah and living space, the interior spaces moved to the edge of the house and are light filled, open and outwardly looking.

'Four Houses' by Dalton & Heathwood, Architects

The publicity surrounding the Plywood Exhibition House proved enormously beneficial for the young practice and commissions followed for houses, flats and commercial fitouts. Four houses by Dalton and Heathwood featured in an article in *Architecture and Arts* in September 1959 including the Semi-Rural House (1956) and Spinks (1956) Houses attributed to Dalton, and the Speare (1958 demolished) and Brennan (1959) Houses attributed to Heathwood.¹⁶ Each project is described through a short text and the 'clean line' drawings adopted by Dalton thereafter for publication of his work. In a preamble on the leading page of the spread, the pair expressed a commitment to 'industrialised building technique' and alongside Brisbane architect, Campbell Scott, they cited Lewis Mumford as influential in the formation of their shared view that 'the Architect's social responsibility is to the future' (Figure 2.2).¹⁷

The acknowledgement of Mumford is an interesting declaration and may have prompted *Architecture and Arts* editor, Kenneth McDonald, to publish 'An Address to Students of Architecture in Rome' – Mumford's synopsis of his thesis in *The Transformations of Man* (1956) – in a subsequent edition of the journal. In his

FIGURE 2.2 'Four Houses by John Dalton and Peter Heathwood Architects', *Architecture and Arts* (September 1959), page 58.

'Address' Mumford warned of the consequences of the ignorant use by humans of their scientifically and technically enhanced powers, arguing that modern humans' capacity to dominate and subdue nature should not confuse the task of architects which is to address the needs of life in all its dimensions.[18] Dalton and Heathwood would also have been aware of the proto-environmentalist writings of Richard Neutra in which he argued that architecture was about the design of 'a properly scaled environment corresponding to the needs of human beings' not elaborate sculptural forms.[19] Karl Langer used Neutra's *Mystery and Realities of the Site: Richard Neutra on Building* (1951) as a teaching resource in his lecture course on garden and landscape design at the University of Queensland and Heathwood and Dalton would have been familiar with it.[20] Whilst Dalton did not have amongst his own books a copy of *Mystery and Realities* or *Survival through Design* (1954) also by Neutra, he did have a first edition of *Richard Neutra: 1950–60: Buildings and Projects (1959)* which included a number of essays by Neutra including 'The New and the Old in Architecture' in which he challenged architects to be alert to environmental stimulii.[21] It is inconceivable that Dalton was not familiar with

Neutra's arguments for architecture to be 'organically oriented' and an 'extension' of humans' physical and sensory system.[22]

A short quote printed in a different font and located in the top left-hand corner of the first page of the five-page spread, 'Four Houses' reads almost as an afterthought. 'Sunlight, shade and shadow are the only constants from which we derive our Architectural form' is the first indicator of Dalton's emerging interest in architecture's expressive capacity. In comparison much of the commentary in 'Four Houses' addresses the practical and programmatic requirements of each individual project, describing in a clipped style how each house utilized proprietary insulation products and addressed the fierce summer sun, heat load and glare or captured the cooling breezes.[23] Particular attention is given to describing the effort taken to achieve cross-ventilation and northern aspect in compact plan arrangements. In the Semi-Rural House, also known as the Head House, the master bedroom steps out to the eaves line to achieve exposure to the north, whereas in the Spinks House the verandah is replaced by a deep corner porch enabling the living room to have some northern aspect. In comparison, the Speare and Brennan Houses achieve cross-ventilation through variation in roof height, ventilating roof forms and the placement of external spaces. The Speare House utilizes a ventilating lantern over an open plan whereas the Brennan House, a comparatively large house with a linear plan of double-banked rooms, a pop-up roof creates a clerestory running the length of the house.[24] A sun-court further assists with cross-ventilation and sun penetration in the Brennan House whilst the sub-floor was excavated for under-floor ventilation.

Only in the description of the Speare house, where fixed lattice panels wrapped around the entire pavilion replacing the Thurlow blinds used in the Plywood Exhibition House, is text expansive, extending beyond the practical to describe how a climate-driven solution might also give rise to a distinctive architectural expression: 'By day the building is a serene and solid mass, at night its full sense of lightness and delicacy is revealed when the light pours through the myriad tiny openings and the great roof lantern floats on a flood of light' (Figure 2.3).[25] The Speare House coincided with Dalton's deepening realization of the significance of the sensory in architecture, the significance of which was assisted by his other activities, most notably his painting.

The Speare House was nominated by Melbourne architect and critic Robin Boyd for inclusion in the Australian Government's 'Domestic Architecture in Australia' exhibition at the Lausanne Fair, Switzerland in September 1960. This important acknowledgement coincided with a deterioration in relations between Dalton and Heathwood. A letter of invitation to Dalton & Heathwood Architects from the Director of Trade, Commonwealth Department of Trade dated April 1960 noted that the Speare House 'represents a good modern version of the Brisbane vernacular'.[26] It achieved the transformation of the local vernacular that Boyd and colleague Peter Newell had anticipated in their article 'St Lucia: A Housing Revolution in Taking Place in Brisbane' published in

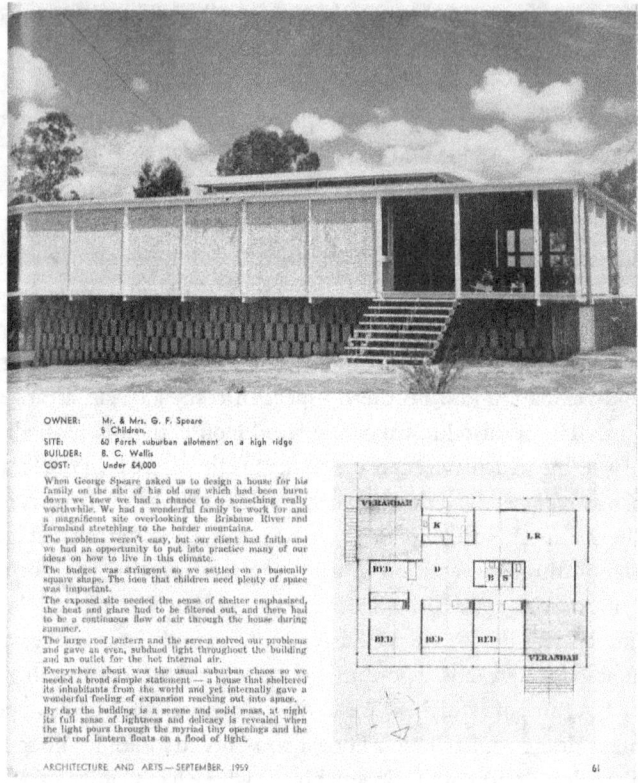

FIGURE 2.3 Speare House, Dalton and Heathwood Architects, 'Four Houses', *Architecture and Arts* (September 1959), page 61.

Architecture in July 1950.²⁷ However, by the end of 1960 only Dalton remained in the Queen Street office to continue practice as John Dalton Architect & Associates.²⁸

The Semi-Rural and Brennan Houses (both demonstrating the 'verandah tradition') and the Speare House by Dalton and Heathwood and Dalton House by John Dalton Architect & Associates (both demonstrating 'tropical and semi-tropical control') were amongst works selected by Kenneth McDonald, to illustrate an editorial essay, 'Post War Domestic Architecture' published in *Architecture and Arts* in June 1961.²⁹ They were presented alongside houses located in Melbourne by David Chancellor, Grounds Romberg and Boyd and Peter and Dione McIntyre and Associates, in Sydney by Sydney Ancher and Harry Seidler, in Adelaide by Lawson, Cheesman and Doley and the ES&A Bank Managers House in Darwin by Stuart McIntyre. All are photographed externally. Editorial commentary links these houses to settler myths: 'If modern architecture has a link with our colonial beginnings than these houses reveal this link'.³⁰ Differences are swept aside in favour of generalizations identifying the shared characteristics of a modernity that might be said to underpin a national 'style'. Despite vastly different climates, editorial attributes 'unmistakable similarities between the architecture of north and south Australia' to 'wide and sweeping eaves' and a 'common regard and sympathy for the use of natural materials – a reliance by almost all on some form of modular planning and expression and provision for some form of indoor-outdoor living facilities.'[31] Adjustments were noted as being necessary only in southern homes in order to accommodate greater variations in temperature. The Semi-Rural (Head) House was very similar to a number of houses by Dalton at this time including the Walker and Spinks House (Figure 2.4). An understated gable structure located in the foothills of Mt Coot-tha in the western suburbs of Brisbane, the Semi-Rural (Head) House was given special attention in 'Post War Domestic Architecture': 'The finest example of the old colonial days, here achieved in a simple, modest but charming little three-bedroom home, which the architects have referred to as "an anonymous design incorporating the local vernacular"'.[32]

'Post War Domestic Architecture' contributed to an on-going debate around the place of colonial architecture in the development of an Australian modernism. Robin Boyd had initiated this debate in *Victorian Modern: One Hundred and Eleven Years of Modern Architecture in Victoria, Australia* (1948) by linking a modern Victorian Type to both a colonial past and, and a regionalist modernism emanating from the Bay Region of California and promoted as a more sensitive alternative to mainstream orthodox modern architecture.[33] In a subsequent essay, 'Port Phillip Idiom: Recent Houses in the Melbourne Region' published in *Architectural Review* in 1952, Boyd aligned Melbourne's domestic architecture with 'New Empiricism', another regionally inflected body of work, this time by Scandinavian architects concerned with an alternative and more humanist modernism. In this essay Boyd differentiates a 'family likeness' that arises from the unselfconscious use of traditional construction techniques in practical and

FIGURE 2.4 Perspective by Dalton of Spinks House, 1956, Dalton and Heathwood Architects. Courtesy of Sue Dalton.

functional ways and the more self-conscious referencing of a 'style' or 'fashion'. Boyd recognized the former approach, as productive of new architecture. It is in the context of this argument that Boyd issued his challenge to Queensland architects to transform the local vernacular through the application of science to produce a truly regional architecture. Interestingly Dalton's Semi-Rural and Spinks Houses share a 'family likeness' with the work of Melbourne architects described by Boyd in his articles, 'Port Phillip Idiom' and the earlier 'Mornington Peninsula' in *Architecture* (1950) rather than the Queensland vernacular. They are long and low, timber framed with gable roof and living rooms opening onto porch and verandah, but they are also 'matter-of-fact-solutions' to local circumstances.[34]

The identification of Dalton's Semi-Rural House with the colonial homestead also occurred in popular press. In 'Simple Dignity in Ranch: New Ideas Enhance the Ranch' in *Australian Home Beautiful,* Eric Wilson' writing about the Semi-Rural House describes the 'ranch house', as a 'favourite form of home with every Australian generation since the foundation of this country'. He promotes it as an ideal solution 'provided it can be oriented with its long front to the north'.[35] The later Stoneham House (1964) by John Dalton Architect & Associates was also described by John Hay in Brisbane's *The Sunday Mail* as a 'ranch-style' house.[36] There is awkwardness to the use of 'ranch' – ranches belong in the American mid-west, whilst rural houses in Australia are commonly referred to as a station or homestead – that underscores the extent to which the popular press in Australia promoted modernism to a local audience by linking it to the highly desirable lifestyle and culture of West Coast USA. It is also clear that Dalton, in allowing the label, wished to identify himself with a national debate.

In 1963, Dalton would be challenged by a commission for a real homestead, 'Morocco' for Stan and Noela Wippell on the Darling Downs between Roma and St George, 500 kilometres west of Brisbane. Until 'Morocco', the idea of the homestead had been sustained through editorials and photographs of houses in the open sclerophyll forest landscapes of the underdeveloped western suburbs of Brisbane – the Semi-Rural, Spinks, Leverington (1961) and Neale (1962) houses. Myth and reality collided at 'Morocco'. Its remote location, a climate vastly different to that of Brisbane, the complexity of the programmatic brief and the problems of building remotely required Dalton to come to terms with the reality of a sometimes hostile outback environment.

The Contemporary Art Society Queensland Chapter

Whilst Dalton and Heathwood Architects were undertaking their early commissions, Dalton was also involved with Brisbane's contemporary art scene, painting and exhibiting his work in group exhibitions. Dalton's arrival in Brisbane coincided with a period of intense activity in contemporary art in Australia generally. In Brisbane Dr Gertrude Langer (1908–84), a strong advocate for modern art, was through her column for the Brisbane *Courier Mail* from 1953 inculcating a modernist sensibility. In 1955 Queensland Art Gallery Director Robert Haines (1911–2005) used his Friday evening radio programme 'Notes from the Gallery' to explain the 'new' modern art to an interested (but largely unconvinced) general audience.[37] Despite these initiatives Brisbane's art scene remained divided between a conservative establishment who identified with associations such as the CTC art school and the Royal Queensland Art Society (RQAS) and who were openly antagonistic to modernism on the one hand[38] and a group of younger artists who identified strongly with modernism in art, design and architecture on the other.[39] In 1961 the latter group would form the Contemporary Art Society Queensland Chapter (CAS). Membership of the CAS was not exclusive of artists and extended to philosophers, writers and academics[40] and this diversity at CAS art events, drawing classes, life classes, balls and bi-annual exhibitions enriched the intellectual and social life of Brisbane's progressives.[41] The CAS deliberately framed its activities in opposition to the RQAS whose annual exhibitions were described by Betty Churcher in her biography of Australian artist Jon Molvig 'as predictable as lamingtons: a tame art, which recorded a comfortable and complacent world'.[42] In turn the CAS were branded by the Brisbane art establishment as 'bohemian'.[43] Unlike the male-dominated architecture profession, the Brisbane art scene was not gendered; artists Betty Churcher (1931–2015), Joy Roggenkamp (1928–99) and Judy Cassab (1920–2015) were not overlooked in exhibitions and reviews whilst art critic Gertrude Langer and independent gallery owners Marjorie Johnstone (1912–94), Verlie Just (1922–2000), Joy de Gruchy (1922–2011) and Dr Ruth Smout (nee Cilento 1925–2016) influenced the reception of modern art and design work in Brisbane.

Also contributing to a lively art scene in the 1950s and 1960s was an extraordinary range of nationally significant artists who were attracted to Brisbane's climate, its tolerant, easy-going and relatively cheap lifestyle and stayed for extended periods of time. This list of artists includes Ian Fairweather (1891–1974) who lived an artist hermit existence on nearby Bribie Island, Ray Crooke (1922–2015), Charles Blackman (1928–2018), Margaret Olley (1923–2011), Andrew Sibley (1933–2015), Sam Fullbrook (1922–2004) and Mervyn Moriarty (1937–2021).[44] Many of these artists held exhibitions at the Johnstone Gallery, which opened in 1950 in rooms in Upper Edward Street, before moving, first to the Brisbane Arcade in 1951 and finally Bowen Hills in 1958.[45] When the author Rodney Hall was asked by art historian Glenn Cooke to comment on 'why Brisbane of the 1950s and 1960s is so much more a vivid presence in art and literature than any other Australian city, with the possible exception of Sydney' he answered: 'the city nourished the imagination of those who lived there then, created a colourful ambience and shaped our sense of the world in ways which would be impossible to analyse'.[46]

Two artists stayed in Brisbane long enough to exert a strong influence over Brisbane's art scene. Roy Churcher (1933-2014) was a graduate of the Slade School of Fine Art who met and married Brisbane-born artist Betty Cameron whilst she was in London studying at the London Royal College of Art on a Younger Artists' Group Scholarship in 1953.[47] Returning for a short stay in Brisbane in 1957, the pair instead chose to stay: Roy was attracted by Brisbane's light and strong colours.[48] The other figure was Jon Molvig (1923-70), a mostly self-taught artist who arrived in Brisbane in 1955 to relieve his friend John Rigby of art classes at St Mary's Church of England, Kangaroo Point, before departing at the end of 1957 on a tour of Central Australia.[49] Both Churcher and Molvig were charismatic, but with different styles and personalities; they respected each other but were not friends.

John and Sheila Dalton joined the Queensland Art Gallery Society 'Friends of the Gallery' in 1952 and in 1961 became foundation members of the CAS. Dalton entered his paintings in art competitions including two works – 'Immediacy at Fingal' and 'Portrait of an Architect' – in the Queensland Centenary Eisteddfod Art Competition of 1959. He also entered the Warana-Caltex Art Prize and the 1959 H.C. Richards and L.C. Harvey Memorial Competitions where his entry 'County Stanley, Parish of Indooroopilly' was singled out by *Courier Mail* art critic Melville Haysom alongside work by Roy Churcher as being 'outstanding in the abstract division' (Figure 2.5).[50] 'Immediacy at Fingal' was exhibited in the Centenary Exhibition at the Queensland National Art Gallery along with work by Margaret Olley, Jon Molvig, Andrew Sibley and Bronwyn Yeates, Betty Cameron (Churcher) and Roy Churcher, John Rigby, and Joy and Kenneth Roggenkamp.

FIGURE 2.5 John Dalton, 'County Stanley, Parish of Indooroopilly' c.1956. Mixed media on hardboard. Reproduced on the cover of *Centre Line*, 1967. Courtesy of Sue Dalton.

Very few architects were engaged with art in Brisbane at this time. The only other architect exhibited as part of the Centenary Art Competition was Colin Munro, an ex-pat Melbourne architect.

From 1961 Dalton exhibited paintings at the CAS bi-annual exhibitions.[51] His entry to the Warana-Caltex Prize, 'South Queensland Landscape – Gympie', featured a spiralling sun in the manner of Jon Molvig, appeared on the front cover of the July 1960 edition of *Architecture and Arts* (Figure 2.6).[52] That year a work by Dalton was selected for the CAS New South Wales Chapter's 23rd Annual Interstate Exhibition at the Blaxland Gallery along with works by John Aland, Maryke Degeus, Roy Churcher, Judy Cuppaidge and Andrew Sibley.[53] By 1965 more architects were involved in the CAS, but notably not members of the local profession. The CAS Autumn Exhibition 1965 Catalogue lists work by architects Graham de Gruchy, recently arrived from South Africa and Barbara van den Broek from New Zealand.[54] It would be some time later that a younger generation of architecture students would become involved including Paul Memmott and Greville Patterson. Dalton remained active in the CAS until its demise in 1972, holding positions on the Executive from 1965, organizing soirees, lectures and making presentations himself. Whenever he could he used his editorial role in the RAIA Queensland Chapter newsletter to promote artists and art exhibitions and to encourage the integration of art with architecture. Events were often held in the apartment he shared with Sue Stirling in Toowong. The New York art critic Clement Greenburg, visiting Brisbane on a lecture tour in 1968, led a discussion at one memorable event in Dalton's living room attended by Paul Memmott.[55] Indeed, Dalton's preference for the company of artists cemented his reputation amongst many in the profession as a radical.

FIGURE 2.6 John Dalton's entry in the 1960 Warana-Caltex Prize, 'South Queensland Landscape – Gympie' c. 1960. Reproduced on the front cover of *Architecture and Arts* in July 1960. Courtesy of Sue Dalton.

The 'verandah series'

Despite this activity, there is little to suggest that art was a part of Dalton's life before he arrived in Brisbane. One watercolour completed by Dalton whilst on his tour of duty in war ravaged Europe survives and depicts a church in Austria. Dalton testified that his family home in Leeds contained no art. In comparison, Dalton and Sue's house and studio in Allora, their flat in Toowong and the Dalton House at Fig Tree Pocket, where Sheila Dalton lived, were lined with sketches, paintings, architectural models and prints by Dalton and others and collected over fifty-seven years. They provide a record of his interests over time.

Two works painted seven years apart provide a window onto Dalton's preoccupations at two different points in time during the 1950s. The first painting titled 'sea-nymph and a sailor' depicting two figures embracing in their own bubble of space is signed and dated 1952 (Figure 2.7). It coincides with Dalton's first year of architecture study. The second, 'Immediacy at Fingal' depicting the structure and material fabric at the edge of a verandah, was painted by Dalton after he had completed his studies in architecture and entered in the 1959 Centenary Eisteddfod Art Competition. It was one of six paintings that he would later refer to as the 'vernadah series'. The 'vernadah series' paintings were never exhibited together but black-and-white reproductions of all six were published in *Architecture in Australia* in 1964.

'Sea-nymph and a sailor' may have been completed by Dalton in fulfilment of the art requirement for entry to the Diploma course at CTC. Highly reminiscent of the collage work of German-French sculptor and abstract artist Jean Arp, in

FIGURE 2.7 John Dalton, 'sea-nymph and a sailor', 1952. Ink and gouache on card. Courtesy of Sue Dalton.

particular collages completed by Arp during the 1920s, it is very much an art project 'in the manner of'. That it is amended with the pencil outline of additional lozenges almost certainly added at a later date (or after assessment), further suggests it was a rehearsal for something. Dalton's selection of Arp for this task is telling, indicating his awareness of Arp's significance to modern architects. He would have known of the 1949 *Architecture and Arts* article, 'Painting toward Architecture', in which Australia's foremost architect Harry Seidler argues for the 'fusion or interdependence' of art and architecture. In this article, Seidler juxtaposes an image of one of Arp's 'free form' sculptures alongside Niemeyer's church at Pampulha, Brazil (1943), which he visited whilst working with Niemeyer *en route* to Australia.[56] With reference to Arp's sensuous forms, Seidler posits the significance of art to the distillation of a visual language for architecture.[57] Dalton's choice of Arp for his scholarly exercise reveals an intent to understand something about the origins of the language of modernism.[58]

The key elements of Arp's work are all present, rendered in primary colours: 'humanoid ovoids', 'gestative shapes', Arp's 'navel'.[59] Forms are fitted closely yet separated from each other by the white space of the page. This has the effect of creating a sense of movement in repose.[60] Even the subject of Dalton's painting evokes one of Arp's bronze sculptures, 'The Mermaid' (1942). But Dalton's composition is an exercise in composition in the manner of Arp; it does not reveal to him new motifs capable of interacting with the sub-conscious.[61] It is also unlike Seidler's interest in Arp, which is purposefully directed at finding the 'universal principles' governing a language of form, which would find expression in his mural for the Rose Seidler House (1949), and the Williamson [Igloo] House at Mosman (1951). If 'sea-nymph and a sailor' was merely a set task for passing Scholarship in Art required for entry to the Diploma of Architecture, it achieved its aim. That Dalton chose to keep it indicates it was somehow significant to him.

In comparison the series of paintings known as the 'verandah series' were purposeful and intentionally directed and did enable the distillation of an abstracted language of form. 'Immediacy at Fingal' is a detailed study of the ordering of structure and material fabric at the edge of a traditional verandah, together with the space of the landscape beyond (Figure 2.8).[62] Timber blind, lattice, post and rail are rendered as horizontal and vertical elements read against a sunlight drenched landscape of sky, sea, sand dunes and wind-ruffled grass. The painting is composed, with form and space organized as a series of flat planes parallel to the picture surface. Yet its subject matter is local and its title confirms specificity. The term 'immediacy' had been introduced into the architectural lexicon by Gordon Cullen writing in *The Architectural Review* in 1953 but its use was hardly widespread[63] whilst Fingal, located on the Tweed Coast in Northern New South Wales, was a favourite beach holiday location. Dalton's painting is transformative, bridging local conditions and modern sensibility.

FIGURE 2.8 John Dalton, 'Immediacy at Fingal', 1959. Acrylic on board. Entered in the Queensland Centenary Eisteddfod Art Competition, 1959. Courtesy of Sue Dalton.

An interest in the figurative and representational is consistent with the preoccupations of artists who exhibited in Brisbane in the 1950s and 1960s and owes much to both Jon Molvig and Roy Churcher. Molvig is described by Betty Churcher as an abstract expressionist working from 'direct experience and personal identification', despite a general shift within Australian art to abstractionism.[64] Dalton's working of paint on hardboard in 'Immediacy in Fingal' echoes Molvig's preferred medium and technique. Roy and Betty Churcher, on the other hand, brought mid-century British art perspectives to Brisbane.[65] Their mode of studio instruction was to allow each artist to find their own way and to bear witness to the richness of the sensory world.[66] In particular, Roy Churcher promoted expressionism in which colour structure communicated sensation and reality. Although it is unclear whether Dalton ever attended CAS studios, he was active on CAS committees with Roy Churcher and his work at this time is consistent with Churchers' emphasis on 'taking hold' of experience through observation and response, invention and constructive simplification.[67] Betty Churcher writes that 'the priorities of artists can be found as readily in what they choose to paint as in how they choose to paint it'.[68] In 'Immediacy in Fingal' Dalton chose to paint the material fabric at the edge of the verandah. He places the observer inside the building line and invites their identification with the registration of light and shadow at the building's edge. In attending to the particularities of material fabric at the edge of building form, the real subject of Dalton's work is revealed – the play of light and shadow that building form gives rise to. These paintings contain the elements that would become associated with Dalton's language of form, and essential to his mantra of 'sunlight, shade and shadow'. But they are concerned with the consequences of form for experience, not form alone. In making these paintings other architectural preoccupations also emerge into view – the role of the building edge not as a conditioning envelope but as mediator between interior and exterior space, the role that material detail plays in the experience of architectural form and the capacity of architecture to orient humans in relation to their sensory world.

Dalton's interest in contemporary art differs from that of his peers in Brisbane. After his appointment as chief architect for the BCC in 1955, Melbourne-educated architect James Birrell (1928–2019) designed a number of innovative projects which integrated contemporary art. Birrell's Wickham Terrace Car Park (1958–60) featured a concrete relief pattern by Melbourne artist James Meldrum. Other instances of the integration of art into architecture include the incorporation of a mosaic mural by Lindsay Edward into extensions to the old Queensland State Library (1959) by Department of Public Works and the incorporation of a stained glass window by Neville Matthews into Mayne Hall (1972) at the University of Queensland by Robin Gibson.[69] But there is little evidence in Brisbane of art intersecting with architecture in the manner advocated by Seidler in his article 'Painting toward Architecture'.

'sun + life + useful form'

From 1960, after the dissolution of his partnership with Peter Heathwood, Dalton sets out his thinking about detail and sunlight, shade and shadow in a series of polemic texts published in *Architecture and Arts* and *Architecture in Australia*. The first of these texts, 'Queensland's Pragmatic Poetry' was published in 1960 in *Architecture and Arts*. It appears between a reprint of Lewis Mumford's 'An Address to Architectural Students in Rome' and a review (written by Dalton) of his own Dalton House, Fig Tree Pocket (1960). Completed around the time that Dalton began practising as John Dalton Architect and Associates, the Dalton House was included in *Architecture and Arts* '10 Best Houses for 1959–1960'.[70]

In 'An Address to Architectural Students in Rome' Mumford reiterates his thesis on the need for developments in science and technology to be bought into alignment with a deeper appreciation and understanding of human life.[71] He argues that 'a good mechanical solution to a human problem can only be a part of an adequate organic solution which meets the needs of life in all its dimensions.'[72] Read against Lewis Mumford's generalized call to architects to deploy humanist values, 'Queensland's Pragmatic Poetry' presents as a situated response. Its central claim is that whilst the appearance of the Queensland house is changing, its 'characteristic qualities' remain, embedded by a reinvigorated language of form. Importantly Dalton does not advocate the stylistic appropriation of familiar elements of the pre-existing Queensland house. Rather the conditions necessary for architecture to impart qualities that are 'familiar' and 'characteristic' are derived from new insights into what constitutes 'useful form'.

> The new image is revealing itself in pragmatic terms and finds delight in the naïve expression of form and function with ever present sunlight animating the simple details.
>
> ....
>
> A constant reference to human values establishes the local idiom and ensures the growth of useful form, while changing social habits, reinforced by the investigation and analysis of the problems of modern life present the basic architectural material.[73]

Dalton's use of the term 'idiom' is also interesting, drawing as it does upon architecture's analogous relationship to language and more particularly to poetry and poetic prose.[74] Its use in relation to architecture was not common at the time of Dalton's writing. That it was used by Robin Boyd in his essay 'Port Phillip Idiom' is significant for Dalton greatly admired Boyd. Boyd's article begins 'A school or idiom of domestic architecture, if not a style, has developed about the city of Melbourne'.[75] How Boyd aligned the modest modernist houses found on Melbourne's Mornington Peninsula with California's 'Bay Region Style' and Sweden's New Empiricism for the benefit of an international audience has been described in detail by Melbourne Professor Philip Goad.[76] Dalton's intentions for 'Queensland Pragmatic Poetry' were less ambitious. He was more concerned to position Queensland's modernist houses within a national debate as a regional modernism.

Boyd's use of the term 'idiom' enabled him to draw a distinction between a 'family likeness' and 'style'. For Dalton 'useful form' – the 'restatement of ... basic needs' – provided the basis for distinguishing between architecture and an aesthetic or 'image'; for he believed 'architecture only occurs if those involved breathe a poetic purpose into their building'.[77] Poetry is revealed when 'useful form' is animated by the 'ever present sunlight'. It was Dalton's belief that such an approach would lead to patterns 'indigenous and regional in character'. Dalton's account of a regional architecture differs significantly from Boyd's more analytical description of the modernist domestic architecture on Mornington Peninsula through its reference to the role of the sun in the expression of a way of life and the sensory experience of form. 'Queensland's Pragmatic Poetry' speaks of a modernist architecture firmly located in Queensland. Dalton's search for an appropriate language of modern form – one that was contemporary but evoked a local patois – became focused in a concern for idiomatic detail capable of imparting delight.

A review of the Dalton House immediately followed this polemic, clearly to impress it in readers' imagination as an exemplar of the new, modern Queensland idiom. Interestingly, text describing the Dalton House focused on the role of detail in technical innovation rather than its poetic consequences – the use of folding walls to link the living space and patio to the garden, clerestory ventilation through a pop-up roof over the kitchen, an excavated sub-floor to

practitioners. They both submitted entries to the competition and formed a pact that if one or other of them won the £3000 prize on offer they would use it to establish a partnership.[5] Heathwood's entry was successful and in late 1956 Dalton & Heathwood Architects opened their office in Queen Street, Brisbane City.[6] The winning scheme was announced in Brisbane's *Courier Mail* newspaper as the 'House of Tomorrow', a by-line appropriated from media coverage of Robin Boyd's 1949 'House of Tomorrow'. It was illustrated with a perspective drawn by Dalton complete with his characteristic *l'homme architecturale*. Dalton documented the winning design for construction whilst Heathwood was on his honeymoon (Figure 2.1) and it was built at the Exhibition Showgrounds, Newstead, in time for the Royal National Show in August 1957.

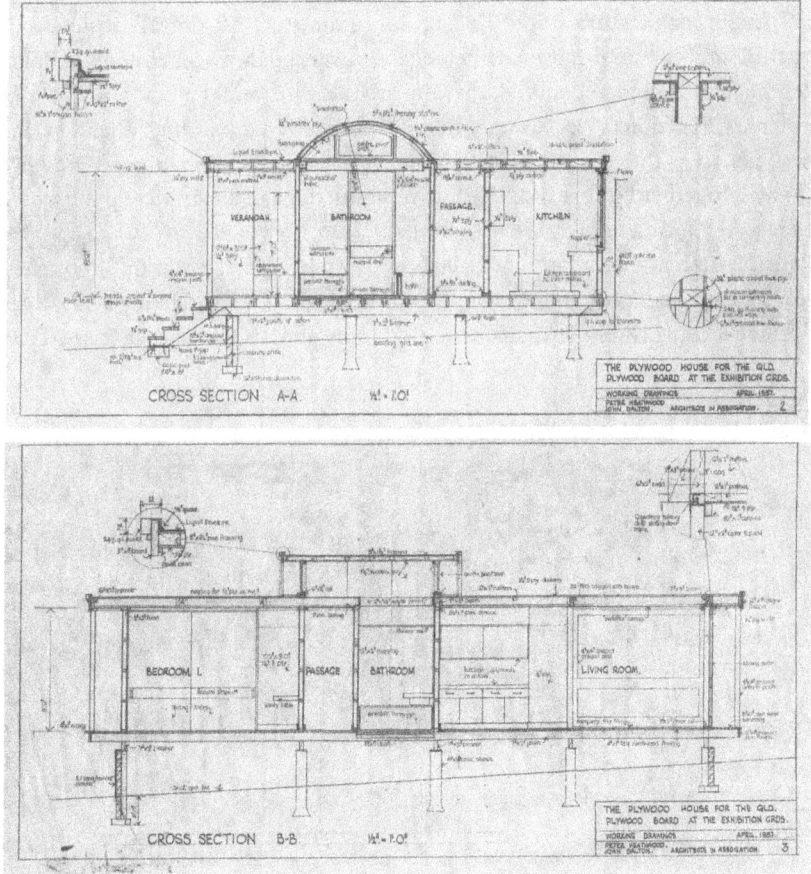

FIGURE 2.1 Plywood Exhibition House, 1957, designed by Peter Heathwood. Sections drawn by John Dalton. Courtesy of Sue Dalton.

The 'verandah series'

Despite this activity, there is little to suggest that art was a part of Dalton's life before he arrived in Brisbane. One watercolour completed by Dalton whilst on his tour of duty in war ravaged Europe survives and depicts a church in Austria. Dalton testified that his family home in Leeds contained no art. In comparison, Dalton and Sue's house and studio in Allora, their flat in Toowong and the Dalton House at Fig Tree Pocket, where Sheila Dalton lived, were lined with sketches, paintings, architectural models and prints by Dalton and others and collected over fifty-seven years. They provide a record of his interests over time.

Two works painted seven years apart provide a window onto Dalton's preoccupations at two different points in time during the 1950s. The first painting titled 'sea-nymph and a sailor' depicting two figures embracing in their own bubble of space is signed and dated 1952 (Figure 2.7). It coincides with Dalton's first year of architecture study. The second, 'Immediacy at Fingal' depicting the structure and material fabric at the edge of a verandah, was painted by Dalton after he had completed his studies in architecture and entered in the 1959 Centenary Eisteddfod Art Competition. It was one of six paintings that he would later refer to as the 'vernadah series'. The 'vernadah series' paintings were never exhibited together but black-and-white reproductions of all six were published in *Architecture in Australia* in 1964.

'Sea-nymph and a sailor' may have been completed by Dalton in fulfilment of the art requirement for entry to the Diploma course at CTC. Highly reminiscent of the collage work of German-French sculptor and abstract artist Jean Arp, in

FIGURE 2.7 John Dalton, 'sea-nymph and a sailor', 1952. Ink and gouache on card. Courtesy of Sue Dalton.

enable underfloor air flow and the insulation of walls.[78] A roof-top sprinkler for bush fire protection operated from a cupboard next to the kitchen was a novel feature that turned the flat roof into a playground for Jane and Amanda Dalton in the heat of summer.[79] In all other aspects, its design reflected the best practice principles of late modernism. It has an economical square plan, lightweight construction and a regular grid, expressed in elevation by cover strips to the fibre cement wall cladding (Figure 2.9). Internal spaces and external courtyards are captured between walls and the horizontal roof extends beyond the building envelope with three-foot overhangs. *Architecture and Arts* chose to illustrate the Dalton House with a plan and section demonstrating sun angles and ventilation, an interior image of open plan living spaces and a view to the house from the north. What was not selected for publication were any one of a number of images demonstrating how interior and exterior spaces were linked through a building envelope that folds open or slides away (Figure 2.10). A photograph demonstrating the most up-to-date cabinet work also draws the bush into close proximity with the kitchen through an opening free of joinery (Figure 2.11). The manner of this photograph is not dissimilar to images taken by Julius Shulman of Neutra's desert houses. It has been noted that Shulman's images, taken under Neutra's direction 'never frame views of the houses, but rather, look through them with dynamic vision'.[80] Schulman's images capture the experience of interior

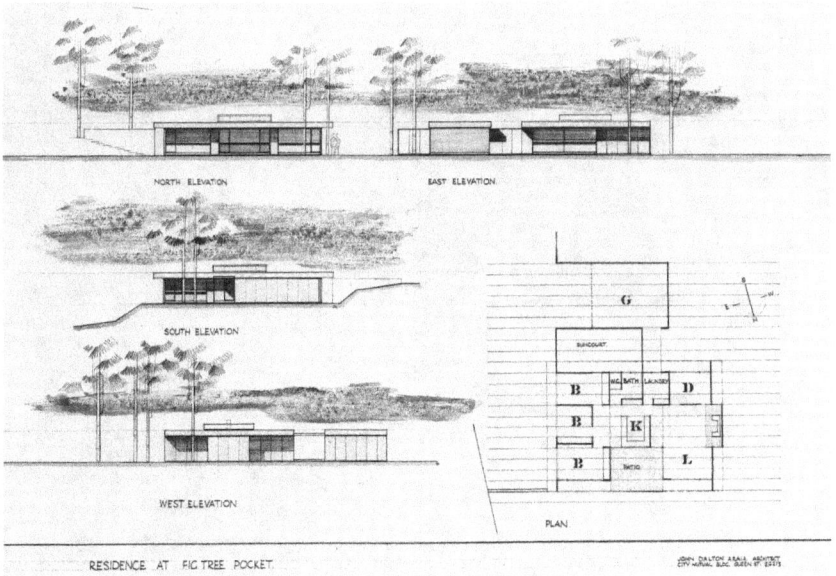

FIGURE 2.9 Design Development. Dalton House, Fig Tree Pocket, 1960. John Dalton Architect and Associates. Courtesy of Sue Dalton.

enable underfloor air flow and the insulation of walls.⁷⁸ A roof-top sprinkler for bush fire protection operated from a cupboard next to the kitchen was a novel feature that turned the flat roof into a playground for Jane and Amanda Dalton in the heat of summer.⁷⁹ In all other aspects, its design reflected the best practice principles of late modernism. It has an economical square plan, lightweight construction and a regular grid, expressed in elevation by cover strips to the fibre cement wall cladding (Figure 2.9). Internal spaces and external courtyards are captured between walls and the horizontal roof extends beyond the building envelope with three-foot overhangs. *Architecture and Arts* chose to illustrate the Dalton House with a plan and section demonstrating sun angles and ventilation, an interior image of open plan living spaces and a view to the house from the north. What was not selected for publication were any one of a number of images demonstrating how interior and exterior spaces were linked through a building envelope that folds open or slides away (Figure 2.10). A photograph demonstrating the most up-to-date cabinet work also draws the bush into close proximity with the kitchen through an opening free of joinery (Figure 2.11). The manner of this photograph is not dissimilar to images taken by Julius Shulman of Neutra's desert houses. It has been noted that Shulman's images, taken under Neutra's direction 'never frame views of the houses, but rather, look through them with dynamic vision'.⁸⁰ Schulman's images capture the experience of interior

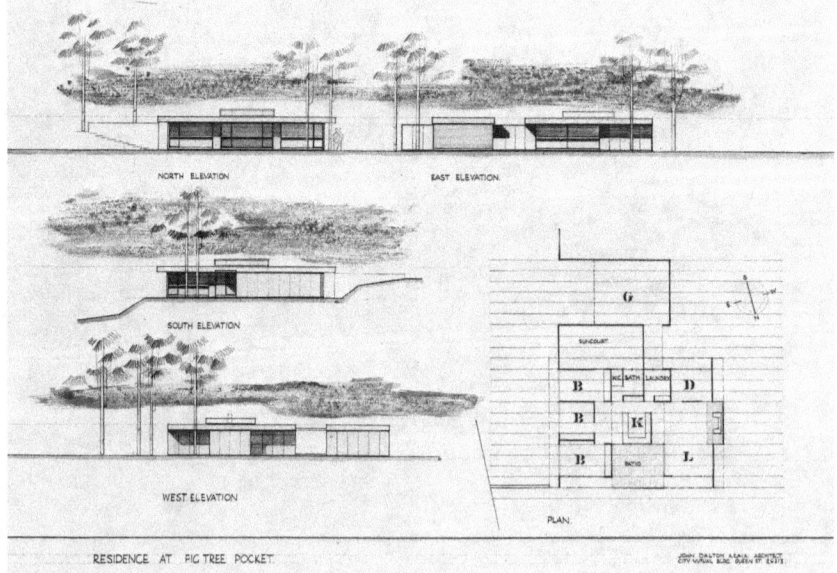

FIGURE 2.9 Design Development. Dalton House, Fig Tree Pocket, 1960. John Dalton Architect and Associates. Courtesy of Sue Dalton.

FIGURE 2.10 View from kitchen north to bushland. Dalton House, Fig Tree Pocket, 1960. Photo credit Geoff Dauth. UQFL499, John Dalton Papers, Fryer Library, University of Queensland.

FIGURE 2.11 View through sun-patio to living room. Dalton House, Fig Tree Pocket, 1960. Photo credit Geoff Dauth. John Dalton Papers, UQFL499, Fryer Library, University of Queensland.

space linked to exterior space as an extension of the same setting, a constant in Neutra's work. Instead of images linking interior and exterior spaces, the north elevation of the Dalton House became, through repetition in books and journals, the image most associated with this house (Figure 2.12). This image was used in the very next edition of *Architecture and Arts* to announce the Dalton House amongst 'The ten best houses for 1959–1960'.[81]

The publication of another project, the Tremont Flats in Toowong, also listed by *Architecture and Arts* as one of '1959–1960 10 Best Buildings' provided another

FIGURE 2.12 North Elevation, Dalton House, Fig Tree Pocket, 1960. Photo credit Geoff Dauth. Courtesy Sue Dalton.

occasion for Dalton to promote the opportunities of design for sunlight (Figures 2.13 and 2.14). The publication of this project was accompanied by text taken from an address Dalton delivered at the 1961 Australian Architecture Students Association (AASA) Symposium. Comprising five units and caretaker's accommodation, Tremont Flats is an exercise in *existenzminima* planning to achieve cross-ventilation, northern light and a garden adjacent all living spaces. The published image of the western elevation reveals a composition of breezeblock walls, screens, horizontal and vertical elements with sunlight revealing space and form. Dalton's address to the Symposium 'What is wrong with the Diploma course' was an appeal to part-time architecture students to recognize and be excited by the potential of their chosen profession:

> This love of life and architecture should be an inseparable partnership which can turn the base metal of our experience into the richest fabric our society has even known. We are the Magicians and architecture is our Magic ... ... The exquisite qualities of space and light are the instruments which delight our fancy and this all-consuming experience of architecture should be our ultimate desire.[82]

The text submitted by Dalton for publication in *Architecture and Arts* is a more succinct précis of this address. 'Sun + Life + Useful Form = Architectural magic' is read against black-and-white images in which the blockwork screen walls of the Tremont Flats feature prominently and reads:

> ... for us, life in the sun is a reality, and we who build in the sunlight sense the joy of space and light. It is our delight. The magic of shade and shadow capture our senses and direct us towards our purpose, which is to dispense comfort and happiness through useful form ....[83]

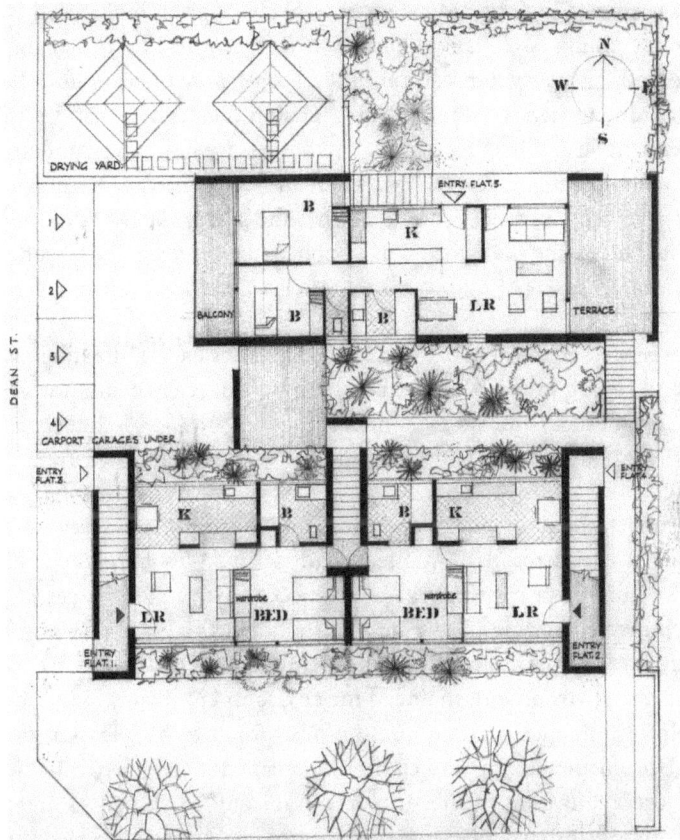

FIGURE 2.13 Plan, Tremont Flats, Dean Street, Toowong, 1960. Courtesy of Sue Dalton.

FIGURE 2.14 Street view, Tremont Flats, Dean Street, Toowong, 1960. Courtesy Sue Dalton.

This text is similar in tone and expression to advice given by Richard Neutra in 'Notes to the Young Architect', published in *Perspecta* in 1957: '"Delight" is after all not something apart from natural "utility" and, more than comfort, happiness itself is laid in our hands.'[84] From Neutra, Dalton understood that delightfulness was dependent on architecture harnessing the sensory in settings for daily life. He also understood that in Queensland – where the sun is the 'mainspring of magical qualities' – an acute awareness of the diurnal and seasonal passage of the sun was essential to harnessing the sensory. In a public radio broadcast in 1964 he advised Brisbane's citizens:

> This ever present constant of our day-by-day experience of the sun rising in the East and setting in the West is something we can really count on. The reality of the Queensland climate must dictate the methods we Architects employ to design the houses offices City Halls and the whole complex of cities.[85]

The conventional view of 'environment' at this time is captured in a 1941 lecture delivered by architect and soon-to-be appointed Professor, Robert E Cummings in which he introduced 'environment' a set of discrete and disconnected settings – the home, the hotel, the place of work, the city, suburban streets, parks, countryside.[86] Cummings addressed the need for variety in the environment, the need for environment to suit the occasion and be a 'helpful influence' in daily life the need for it to be 'pleasant to look at' because it is encompassing and cannot be escaped, that it be treated in design through the application of the principles typically attributed to architectural form – composition, balance, contrast. Cummings' conception of environment is ocular-centric; removed from the sensory. It does not envisage a continuity between architecture and its surroundings, or architecture's capacity to enhance the individual's sensory engagement with their surroundings. In comparison, Dalton's polemical text grounded such ideas in the particular circumstances of Brisbane, Queensland.

The 'verandah series' paintings finally appeared together in an article, 'the verandah' published in 1964 in *Architecture in Australia* (Figure 2.15). In 'the verandah' Dalton's musings on the role of detail and light and shadow in architectural experience are presented together with a photograph of a single room settler's cottage and black-and-white reproductions of all six paintings, their saturated blues, ochres and browns now rendered in terms of texture, shape, pattern and contrast.[87] On quick reading the detail of individual paintings conflates to produce a single impression of a 'verandah' experience – a pattern of light and shadow, with details giving scale and texture. The image of a cottage is offered as a touchstone whilst accompanying text invokes the experience of vernacular form.

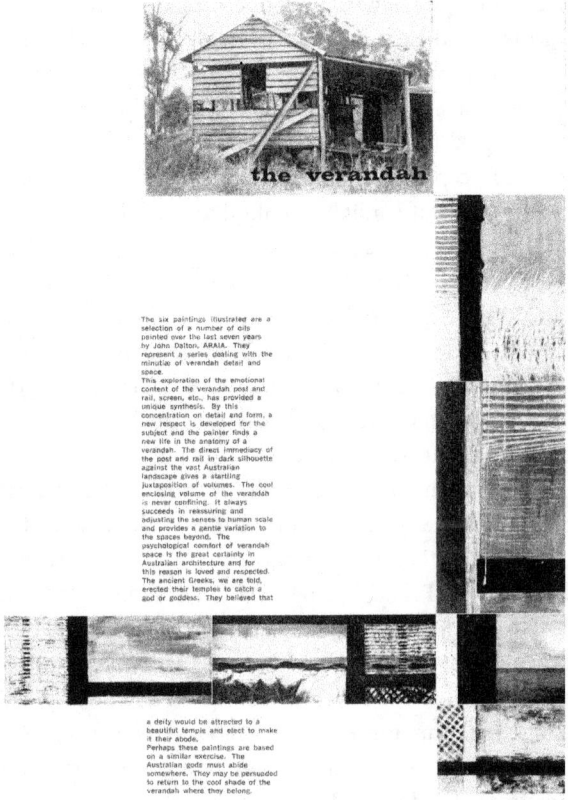

FIGURE 2.15 'the verandah' as it appeared in *Architecture in Australia* in March 1964.

By this concentration on detail and form, a new respect is developed for the subject and the painter finds a new life in the autonomy of the verandah. The direct immediacy of the post and rail in dark silhouette against the vast Australian landscape gives a startling juxtaposition of volumes. The cool enclosing volume of the verandah is never confining. It always succeeds in reassuring and adjusting the senses to the human scale and provides a gentle variation to the spaces beyond. The psychological comfort of the verandah space is the great certainty in Australian architecture and for this reason is loved and respected.[88]

Initially an investigation of detail, paintings had by 1964 become implicated in authenticating the experience of verandah space, as an essential space and the means by which humans 'adjust their senses' and mediate their relationship with their wider environment. Dalton draws attention to memories evoked by the sensory experience of space, and not from criteria associated with physiological comfort such as those identified by Karl Langer: 'the avoidance of fatigue', 'the provision of light and avoidance of glare' and 'economy'.[89] He is not advocating for a recovery of the vernacular house form, its structural or constructional systems but for a reimagining of its key space in new ways.

Most successful in capturing the essence of Dalton's polemic is Harry Sowden in his iconic photograph of sunlight falling into the atrium space of the Wilson House (1964) (Figure 2.16). This image was taken by Sowden to illustrate *Towards an Australian Architecture* (1968) and is accompanied by text taken from 'the verandah'. It depicts the timber rail and mullions of a flyscreened enclosure in dark relief against the hazy bushland beyond.[90] A chair invites the viewer to identify with the experience of the atrium bathed in morning light. Constructed as a view from the inside out, Sowden's photograph captures the experience of a verandah as a space separated from but connected to its bushland setting.

Dalton would express his views about the significance of 'experience' on many occasions. One early instance occurs in a letter to the editor of *Architecture in Australia* in which he criticizes an appraisal of the state of architecture by W H Nankivell titled 'Organic Fallacy' (1964). Dalton describes Nankivell's method of analysis on the basis of form as 'old hat techniques [that] have little relevance for today'.[91] Evoking the legacy of John Dewey and Herbert Read he writes: 'architecture as experienced is more than the sum total of its parts and therefore the distinctions that a critic should make are those that relate to superlative degrees of experience'.

By 1963 Dalton's position on architecture had come more clearly into focus, drawn together from insights made whilst reading and painting. He may have sought recognition as an artist by exhibiting his work and may even have been encouraged by favourable reviews, but it is as an architect of climate-responsive

FIGURE 2.16 Atrium, Wilson House, Mt Coot-tha Road, Toowong, 1964. Photograph taken by Harry Sowden for *Towards an Australian Architecture* (1967). Reproduced courtesy Harry Sowden.

modern houses for the subtropics that his reputation had by the early 1960s became firmly established. Haig Beck and Jackie Cooper have described Dalton as 'an abstract expressionist who used his paintings to explore the qualities of Australian light' and who by 'seeing things though artists eye's' perceived new possibilities for Queensland architecture.[92] Renowned Australian art dealer and gallery director Ray Hughes (1946–2017) maintains that Dalton was 'too timid' about his art; that it was overly concerned with 'decorative' values.[93] Nevertheless, Dalton was drawn to the company of artists and participated in their forums. He continued to enjoy painting and drawing, although after 1965 he chose not to exhibit. The extended network that gathered around Brisbane's art scene would provide an important client base leading to numerous commissions and Dalton's houses were particularly well suited to the display of contemporary art. Published images frequently reveal interiors filled with contemporary works by artists represented by the Johnstone Gallery, Gallery One Eleven and Ray Hughes Galleries and furnishings from Joy de Gruchy's (1921–2011) Craftsman's Market.

What then was the purpose of his painting? Dalton's explorations were intentionally directed, influenced by his friendship with artists, and informed by his reading of Herbert Read and John Dewey. Certainly, painting contributed to his mindfulness of a distinctly Queensland condition and to an awareness of how architecture might generate a distinctly Queensland experience of modern space. Painting identified the idiomatic detail and encapsulated the role of building envelope in linking interior and exterior spaces and in orienting occupants to the sensory. Polemical texts situated or 'made local' ideas garnered from the writings of Neutra and Mumford – ideas relevant to a design process that places humans and their experience of daily life as its focus, that positions daily rituals in relation to the diurnal and seasonal passage of the sun in a specific locale and that acknowledges the sun as the source of delight. Dalton's activities shifted his perspective on architecture and building from opinions first expressed in 'Four Houses by Dalton and Heathwood Architects'. The call for the 'advent of industrialised building technique' had developed into an appeal for 'idiomatic detail'. But it would take some time for these perspectives to be fully realized in built work. A disconnection between disciplinary domains remained to separate Dalton's early writing and painting from his architecture. Commissions for houses by John Dalton Architect and Associates were still very modest and insights into the experiential dimensions of architecture needed to be negotiated against the effort required to achieve a rigorous and aesthetic form within extremely tight budgets. Nevertheless, over the next decade, Dalton would continue to work with idiom and sun to create shade and shadow bringing delight. His reflective practice would ultimately lead to what would become known as the 'Dalton House'.

3 FORM AND ITS EXPERIENCE: DESIGNS FOR 'SUNLIGHT, SHADE AND SHADOW'

During the 1960s John Dalton Architect and Associates was very busy with numerous commissions for relatively modest domestic projects. There is a consistency in the work from the early part of this period reflecting the type of client – young professionals at the start of their careers – and sites – predominantly locations in the foothills of Mt Coot-tha to the west of Brisbane – but also the way that a small practice might manage a large number of modest commissions. Of the more than 100 domestic projects completed by Dalton between 1956 and 1986, sixty-two are located within an area of less than 100 square kilometres. These houses were published widely in Australian journals and popular magazines and came to be associated with modern living in the subtropics. Dalton assumed the manner expected of Brisbane's foremost architect of modernist houses, dressing stylishly and driving an expensive and rare British car, a V8 Daimler. It was during this period that Dalton's painting and reading activities began to impact his design practice in more productive ways and between 1964 and 1966, Dalton's interest in a regionally inflected modernism became increasing implicated in broader questions about Australia's cultural identity and the search for an Australian architecture. Less obvious perhaps than a shift in architectural expression are the steady, subtle and incremental changes that reveal an increased gearing of building to specific site and micro-climate.

Brisbane's climate 'stated in detail'

Architects trained during the 1950s and inculcated into the view that climate was pivotal were beneficiaries of the research around climate-responsive design conducted by State and Commonwealth agencies from the 1940s.

Government-funded research projects were directed by the need to improve housing standards in the post-war era and were complicated by the scale of enterprise, the variety of climate zones and the need to find solutions that were economically viable even in remote areas. Such complexity encouraged the development of generic housing models applicable to the widest range of circumstances. Research was underpinned by climate data and the way this data was interpreted had consequences for the delineation of climate zones and the recommendations for design that flowed from research. Distinctions between humid and dry categories within tropical and sub-tropical climate zones, based on degree of seasonal and diurnal temperature change, were overlooked in the design of the model generic 'tropical house'. Instead the Commonwealth Experimental Building Station (CEBS) considered it acceptable that variation be addressed with the addition of insulation and sun-shading as required for hot dry or hot humid conditions. Compromise is evident even in Brisbane, now understood to have the characteristics of a transitional climate – subtropical for most of the year but with cool episodes during winter months. Langer's seminal publication *Subtropical Housing* cemented the prevailing view by adopting the zoning identified by Dr Douglas Lee, Professor of Physiology at the UQ and a member of the QTHC. Derived from temperature data and pressure systems Lee located Brisbane in the humid subtropics.[1] Lee's assessment was confirmed by J.W. Drysdale in his seminal *Climate and House Design* (1949) for the CEBS. The use of climate data to establish the classification of climate and the definition of comfort for the purpose of housing research also meant that the effects of localized factors were overlooked. The impact of topography and distance from the sea make the climate of Brisbane's western suburbs in the foothills of the D'Aguilar Ranges subtly different to that of the Brisbane River floodplain or the suburbs fronting Moreton Bay. Lost was any encouragement to reflect on the actual conditions of site and the opportunities these might provide for architecture. Instead research into climate-responsive housing established a set of design principles and generic house solutions for tropical zones. Generalizations about Brisbane's climate supported the development of a particular form of modernism – lightweight, timber pavilions orientated north-south, elevations shaded through overhangs and screens to reduce solar heat gain and glare in summer, and openings located to maximize cross-ventilation.

The science underpinning the classification of Brisbane's climate as subtropical climate was not scrutinized until research conducted by architect and UQ lecturer William Greig in 1965. In a dissertation, supervised by Professor Cummings and Bruce Lucas, with input from staff in the School of Mechanical Engineering and the Commonwealth Bureau of Meteorology, Greig observed that whilst many may argue Brisbane's climate 'has been overstated, it had in fact, not been stated in detail at all'.[2] Greig adopted the methodology developed by the pioneers of bioclimatic design research, Victor and Aladar Olgyay, of plotting dry bulb temperature against relative humidity on a psychrometric chart. Using data provided by Lee and MacFarlane and the Bureau of Meteorology, Greig confirmed that in Brisbane 'ideal comfort zone conditions exist for short periods only'[3] and that Brisbane's climate relative to human comfort is characterized by high summer humidity, and uncomfortably low winter temperatures for two months of the year.[4] Brisbane's high diurnal temperature range in winter, particularly pronounced in its western suburbs, meant that houses were uncomfortable in the cooler months and made the use of mass elements – masonry or concrete elements with a higher specific heat capacity than timber– to catch and store the sun's energy, desirable. After the CEBS issued a bulletin on the heat capacity of certain materials, Dalton tested the use of mass elements in the Leverington House (1961). In houses that followed, masonry east and west end walls and chimney elements created cosy living arrangements for cool winter evenings. Dalton's Leeds training ensured his chimneys always drew properly. Masonry elements also appeared in work by other Queensland architects including John Railton, and Maurice Hurst and later Gabriel Poole, Peter O'Gorman and Patrick Moroney. Even Robin Gibson utilized masonry in his award-winning Mocatta House (1966).

The association of climate-responsive design with modernism in the minds of Brisbane's more conservative practitioners, prompted a debate in the pages of *Cross-Section* in 1965 as to whether attention to climate was an 'absolute' or an 'artifice'.[5] As Queensland's contributing editor to *Cross-section* Dalton defended climate as a primary design consideration. But he was equally disparaging of work that uncritically adopted the language of a tropical modernism, well-known to local architects through international journals such as *Architectural Review* and *L'Architecture d'aujourd'hui* and publications such as those by Maxwell Fry and Jane Drew and characterized by elements such as breeze-block screens and walls, pilotis and brise-soleil. Dalton's review of the University of Queensland Student Union Building (1960) by Fulton Collin and Partners for *Cross-Section* was censorious: 'Concrete sun screen walls set promiscuously around the perimeter of the building with 11 inch cavity walls set immediately behind. Design for climate is reduced to a euphemistic prattle.'[6] As far as Dalton was concerned, the architect had applied the lessons of a different type of tropicalism – hot and dry – and was guilty of 'stylistic formalism'.[7] Dalton's critique may seem a little unfair considering his own use of breeze-block screens in the Tremont Flats (1960), Toowong, to privatize external courtyards and circulation spaces (Figures 2.13 and 2.14). These screens did not however act as heat sinks to occupiable spaces behind.

Climate science intersected with Dalton's fascination with 'sunlight, shade and shadow' further reflecting his awareness of global discourse. A number of influential twentieth-century architects including the Olgyay brothers, Jane Drew and Maxwell Fry, Frank Lloyd Wright, Marcel Breuer, Louis Kahn and Harry Seidler had already argued that technical precision in the design of sun-shading devices does not by itself deliver architecture.[8] They argued pragmatic questions about shade introduce a range of options for the ordering of sun-shading elements, each generating a different patterning of shadows with implications for the expression of architectural form, from which the architect as artist must make a selection.[9] Dalton's phrase 'sunlight, shade and shadow' also reflects an awareness of established conversations in Australia around the consequences of sunlight for architecture. The Australian architect and artist, William Hardy Wilson (1881–1955) was perhaps the most renowned advocate for the inspirational quality of light in Australia and its role in revealing the architectural form of colonial buildings.[10] Similarly for ex-pat Englishman Dalton, the sun was something to be harnessed, but the patterns of sunlight and shadow generated by architecture had to reflect patterns of living; it was not merely a question of aspiration to form. Dalton also clearly understood the power of the black-and-white photograph to capture light and enhance shadow and contrast, rendering material, texture and form. His early and persistent use of professional photographers to carefully document his practice's work in black and white helped build his reputation locally and nationally. Photos of Dalton's houses by the Keane and Dauth brothers, Harry Sowden or Richard Stringer accompanied articles in professional journals, whilst the colour images preferred by popular magazines were not encouraged.[11]

That Dalton chose to include both 'shade' and 'shadow' in his maxim is also significant. In skiagraphy, 'shade' and 'shadow' reference slightly different concepts that are often conflated in discussions around the topic.[12] Shadow is cast by obstruction of the sun's light by a specific object; in architecture it is both a property of and revelatory of form. Shade refers to the area of darkness cast and the properties of that darkness. It brings with it expectations of cool; that is, it is evocative of an experience. These two meanings intersected in the mid-twentieth century, when scientific research confirmed that shade impacted temperature, humidity and air movement; it was not just the absence of light and heat. At this time design for shade became a task critical to climate-responsive design.[13] Dalton, however, was interested in the phenomenal and physiological, the poetic and the pragmatic dimensions of shade and shadow.

Evolution of the Dalton House 1: The linear house

A series of commissions from young professionals with sites in the western suburbs of Kenmore and Chapel Hill followed construction of the Dalton House in Fig Tree Pocket. Many of these commissions were the result of connections made through jazz and bushwalking or through networks of academics at the University of Queensland and the CAS, although the Roberts House (1964) at Buderim was the result of a recommendation from Robin Boyd.[14] These houses adopted an economically and materially efficient linear plan form and explored its potential for maximizing cross-ventilation and northern light. The major rooms of these houses were located on the north side of the plan with service rooms, bathrooms, minor bedrooms and the kitchen and dining rooms, on the southern side. In such a configuration, kitchens and dining rooms on the south were able to take advantage of open planning for northern light and breezes. Clients' limited budgets favoured tight planning solutions and taut building envelopes. Roofs were emphatically flat or had very low-pitched gables. The Masters (1960), Kelly (1960), Farbach (1960), Brick Manufacturer's Competition (1961), Leverington (1961), Crozier (1961), Neale (1962), Magee (1963), Robert (1964), Stoneham (1964), Wareham (1964), Belagoi (1964), Buckely (1965), Barrett (1966), Korab (1966–7) and Whitehead (1966) houses all follow this pattern. Given the number of commissions it is unsurprising that there is a consistency of design solution. Most of these early houses were published individually in journals and illustrated with black-and-white images taken by professional photographers commissioned by Dalton. Some also appeared in popular magazines with national circulation where colour illustrations were expected. The label 'ranch-style' used in magazine spreads in relation to these houses to establish links with American models,[15] was replaced over time by 'Australian' as images of an Australian architectural identity came to be preferred.[16]

The competition-winning Brick Manufacturer's House design, built at the brickworks site in Darra, an industrial suburb of Brisbane, proved to be a watershed design, the first to incorporate brick cavity wall construction (Figure 3.1). Walls extend beyond the line of the plan, delivering a separation of the elements of structure, but also judiciously capturing territory close to the house for indoor-outdoor living. Having previously utilized timber floors over excavated sub-floors, Dalton also began to trial the heat capacity of concrete slabs to alleviate discomfort during cool winter nights and early mornings.[17] The Leverington House, Chapel Hill and the Wippell Homestead, 'Morocco' (1963), at St George both utilized slab-on-ground construction to store the sun's heat for cold winter nights. St George, 500 kilometres west of Brisbane and 200 metres above sea level, experiences a greater diurnal and seasonal temperature range than Brisbane. The effectiveness of this heat sink strategy in St George's colder winters is recalled by members of the Wippell family.[18]

The Leverington House, which was included in the 1961 *Architecture and Arts* list of '10 Best Houses', is notable for other innovations in relation to climate.[19] Published photographs of this house focus on a breezeway space with floor to ceiling white glass (vitrolite) louvres (Figure 3.2). Timber-framed sliders in the living spaces could be completely removed from their tracks to create a single, large indoor-outdoor room, reflecting the new expectation for outdoor living spaces in Australian domestic architecture in the 1960s.[20] Opaque glass was also used in louvres below sill level, enabling air to circulate over floor surfaces to remove stored heat and to optimize cooling, again in line with CEBS research findings. In copy for this house, Dalton picked up on two themes. Firstly, the

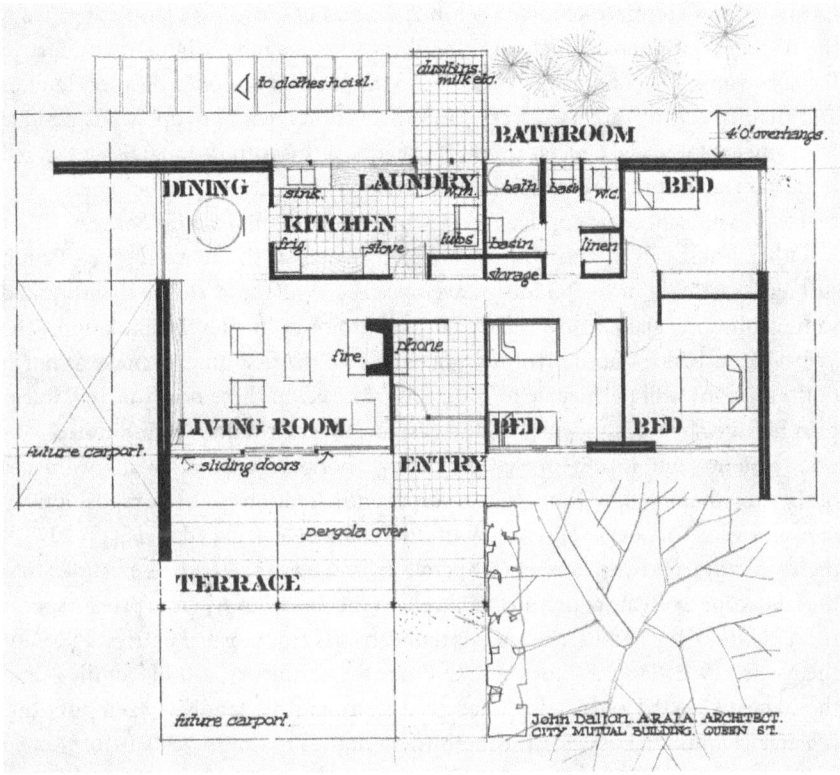

FIGURE 3.1 Plan, Brick Manufacturers of Queensland Competition, 1962. First Prize design, John Dalton Architect and Associates. Courtesy of Sue Dalton.

FIGURE 3.2 Breezeway, Leverington House, Kenmore Road, Kenmore, 1961. Photographer unknown. Courtesy of Sue Dalton.

introduction of a micro-climate: 'Set in 2 ½ acres of bush this plan springs from the demands of micro-climate and the sympathetic study of human comfort in the sub-tropics.' Secondly, local idiom: … 'the local idiom of "iron roof, louvres and chamferboards" are used freely, and there is no attempt to apply cosmetique [sic] veneers for visual effects. This is another basic essay in regional design which reiterates the Architect's conviction that "Pragmatic" solutions can be "Poetic" and that this forthright basic approach will prove a most significant influence.'[21]

Other houses from this time also experimented with enhancing ventilation through treatment of the building envelope. The Whitehead House incorporated sliding obscure glass below sill height to promote low-level ventilation. The Wilson House introduced pivoting wall panels for the first time, to make as much of the leeward wall permeable to breeze as possible. In these north-facing, linear plan houses openings to walls on the east and west elevations were limited – or non-existent – and if present were shaded by roof overhangs or awnings. Images of the Stoneham and Wilson Houses reveal end elevations to be compositions of masonry wall, roof beam and roof with each element articulated and expressive of their structural and environmental operation. End walls and screens extended into the landscape to create courtyards adjacent to the house, to separate private spaces from public spaces, and service yards and carports from formal entries. Plans for the Neale (1962) House – for the UQ Professor of History and his family – and the Magee (1963) House – for a jazz musician and his family – exemplify this practice (Figures 3.3 and 3.4). In both these houses masonry walls incorporated

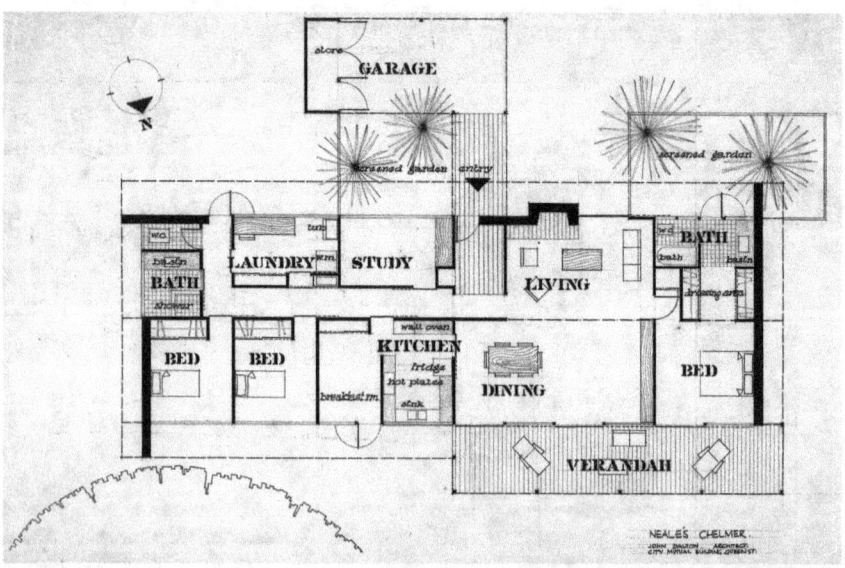

FIGURE 3.3 Plan, Neale House, Rosebery Street, Chelmer, 1962 (demolished). Courtesy of Sue Dalton.

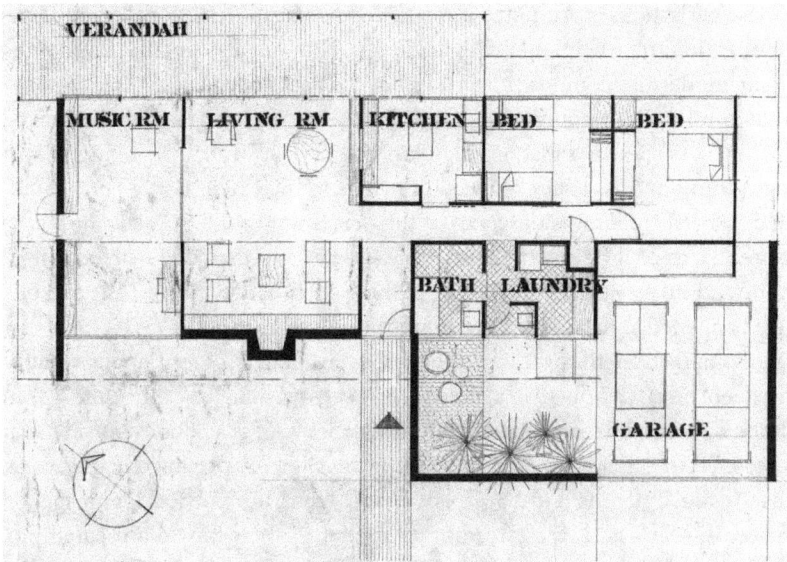

FIGURE 3.4 Plan, Magee House, Woodfield Road, Moggill, 1963. Courtesy of Sue Dalton.

FIGURE 3.5 Magee House, Woodfield Road, Moggill, 1963. View from the street of the south elevation. Photo credit Camera Craft Pty Ltd. Courtesy of Sue Dalton.

the chimney of a fireplace to the living room as a vertical element signifying entry in an otherwise horizontal composition (Figure 3.5). Brick masonry when used was always double skin and increasingly from the mid-1960s, roughly rendered and painted white. Dalton never utilized brick veneer construction and refused to entertain the suggestion if it was raised by potential clients.[22] The role of white walls in reflecting light and heat and mediating indoor temperature cannot be ignored, but they also have significance in a language of modern architecture that distinguishes technology from nature.

These early houses are notable for their formalism, functional planning and their attention to principles of climate design. They are also notable for the clarity of their modernist composition. Haig Beck recalls that Dalton used a viewing device to assist their composition. 'He would hop up on his chair and take his reducing glass … like a magnifying glass but back to front.'[23] Looking at sketch designs through this device reduced drawings to the extent that a *parti* could be seen clearly. The plan was the focus of this scrutiny, not the elevation or sections. Beck recalls that elevations 'fell out of the section' and that 'there weren't any end elevations. End elevations were filling in the section with walls and bits and pieces which happened at the end [of the composition process]'.[24]

Yet composition always carried with it an awareness of spatial and relational consequences. Carefully constructed perspectives made at this time confirm Dalton's ongoing interest in the relationship between inside and outside spaces as mediated through a permeable building envelope. A perspective of the Neale House is illustrative (Figure 3.6). As a view from the outside looking in, this perspective offers an inverse reading of spatial relationships represented in the 'verandah series' paintings. It depicts occupants engaged in activities in living spaces deep inside the plan and reveals the layering of space at the edge of building form, in a manner similar to photographs taken of the Dalton House porch (Figure 2.11).

The Wilson House for Patrick and Pam Wilson is illustrative of the degree to which Dalton's formal and spatial thinking was integrated. The Wilson House was commissioned for a steep east-facing block on Mt Coot-tha to the west of Brisbane. Dalton elected not to position the house at the top of the site to capture views east to the distant city skyline, dominated at that time not by tower blocks but by the lonely silhouette of the City Hall tower. Arguing that one gets used to views and that trees grow up to obscure views, Dalton instead sited the house halfway down the slope, away from the traffic noise and surrounded by forest, but also at a location where a north orientation was achievable on the site. Photographs of the end elevation of the Wilson House confirm that Dalton was not afraid to

FIGURE 3.6 Perspective drawn by John Dalton of the Neale House, 1962, viewed from the north. Courtesy of Sue Dalton.

combine a wide palette of materials. The major elements of form – walls of split faced concrete blocks reflecting the shale substrate in colour and texture, walls of regular concrete blocks painted off-white, panels of oiled chamferboards lapped vertically, pivoting fibre cement sheet panels painted bright orange-red, two roof planes separated by a clerestory of glass louvres and exposed eighteen-inch deep timber beams painted black – are individually articulated and elegantly composed (Figure 3.7). Photographs of the living room interior depict the same elements – the hovering roof and beams painted black leading the eye into the landscape. Also evident are the pivoting panels, clerestory lights, windows that extend horizontally and slide away and built-in joinery creating a deep window sill. But what is most present in photographs of this space is the bush (Figure 3.8). There is the sense of a minimum enclosure and of being suspended in a bush setting. Interior colours reflect the tones of the surrounding vegetation with brown, oatmeal, off-white, bone and green accents drawing inside and outside into further proximity.[25] The living room is furnished with pieces commissioned from a local joinery company recommended by Dalton to many clients, Quality Danish Furniture. A fireplace comprising concrete block and steel canopy flue painted white, pottery and large rough finished earthenware pieces and paintings by Australian artists Charles Blackman and Jon Molvig completed a quintessentially modernist interior also emblematic of 1960s life in Brisbane.

With the exception of the living room and the corridor to the atrium – an outdoor living room in the centre of the house – the Wilson House was flyscreened throughout with aluminium gauze.[26] The initial decision to omit the use of flyscreen in the major living spaces where continuity with the bush was desired

FIGURE 3.7 East elevation of the Wilson House for Patrick and Pam Wilson, Mt Coot-tha Road, Toowong, 1964 (demolished), demonstrating how the end elevation is arrived at by 'filling in the section'. Photographed in 1967 by Harry Sowden. Copyright Harry Sowden.

FIGURE 3.8 View of the living room interior, Wilson House. Photographed c.1965 by John Dalton. Reproduced courtesy of Sue Dalton.

was revisited after completion of the house when a voracious insect life at sunset made enjoying the atrium – or 'lanai' as it was also known – impossible. The initial design intention of an uninterrupted connection to the bush was modified with a screen to the lanai constructed from a rhythm of timber verticals and horizontals to which flyscreen was fixed. This different relationship is captured in the iconic photograph taken by Harry Sowden for his publication *Towards an Australian Architecture*. The increasing desirability of flyscreens presented significant problems for achieving open plan relationships between inside and outside spaces. It was a problem Dalton continued to wrestle with over the years.

By end of 1964 the Wilson House was also transformed by the construction of a landscape, including a BBQ pit [fire-pit] and outdoor dining setting, designed by East German trained landscape architect, Arne Fink (1930–93) (Figure 3.9). Notably Fink's design was for a naturalistic 'bush garden' not the gardenesque style popular with Brisbane's citizens and characterized by plantings of exotic specimens such as palms or poinciana and jacaranda trees and banks of azaleas and bougainvillea. Fink complemented the existing eucalypts and wattles with lemon-scented gums and sheoaks. His design included elements that would become hallmarks of his distinctive style, and that found their way into the many landscapes he created for Dalton's houses, including log retaining walls, steps constructed from railway sleepers with gravel infill between risers, and in-situ concrete stepping pavers with smooth edges and rough textured faces. At the Wilson House, texture was created by imprinting gum leaves into the drying surface of concrete pavers.[27] Water-intensive subtropical plantings, not native to the sclerophyll forest setting, were restricted to an entry courtyard, which also included an essential ornament of modernist design, the fishpond. The Wilson

FIGURE 3.9 Pam Wilson and her son in her bush garden designed by Landscape Architect, Arne Fink. Photographed c. 1965. Photo credit Photo Camera Craft Pty Ltd. Reproduced courtesy of Sue Dalton.

House was an exemplar of the most cutting-edge thinking about the marriage of house and garden. Ultimately the location of the Wilson House on a 2405m^2 site only six kilometres from the Brisbane CBD meant its existence in the long term was tenuous. It was sold in the 1980s as a development site and the house demolished sometime after.

Whilst most houses by Dalton from the 1960s were published, the 'Morocco' Homestead on the Western Darling Downs for the Wippell family was not. The commission for Morocco was the initiative of Noela Wippell, who approached Dalton after reading about his climate-responsive design in the popular press and who found the existing elevated farmhouse draughty and cold in winter and uncomfortably hot in summer. The programme for living at 'Morocco' was extensive and included in addition to space for a family with small children, separate entry for shearers from the yard to the farm's office, and enough storage space to enable self-sufficiency for a farming community for extended periods, especially during the summer wet. Dalton's solution involved wings separated by courtyards and oriented east-west with long elevations facing north. This configuration enabled the separation of farm operation from family, and dirty spaces from clean spaces. A string of services and storage spaces extended the length of the south elevation and living space was large enough that the dining table and billiard table could be cleared, and the space used for church services. Twelve-foot-deep north-facing verandahs screened with flyscreen gauze ran the length of the living space. Here shearers held meetings and children played or were home-schooled. Flyscreened porches were already a well-tested response to building in the hot dry tropics of Australia and for keeping reptiles and insects at bay. This solution, which Dalton adopted to solve a problem at the Wilson House, would become a trademark form-giving device used in his later houses.

The remoteness of 'Morocco' brought complexity. Costs for the transportation of building materials were a major consideration for construction in Australia's remote and regional locations. 'Morocco' was commissioned before the construction of key road infrastructure and access to the site from Roma was over black soil tracks that were dusty in the dry and heavy after rain, through paddocks, carefully opening and closing gates along the way. Dalton was resourceful with his client's budget. Structural timbers came from trees felled and milled on site by the Wippells using machinery previously deployed to build the original farm buildings on site including the elevated farmhouse. The fireplace, chimney and masonry walls on the east and west elevations were faced with field-stones sourced from Wayamba, fifteen kilometres way. The low-pitched gable roof extends well beyond these walls protecting them from solar heat gain in all but the coldest months. A long low house nestled into its site, with eaves casting dark shadows on stone walls, timber beams and eaves picked out in white paint and verandahs promising cool, it is the result of design decisions addressing prosaic matters such as the maximization of cross-ventilation, the application of sun path data for summer and winter and the control of insects and wildlife rather than the imposition of any pre-determined form (Figure 3.10). Noela Wippell consulted with Dalton over the selection of modern interior joinery and finishes which were far less problematic for transportation. Dalton insisted on supervising and made six site visits during construction, flying into Roma where he was collected by Noela Wippell for the journey out to 'Morocco'. His files contain photographic negatives of the landscapes he encountered on these journeys.

Until 'Morocco', the idea of the homestead had been sustained through editorials and reviews of houses such as the Head, Spinks and Robert Houses

FIGURE 3.10 'Morocco' Homestead for Stan and Noela Wippell St George, 1963. Original timber homestead is visible in the background. Photograph by John Dalton. Reproduced courtesy of Sue Dalton.

and photographs of houses in the bushland settings of Mt Coot-tha and Chapel Hill. The 'Morocco' commission provided an opportunity for Dalton to design for the circumstances of a real remote interior site and climate rather than to romantic notions of an Australian architecture. However, the anticipated experience of interior space extending uninterrupted to the horizon was spoiled slightly for Dalton, when Noela Wippell insisted on fencing a yard close to the house for the safety of her children. Their compromise solution was a chain wire fence.

Experiencing the 'Hot Humid Zones'

Evidence of how the different strands of Dalton's thinking on form and its experience were converging is found in an article that appeared in *Architecture in Australia* in 1963, titled 'Houses in the Hot Humid Zones'.[28] Dalton chose to introduce this article with a gouache of a Queenslander cottage thereby establishing the vernacular house as the touchstone and measure for innovation. Over the following six pages, Dalton carefully choreographed a photographic survey of local work by Brisbane-based architects including Eric Buchanan, Peter Heathwood, Hayes and Scott and J. van den Broek as well as images of work from his own practice. Images of individual houses, some severely cropped, are given attribution but not described in detail. Nor are they grouped through attribution to an individual architect. Rather they are read as an experiential sequence, moving from external images to those taken internally looking out to landscape (Figure 3.11). Accompanying text promotes climate design as the 'prime mover in the search for form and expression' but images link architectural expression to patterns of light and shade at the edge of the house. Images, mirror the earlier 'verandah series' of paintings revealing simultaneously the detail treatment of space and material fabric at the building edge and the consequent spatial and architectural expression.[29]

Notably, the majority of cropped and juxtaposed images illustrating 'Houses in the Hot Humid zones' do not leave the reader with any clear idea about overall form. Roofs if depicted at all are flat or very low pitched. Prominent in these images is the role of the zone at the edge of building form in linking interior space to wider landscape and garden setting – the mediating zone of space that Dalton described in his polemic 'the verandah' as necessary 'for reassuring and adjusting the senses'.[30] Most images depict shadows generated at the edge of the building envelope providing shade for the rituals of daily life. A blockwork screen wall in an image of the street elevation of a house by Hayes and Scott House is balanced a few pages later with an image of a different blockwork screen wall this time in a house by van den Broek viewed from inside with the

FIGURE 3.11 Two pages from 'Houses in the Hot-Humid Zone', *Architecture in Australia*, March 1963. Pictured are pages 76 and 78.

landscape beyond. Similarly, a view to a pergola by Eric Buchanan is balanced on the opposite page by a view taken from under a pergola of a house by Dalton looking out to the landscape. Images depict patterns of shade and shadow created by sunlight falling on pergolas, screens and vegetation. There is evidence as to the occupation of spaces – a child's tricycle, a kitchen stool in the sun, a family in dappled light viewed from a darkened interior. Although images belong to different works, they are conflated through their reading into a single impression of life in an ideal modern house for the subtropics. As a set, they illustrate the experience of interior space linked to exterior space – a spatial adjacency understood as characteristic of the verandah in the traditional Queensland house – but here promoted as essential for modern living. The introductory image of a cottage is deliberately childlike as if to remind the reader that being regional and modern does not imply the recovery of traditional form per se but rather the appropriation of characteristic elements and their transformation, reinterpretation and reuse in new ways in response to the patterns of modern life. 'Houses in the Hot Humid Zones' is an explicit representation of Dalton's thesis on idiom and the idiomatic.

The particular focus of Dalton's article is drawn further into sharp relief when compared with reports on research into climate-responsive housing for the hot dry tropics by climate design researchers Balwant Singh Saini and Robert Shand, both based at the University of Melbourne and featured in the same issue of *Architecture in Australia*.[31] Saini, who would later be appointed as Professor at the University of Queensland, and Shand elucidate data for effective design – heat gain, sun control, transmission of light and radiant heat, heat storage capacity for each element of design, and passive and active climate controls – whereas Dalton draws attention to the potential of a language of post and rail, pergola and blind for light and shadow.

In national debates around climate and architecture, Dalton wished to position himself like Seidler, as an artist integrating scientifically validated principles, but unlike Seidler his arguments supported a regionally inflected modernism. In unpublished text describing the Leitch House (1967) Dalton linked its design, for a couple recently retired from their life in western Queensland's pastoral industry, to their way of life – 'a form that succeeded in relating to the personal and private lives of the occupants'. But he also listed the elements he now considered characteristic of a regional modernism: '8ft wide verandahs, galvanised steel hoods over the windows, batten screens to verandah ends, roof cripples to accommodate high internal ceilings and low verandahs, all naturally evolved out the client's needs.'[32]

Evolution of the Dalton House 2: Crippled + split skillion roof forms

From 1963 the appearance of Dalton's houses changed, with change registering most prominently in a shift from flat or low-pitched gables to steeper pitched skillion roof forms, whilst plan forms remained relatively unaffected. The change in roof form in Dalton's domestic work from flat or very low gable to skillion is most often explained in terms of the failure of flat roofs in Queensland's tropical downpours. As an intern, Haig Beck remembers phone calls from clients whose roofs had failed after a major rain event.[33] After one particularly wet week-end in 1963, a decision was made to discontinue the use of flat roofs.[34] Dalton provided his preferred alternative: a photograph of a simple shed with a gable roof that adjusted roof pitch over the verandah, which was located on a property across the road from Dalton's house in Fig Tree Pocket. When designs for the Wilson House were underway it was Beck who reminded Dalton that they had been planning to do something different with roof forms.

Experimentation with roof forms would eventually lead to the development of a split skillion in Dalton's domestic architecture – and to its corollary, the 'Dalton section'. A number of architects in Australia were already exploring the use of skillions in response to a variety of imperatives including siting, light, program and climate but also fit with the Brutalist aesthetic.[35] In 1962 Ken Woolley and Michael Dysart produced a design for project home company Pettit & Sevitt that included a split skillion roof form over the entire plan, not as a response to climate but as a device for accommodating a transferable house solution to a range of site gradients.[36] In 1962 Woolley was awarded the Wilkinson Award for his own house at Mosman, Sydney, constructed in clinker brick and stained timber as a series of skillion roofs over a plan of split floor levels. This was followed in 1963 by Peter Johnson's house at Chatswood under a single skillion. In both the Woolley and Johnson houses, the living platform steps down over steep topography with the roofline parallel to slope.[37]

In Queensland the skillion was easily normalized because of its suitability in high rainfall conditions and was used in houses designed by John Railton, Maurice Hurst and Patrick Moroney. All were featured in *Cross-Section* with Dalton's editorial commentary addressing their suitability for climate and their brutalist aesthetic. In 1963 Railton's House and Studio in Spring Hill (1963) is described as 'an almost Baroque series of interior volumes, airy, spacious and well-suited to the hot humid summers of Q'land'.[38] In 1965, skillion roofed houses by Maurice Hurst at Indooroopilly and Kenmore are described as 'Brutalist'.[39]

Dalton's roof forms developed in a series of stages from asymmetrical gable, to opposing skillions to split skillions as his house commissions became larger and more complex. In the early linear houses, the leaves of gables were not always at the same pitch whilst the plate heights of walls remained constant. The difference in pitch – imperceptible to the eye – accommodated an imbalance in the plan arrangement resulting from a concern to maximize the exposure of living spaces to the more favourable north. Such suppressed asymmetrical gables are evident in the Masters, Crozier, Buckley and Korab Houses. Whereas in the Wilson, Stoneham and Leitch (1967) Houses, roof asymmetry is expressed.

From 1964, houses featured two opposing skillions with an opening vertically between the two leaves sandwiching a layer of space extending the length of the plan, ventilating not just one room but the entire house.[40] Once arrived at, this split skillion solution was fine-tuned, with experimentation directed at improving ventilation. Split skillion roofs were utilized in a variety of houses from 1964 including the Wilson, Graham (1966), Rabaa (1967) and King (1967) Houses. In the Wilson House (1964), the skillion roof sits over bedrooms at the back of the house with a flat roof section over the living spaces to the north (Figures 3.12). The roof opening to the north occurs along a corridor line where it increases ventilation and light penetration to bedrooms behind with cross-ventilation achieved using eight-foot-long metal blades.[41] The expression of this skillion is subordinated to the horizontal lines of the roof of the living room on the north.

In the Graham, Rabaa and subsequent houses a larger skillion roof sits over the living spaces to the north with a shorter one over bedrooms and service

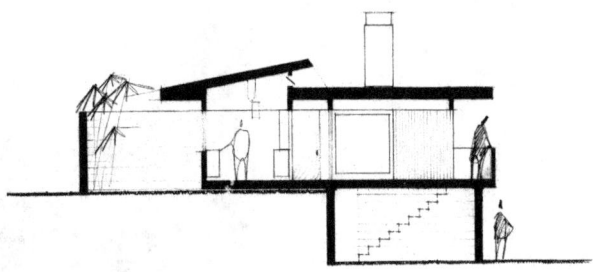

FIGURE 3.12 Section of the Wilson House, Mt Coot-tha Road, Toowong, 1964 (demolished). Reproduced courtesy of Sue Dalton.

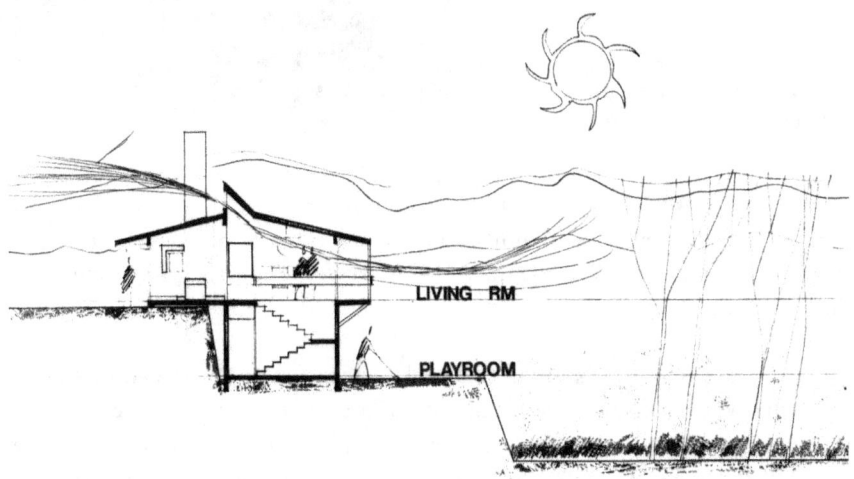

FIGURE 3.13 Section of the Graham House, Gower Street, Taringa, 1966. House. Reproduced courtesy of Sue Dalton.

spaces behind. The resulting section – the 'Dalton section' – generated the north and south elevations whilst end elevations demonstrated adeptness at 'filling in the section' with compositions comprising white painted brickwork, creosote-stained weatherboards and fibre cement sheeting (Figures 3.13 and 3.14). The end elevation is also where the 'Dalton detail' can be found – a detail for reducing the amount of shadow line at the edge of a skillion roof, made by cutting bricks in the external skin of a cavity brick wall neatly to the underside of roofing tiles.[42] This detail owes a great deal to Dalton's analysis of work by Alvar Aalto.

The Hughes House (1966) comprised two skillion roofed volumes organized symmetrically about a central service core and separated by a pergola-covered

FIGURE 3.14 East elevation of the Graham House, Gower Street, Taringa, 1966. Photo credit David Knell. Courtesy Sue Dalton.

courtyard and a low roofed family/service zone (Figures 3.15 and 3.16).[43] The result is not unlike a split gable. In a 1967 letter to the editor of *Architecture and Arts*, Dalton writes:

> This house is an indication of this Architect's return to Australian traditional forms, which incorporates raking roofs over deep verandahs, steeper roofs for airy large volume interiors, lattice and louvred [sic] sun screens etc., A return to an 'Australian Domestic Style' seems inevitable and this Architect's design is a significant contribution. The imaginative use of 'Space,' 'Volume,' 'Shape,' 'Form' are the new key words to describe this house ('Colour,' once the darling of the 50's, is now taboo).[44]

Dalton's reference to 'Australian Domestic Style' recalls Robin Boyd's oft repeated assertion that Australian architects had not succeeded in producing an 'Australian style', first articulated in *Australia's Home* and maintained in his 1967 survey 'The State of Australian Architecture'.[45] An elaboration in the Hughes House roof would became another Dalton trademark. In the vernacular, a change in the pitch of a roof is typical over a verandah and results in a crease in the roof plane along the plate line of the wall to the house core – a cripple.[46] Although a cripple crease was not always associated with a verandah in Dalton's Houses, it was used in the Hughes and Rabaa Houses. In the Graham House the change in roof pitch occurs over an internal corridor. In either circumstance it is clear that Dalton intended his 'crippled' roofs to denote verandah spaces.

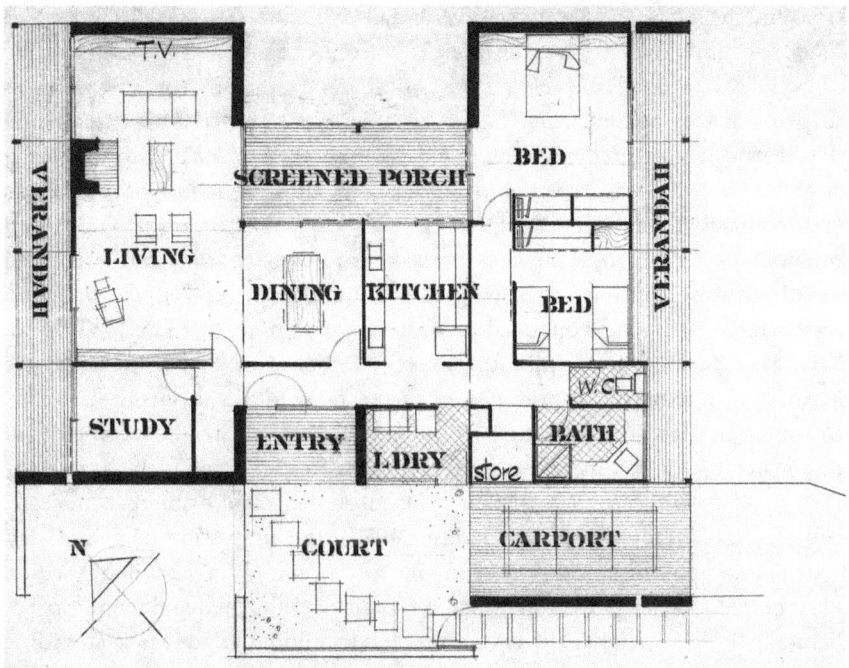

FIGURE 3.15 Plan of the Hughes House for Professor C Hughes, Brookfield Road, Brookfield, 1966. Reproduced courtesy of Sue Dalton.

FIGURE 3.16 View to Hughes House Brookfield Road, Brookfield, 1966. Photo credit Richard Stringer. Copyright Richard Stringer.

From the mid-1960s a narrow verandah extended the north elevation of houses – sometimes partly as in the case of the Graham and sometimes fully as in the case of the Rabaa House – its width determined by winter sun angles to living spaces behind. After 'Morocco' this interstitial zone was frequently flyscreened at its outer most edge. Flyscreens were fixed using the typically straightforward 'bush-carpenter' detail developed for the atrium of the Wilson House; black aluminium flyscreening was 'clouted' to vertical hardwood mullions. A kickboard at the floor level reduced damage from foot traffic and a mid-rail was positioned to lean against. Detailing enabled easy cleaning and replacement. Verandahs operated as a breezeway in much the same way as the 'fernery' in the Plywood Exhibition House, a timber equivalent of an occupiable brise soleil. A range of solutions now occurred along the north-facing elevations of Dalton houses. In the Dunlop House (1970) a double height screened void on the north-east became an actual fernery (Figures 3.17 and 3.18). A watering system fixed to the soffit to irrigate planting established a micro-climate by cooling air. Later, in the Chick House (1977), the suggestion of a verandah was maintained through a screened 'lanai' – a room, not a verandah – with a deep pergola-like edge treatment that also embraced kitchen and family spaces behind. The greatest benefit of the screened building edge was that sliding windows and doors behind remained uncluttered by screens and room spaces extended visually and experientially beyond their perimeter.

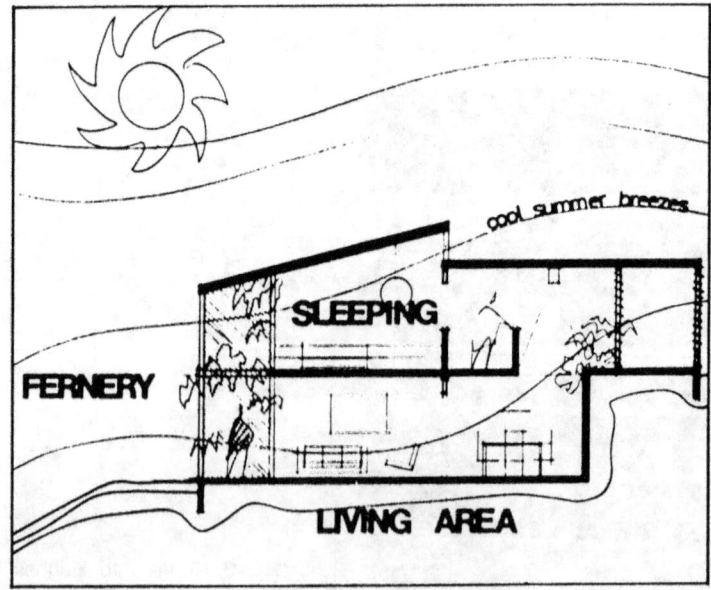

FIGURE 3.17 Section of the Dunlop House, Jesmond Road, Fig Tree Pocket, 1970. Reproduced courtesy of Sue Dalton.

FIGURE 3.18 View to north elevation of Dunlop House, Jesmond Road, Fig Tree Pocket, 1970. Photo credit Richard Stringer. Copyright Richard Stringer.

The Bucknell House (1968), for a narrow, west-facing site on the upper reaches of the Brisbane River, is an anomaly in the development of the Dalton House. In the Bucknell House the skillion is reduced to pop-ups located over major spaces, operating as light scoops and exhausting hot air rising in the house through operable louvres (Figure 3.19). In elevation these pop-ups are subordinated to the horizontal lines of a deep fascia concealing the roof falls necessary for Brisbane's summer downfalls. As a result, the house adopts a more monumental presence in its landscape setting than is typical of Dalton's houses.

Coincident with the development of the Dalton House was a series of houses referred to by Dalton as his 'budget houses'. Dalton's 'budget houses' deployed a New Zealand construction system, the Lockwood System, and the Salter (1970) and Strugnell (1971) Houses are the finest examples of the complete use of this system. An interlocking post and beam construction system, ordered from plan and delivered to site ready for assembly, the Lockwood System was quick and efficient to erect leading to savings in labour costs and very little material wastage. The system comprised western red cedar posts notched to receive beams and planks, and all timber members machined and predrilled to take services and joinery. Allowances were made to incorporate vertical tie rods. Wide cedar boards were used as lining throughout, including on raked ceilings. In the Strugnell House for theologian and UQ academic Reverend Dr John Strugnell and his wife Maureen, cedar structure and linings contrasted with a white brickwork fireplace, imparting a rustic, farmhouse aesthetic (Figure 3.20). This aesthetic proved popular and was recreated in several subsequent projects; some utilizing components but not the entire Lockwood system. Western red cedar boards lined raked ceilings at Los Nidos Resort in Noosa (1972) and the Vice-Chancellor's

FIGURE 3.19 Bucknell Residence, Sutton Street, Chelmer, 1968. Photo credit Richard Stringer. Copyright Richard Stringer.

FIGURE 3.20 Interior, Strugnell House, Grandview Road, Pullenvale, 1971. Photo credit Richard Stringer. Copyright Richard Stringer.

Residence (1972), whilst the Peden family specifically requested their house have no associations with a 'packing case' aesthetic.

The 'Dalton Section' refined

By 1966 the characteristic elements of the Dalton House had been distilled – white painted brickwork walls supporting dark stained timber framed and clad volumes, a distinctive roof form and section and the control of shadow lines through devices such as a distinctive roof edge tile detail and sill line datums. That this language did not alter dramatically was the source of some criticism but suggests that Dalton no longer sought new forms but rather a more focused use of this existing palette of elements.

The Graham (1966) and Rabaa (1967) Houses represent the culmination in development of the 'Dalton section'. Both were widely published. The Graham House, with a north-facing skillion cranked steeply along its back edge over the central corridor,[47] was awarded an RAIA Queensland Chapter Bronze Medal for residential work and was selected by Robin Boyd for exhibition at the Japan Expo, Osaka in 1970.[48] In *The Architectural Review* it was described in terms of response to climate:

> John Dalton's prize-winning passage-down-the-middle house near Brisbane is much more interesting than the plan suggests. Perched on the edge of a sharp drop, it is brick where it rests on solid ground and timber where it is suspended in the air. The problem of joining one with the other is resolved by a kink in the roof providing essential ventilation .... the silhouette reflects climatic needs.[49]

It should be noted here that the Graham House demonstrates Dalton negotiating climate design principles against issues such as siting and buildability for it is oriented on its very steep site to favour slightly the less desirable north-west, rather than the preferred north-east. Further indicating that debate had moved on from climate and in comparison with comments in *The Architecture Review*, judges' comments on awarding the Graham House the 1967 Bronze Medallion link its modern form to the Queensland house: 'We find this residence, in its essential form, a truthful expression of architecture in the Queensland idiom.'[50] In an article published in the *Telegraph* newspaper announcing its selection for the Osaka Expo, Dalton explains that buildings chosen for the Australian Pavilion 'have something visually in common with the old colonial buildings' and are 'in the words of Robin Boyd "handsome modern companions to the truly Australian Style"' whilst his use of phrases such as 'dinky-di' reveals a desire to be associated with the prevailing Aussie larrikin culture.[51]

Whilst the crank in the primary north-facing skillions of the Graham and Rabaa houses celebrate the shift in pitch between the verandah and main volume of a traditional Queensland house, the dark understory of the Queensland house was also evoked in different ways; through the introduction of diagonal cross-braces in the Graham House and in the Rabaa House by tapering white brickwork piers that bracket and support a dark timber-framed box housing the living spaces. The key elements of the pre-existing Queensland house – the undercroft, stumps, the verandah, its posts and rails, cross-bracing, shifting roof pitches – were recognizably present. Black-and-white photographs enhance the elemental composition of these houses, white tile roofs, cranked skillions, white brick or block work, timber frames and cladding with recessed space in deep shadow.

Significantly the emphasis in commentary on the expression of characteristic elements of form distracted attention from the spatial volumes contained within. These volumes are revealed in sections which also feature summer and winter sun angles emanating from a Corb-like orb – also reminiscent of Jon Molvig's signature sun – and wind flow indicated in a manner that mimics the swirling patterns of smoke in a smoke tunnel (Figures 3.13 and 3.17). Sections also reveal how the scale of large volumes were mediated through the introduction of white paper balloon lanterns, which became a hallmark of Dalton interiors. Sections were refined through the testing of scaled models in smoke machines at the University of Queensland. Through experimentation it was confirmed that the most effective ventilation was achieved by maximizing openings in the windward wall through combinations of sliding doors, louvres and pivoting walls and reducing openings in the leeward wall to a small vent. Proprietary 'Colt' ventilators were inserted high on external wall surfaces at the back of living spaces to draw and exhaust rising hot air across the major space. Reporting on the Rabaa and Graham houses in *Cross-Section*, Dalton promoted such instances of cooperation between university architecture schools' science units and practising architects.[52] A few years later the generic solution was presented to the general public in a 1970 episode of the ABC television series, *The Inventors*.[53]

Both the Graham and Rabaa Houses were photographed shortly after construction in their undeveloped bushy landscapes. One photograph of the Rabaa House taken by Harry Sowden with a telephoto lens from the Green Hill Reservoir some distance away shows a small white structure against a densely forested hillside and goes closest to expressing the idea of a tenuous foothold in the Australian landscape (Figure 3.21). This view is a fiction; it disappeared very quickly as the suburb of Chapel Hill was filled in with housing, lawns and garden beds. Another image, also taken by Sowden, depicts the Rabaa House through a screen of foliage with house and foliage drawn into proximity through foreshortening. This image, closely cropped by Dalton, was used to illustrate a pamphlet written to introduce new clients to the architect's services and appears on the cover of this book.

In Dalton's houses from the 1960s we see how principles of climate science interacted with disciplinary debate around identity in the distillation of a distinct language associated with the Dalton House. Explorations conducted in section reveal an evolutionary process engaging a number of different preoccupations – an interest in vernacular form, a concern for space and volume, an awareness of the relationship between interior and exterior space and the role of building edge in 'adjusting the senses' of occupants to their wider settings.

FIGURE 3.21 Rabaa House, Kimba Street, Chapel Hill, 1967. Photograph taken from Green Hill Reservoir by Harry Sowden and cropped by John Dalton. Copyright Harry Sowden.

Links between Dalton's practice and climate science are most evident in his early houses, particularly in those with linear plan forms. He was most adept at incorporating climate research findings into these modest houses in innovative ways. From the mid-1960s an increasing tendency to reference vernacular precedent and commentary in journals and newspaper articles reveals an increasing complicity in debates around regional and national identity. However, whilst he willingly engaged with debate as one dimension of a disciplinary culture, Dalton's primary declared motivation was not a 'style' but a desire to harness 'sunlight, shade and shadow'. A quote from Dalton in the 1970s is significant: 'design for climate is the prime expression – the sun being a constant, regardless of technological and social change.'[54] This position is repeated by Dalton in 1999, when asked to reflect on his career:

If someone backs me into a corner and says, 'What do you stand for?' When you've seen all the other parades of art and cultures and things, I say I'm still for design for climate because it works! The rest comes and goes, it's a chimera, it doesn't hang around all the time.[55]

Dalton's opinion on both occasions was expressed at a time of change within the discipline – in the 1970s when the discipline was broadening its interest to include the recovery of the vernacular and of history in general, urbanism and the problems of the contemporary city whilst 1999 marked the dawn of the new millennium. His position does not preclude the 'rest' – the succession of movements and styles that characterized late twentieth-century architecture. Rather it acknowledges their fleeting nature. For Dalton, whether architecture reflected Bauhaus sensibilities or Brutalist ones was not important. What was important was the timeless and universal certainty of the sun's movement, rendering shadows sharp and shade cool. For Dalton, the sun in Brisbane was not merely a source of unwanted glare and solar heat but was generative of an expressive and delight-filled architecture befitting the Australian way of life. Furthermore, he believed that attention to design for sunlight shade and shadow would deliver an authentic Australian architecture. Over the following years, increasingly disturbed by the poor design of Brisbane's city, he would extend his arguments for architecture to advice for the design of Brisbane city. Dalton's catchphrase sunlight, shade and shadow attracted many clients to his practice over the years. It could only be as successful as it was if it reflected the reality experienced by the readership of popular press.

4 ENVIRONMENT AS PROVOCATION AND NARRATIVE: DALTON THE ACTIVIST

By the end of the 1960s, Dalton was maintaining a successful professional practice, sustained by commissions from a mostly young professional clientele, whilst keeping alert to new ideas. He continued his involvement with the Contemporary Art Society, editing its newsletter and serving on its executive until 1970. Between 1963 and 1971 Dalton accepted sessional teaching appointments at the University of Queensland, and in 1969 he was appointed to the Board of the Faculty of Architecture. It was a time of reckoning in the education sector, under pressure from emerging social and environmental forces. Students across the country protested the state of their education, conscription for the Vietnam War and the 1971 Springbok Rugby Union tour, and in Queensland students protested the increasingly repressive rule of Premier Johannes Bjelke-Petersen. Whilst architecture students at the University of Sydney went on 'strike' in 1972 in protest at the inadequacy of their education for the new age, two students at the University of Queensland responded to the appetite for change by instigating their own review of curriculum. Between 1969 and 1971, having completed their third year of study, Peter Bycroft and Paul Memmott, researched, published and presented 'Towards an Understanding of Architectural Education: A Student Report', their argument for generalization and interdisciplinarity in architectural education framed by the psychology of learning.[1]

At this time, Dalton aligned himself deliberately with students and their activities, whilst also producing some of his finest houses and a number of interesting institutional buildings that demonstrate his attention to the social and political dimensions of architecture. His concern with designing for an 'authentic life' and his dismay at the proliferation of meaningless environments in Brisbane – the result of its too rapid growth – encouraged Dalton to extend his interest in the sensory dimensions of architecture to city planning. His environmentalist perspectives are evident in letters to editors and articles for newspapers and journals, lectures and public addresses in which he expressed his alarm at poor planning decisions and the mindless individualism of suburbia.[2]

The quality of urban environments was the subject of much speculation globally during the 1960s. The impact of modern planning and development on the life of cities had been described by Jane Jacobs, Lawrence Halprin and Jan Gehl who argued from within their different fields, for diversity and the re-injection of a human scale into city fabric.[3] Around the world, cities choked by pollution, urban blight and social disjunction were becoming major catalysts for and incubators of environmental consciousness. Even in Australia with its much lower population, cities were subject to conflicting interests, social unrest and environmental decline. Responding to this worsening situation the RAIA hosted a convention in Sydney in 1971 titled 'The Consequences of Today' with speakers from fields as diverse as sociology, biology and microbiology, planning, economics and commerce, addressing the discipline's responsibility to the future well-being of planet Earth. Keynote speakers included landscape architect Ian McHarg, who founded the department of landscape at the University of Pennsylvania and whose 1969 publication *Design with Nature* established basic ecological planning methods. Sir Robert Matthew and Fumihiko Maki were also keynote speakers, and Serge Chermayeff delivered the A.S. Hook Memorial Lecture, in which he adopted an ecological metaphor to define an 'urban system' as 'the product of a dynamic order, in which interaction between events of growth and change represent a continuous process .... a diversified activity of enormous complexity'.[4] The apocalyptic sentiment expressed by many at this conference is best captured in a presentation by biologist Stephen Boyden, who warned that unhindered and unrestrained growth was incompatible with the long-term survival of human civilization. Humans, he postulated, were now confronted by two possible futures: one conditioned by continued economic growth based on industry and technology – the dominant doctrine of Western society – or one conditioned by an ecological viewpoint.[5] 'The Consequences of Today' convention is a useful milestone; it confirms that by 1971 environmental consciousness had become mainstream within Australia's architecture profession.

In 1965, Brisbane was a city with a population nudging 700,000, unprepared for the changes brought about by rapid urban growth. The lack of a gazetted city plan meant that housing development had progressed unchecked and critical infrastructure lagged.[6] Urban sprawl, a lack of public transport and increased automobile ownership led to commuter traffic issues. There were problems in the provision of electricity and water supplies, sewerage and properly sealed roads. Large portions of Brisbane remained unsewered in 1968. The rapid expansion of the city brought into sharp relief the urgent need for qualified landscape architects and designers. In 1965, Dalton actively campaigned for the introduction of landscape courses at the University of Queensland[7] and petitioned Brisbane's Mayor Clem Jones[8] and the Under Secretary, Department of Works, Sir David Longland[9] for the appointment of qualified landscape architects, arguing that such appointments were 'critical' to the success of urban infrastructure projects and, furthermore, that such projects would not proceed elsewhere in the world without the services of landscape architects.

Unfettered and poor urban development provided the context for a series of articles and letters written by Dalton from 1965 criticizing developer-driven procurement practices,[10] the demolition of significant colonial buildings[11] and the pressing need for a new art gallery.[12] Along with Robin Gibson he campaigned for the conversion of Queen Street, Brisbane's prime shopping street, to a mall.[13] His criticism of the proposal for completion of St John's Anglican Cathedral almost certainly cost him one project – a commission to build his first prize scheme for the Kenmore Anglican Church, which was featured in *Architecture and Arts* in 1964.[14] He wrote against the extensive freeway system proposed by the American consultants Wilbur Smith that would have seen the inner-city suburbs of Woolloongabba and Bowen Hills destroyed, rebuking the uncritical acceptance of data generated by computers from traffic surveys as the justification for such 'development'.[15] Dalton based his arguments on matters of city form and structure around improving the civic experience of Brisbane's citizens rather than traffic and carparking needs. In a feature article published in the *Courier Mail* in July 1965 entitled 'We Should Build to Suit the Climate: Houses and Office Blocks Criticised', he extended his crusade for a delight-filled architecture to the urban realm. In this article, which opens with the by-line 'Too few of the buildings going up in Queensland, particularly Brisbane, are designed to suit the climate, declares Brisbane architect, John Dalton', Dalton described international-style corporate buildings erected in Brisbane as pedalling the 'British Company Image', an 'un-Australian activity' and 'subversive'. He writes: 'The reality of the Queensland climate must dictate the methods we architects employ to design the houses, offices, city halls and the whole complex of cities ...' Once again Dalton links climate to life in the sun, and he draws on historical precedents to provoke images in readers' imaginations of what this might look and feel like:

> The shape of Queensland tomorrow can be as wonderful as the Courts of Cordoba, the Seraglios of Constantinople, of the mysterious glories of Samarkand. Fountains and shaded piazzas will be integral parts of our new cities.

> Imagine a city office building rising from the city streets not in glass and aluminium but softened with green lush vegetation at each floor covering and enclosing the building with a soft veil of ever-changing organic life.[16]

In making this and many similar pronouncements, Dalton wished to draw citizens' attention to the functionally driven planning and developer-led procurement processes then driving Brisbane's city development and which he set against the city's abundant natural attributes – the sun, the river, water and vegetation – available to make something memorable and 'authentic'. He was seeking to galvanize the public's interest in their city and its civic identity at a critical time. Colonial buildings were being demolished and city blocks consolidated to make way for the office towers, considered by Premier Bjelke-Petersen as emblematic of a modern progressive state.

Dalton matched statements in the public realm with informed opinion pieces published in professional journals. Several CBD sites had become available through demolition and relocation of infrastructure, and designated civic spaces were as yet incomplete. Plans for a new civic square fronting the City Hall (the future King George Square) were contentious. The relocation of the Roma Street Municipal Markets released a site offering opportunities for the public realm, and attracted proposals from business organizations, individual practitioners and through a design competition organized by the Queensland Chamber of Commerce.[17] Whilst supportive of such initiatives, Dalton also argued for a memorandum to assist councils in managing the particular problems that arise when large and valuable central city sites become available, recommending as a guide 'Methods of Tendering for the Redevelopment of Central Areas', a document prepared by the RIBA and Royal Institute of Chartered Surveyors in the UK.[18] In an article published in *Architecture in Australia* and *Queensland Master Builder* in 1966 he argued that an expression of interest process that required an architectural solution to be tendered with a financial offer was open to corruption, rarely proceeded from a sound understanding of the larger planning issues and led to 'piecemeal and haphazard' outcomes for the city. If Dalton was hopeful of receiving a larger commercial commission, he would be disappointed for he was too closely identified in the public imagination as an architect of houses. He had by this stage already rejected the ideal mechanism by which an 'outsider' might attract larger commissions in Queensland, by pulling out of negotiations to enter an arrangement with the established practice of Hassell, McConnell & Partners Architects, Adelaide and Melbourne.[19]

Dalton sought to normalize critical debate on architecture within the local profession. In a paper delivered at the RAIA Queensland Chapter Convention in 1965 he advocated for rigorous criticism and defended the role of *Cross-Section*, a newsletter published by the Department of Architecture at the University of Melbourne to which he was the supposedly 'anonymous' – but readily identifiable – Queensland contributor. In his address he cited the opinion of much of the profession about *Cross-Section* including that it was an 'unsavoury University publication that is circulated throughout the Commonwealth', that its editors were guilty of '"unsettling" blatant mischief making' and 'guaranteed to render the profession a disservice and as a consequence unethical'.[20] Dalton expressed his affront at the stymying of debate on matters of architecture and design within the local profession. His plea for more robust debate followed an exchange with the Queensland Chapter Council RAIA over his critique of Queensland Newspapers Building by 'establishment' firm Conrad and Gargett, which appeared in the January 1964 edition of *Cross-Section*:

> A skilful handling of good forms, a sensitive respect for materials (not to mention poetic insights) are generally expected to be attributes of architects. In Q'land this is rare. The large majority … still hold fast to their thin and wearisome diet of apathy and disinterest and it is unreasonable to expect any improvement in Q'land architecture while this cultural lethargy exists.[21]

In response, Dalton received a letter dated 31 January 1964 from the Queensland Chapter Council invoking disciplinary action for undermining the standing of the profession under Article 52 of the RAIA Charter.[22] Dalton forwarded this letter onto Neville Quarry, then editor of *Cross-Section*, who replied a few days later: 'It seems to me that the Qld Chapter Council, after a number of fruitless sallies in the past are either out to put the stopper on you personally, *Cross-Section* generally or both.'[23] Sometime later, in reference to the Good Shepherd Chapel, Ascot, also by Conrad and Gargett Architects, Dalton would write provocatively: 'An amazingly accomplished plagiarism on FLW's Unity Chapel. … Since most architecture in Australia is more or less derived at third or fourth hand from various Masters' works, should we complain when someone swings close back to the source?'[24]

Dalton's activism, which unsettled members of the more conservative establishment practices, was double-edged, for it frustrated his attempts to implement real change after being elected to the Chapter Council of the RAIA in 1966. Although he was not successful in his efforts in 1969, to have a student representative included on the Chapter Council, he was successful in his campaign to have a new library to be housed at the Queensland Chapter Offices named in honour of Bruce Lucas, the F.B Lucas Library.

There were at this time in Australia architects who were far more purposeful and directed than Dalton in their environmental and social advocacy. Sydney architect and Dalton's friend Don Gazzard (1929–2017), together with his wife, sculptor and ceramicist Marea Gazzard (1928–2013) and fellow architect Bill Lucas (1924–2001), founded the Paddington Society to protect the historic fabric of the inner-city suburb of Paddington from development.[25] Miles Dunphy (1891–1985) lobbied relentlessly for more national parks to connect Australian citizens with nature and Barry McNeill (1937–2014) in Tasmania and Colin James (1936–2013) in Sydney worked to radically reshape architectural education to reflect the discipline's broadening interests. Dalton's activism was different; broader in its reach and often reactionary in character, he did not stay with a single issue for long; there were far too many. But frustration at the paucity of debate did ultimately lead to his decision to write and publish two handbills, *Broadside* and *diametrix*. They are a record of his navigating architecture's intersection with a wide range of political and social issues and reveal something of the circumstances surrounding the emergence of an environmental awareness in Queensland. They also provided Dalton with a diversion from the polite conventions of his practice, which was beginning to attract an increasingly affluent clientele.

Action and reaction: *Broadside* and *diametrix*

Dalton observed that professional apathy had its origins in student apathy. In his invited address to the Australian Architecture Students Association (AASA) Symposium in March 1961 titled 'What is wrong with the Diploma Course?' he sought to galvanize students writing that 'the basic problem inherent in our system of Architectural schooling is student apathy …. Rather than bemoan the curriculum and teaching staff which saps the energy and leads to lethargy and cynicism' he suggested students take control of their experience to better prepare themselves to change their world.[26] It was in his capacity as a member of a faculty level curriculum review panel in 1969 that Dalton wrote a paper, 'Thoughts on Architectural Education' in which he argued for the need to regularly review content and mode of teaching; 'the "change" thesis as being mandatory to teaching methods in the second half of this century. There is a need to educate for "NOW" and the future. [Or] Architects are relegated to a position of Historians always evaluating the past.'[27] Dalton's criticism was directed at the Joint Board of Architectural Education established in 1950 to administer the RAIA Education Policy and accredit schools of architecture. The Board was dominated by established professionals concerned more with maintaining standards for admission to the RAIA than it was about the educational direction of schools.[28]

From the mid-1960s Dalton supported the efforts of the Queensland Architecture Students Association (QASA), and attended the Australian Architecture Students Association conventions which he held to be more interesting than the professional equivalent.[29] During the Moratorium protest era, he and fellow UQ academic Bill Carr marched with the student body in demonstrations.[30] As a member of the RAIA Queensland Chapter Council and Chair of the Queensland Chapter Publications Committee,[31] he campaigned unsuccessfully for student participation on committees of the RAIA, later describing the Queensland Chapter Council as a 'cabal' in a private file note on the matter.[32] In a letter to the Queensland Chapter News after the failure of this initiative, he quoted from noted classicist, friend and fellow ex-pat Dennis Pryor who in an address to an RAIA convention had described students as engaged in 'an ethical revolt against the quality of life that surrounds them', a revolt which would 'inevitably be resisted out of fear'.[33] He supported and wrote text for student magazines, hosted open house in his office during the 1967 AASA 'City Synthesis' conference in Brisbane, judged design competitions for the AASA and contributed to panel discussions at their conferences. At the Adelaide AASA Conference (1969) he connived, together with students in the Queensland cohort, to stage an 'intervention' that interrupted the opening key note speaker, who was an unpopular choice forced on the organizing committee by their Dean.[34] Queensland student delegate Paul Memmott describes how the keynote address on the topic of English town-planning had only just begun when Dalton rose to deliver an unsolicited question from the floor. Before his question was complete it was taken up by a student delegate in another part of the auditorium, followed by another. A succession of student delegates each contributed to an endless question that degenerated into nonsense. There was outrage and the keynote had to be abandoned. Memmott recalls students spent much time conceiving interventions for AASA conventions. The intervention performed at the Brisbane conference(1967) and remembered as 'Two Dead Chickens' was the most notorious of these.[35]

When in 1966 Dalton launched *Broadside*, writing, publishing and distributing it himself to students at both the University of Queensland and the Queensland Institute of Technology[36] he was not addressing a deficiency – cohorts of students were already engaged in a range of extra-curricular activities. *Scarab* was published by QASA between (May 1965 to May 1966), and *ASM* (1967–8) and *MKII* (1970–1) by 'architecture students promotions'. Student magazines appeared on an irregular basis and relied heavily on content provided by academic staff including Dalton. In his contribution to the first edition of *Scarab*, titled 'feeding the psyche', he advocated involvement with the fine arts as 'paramount', apposite advice given the insights he had garnered from his involvement with the CAS.

> We all know that a tree's branches extend only as far as the spread of its roots. This is true of an architectural student's development. If a student wants to develop 'architecturally' he must send his roots deeper & deeper into life and culture that surrounds him.[37]

Some were critical of the students' efforts. *Scarab* editor Robert Riddel published in full a letter from UQ academic Graham de Gruchy accusing students of being pusillanimous in their choice of material and observing that the 'percentage of astute and informed criticism [was] too low to balance the poorly conceived polemic and the comic book and lavatory wall art section'.[38] Dalton did not seek to compete with existing student magazines. He was clearly excited by the prospect of being involved in debate, of the potential of a newssheet for his own professional development and as an opportunity to collage (Figure 4.1). In correspondence with NSW Institute of Technology fourth year student Andrew Metcalf, he described *Broadside* as 'my

practitioners. They both submitted entries to the competition and formed a pact that if one or other of them won the £3000 prize on offer they would use it to establish a partnership.[5] Heathwood's entry was successful and in late 1956 Dalton & Heathwood Architects opened their office in Queen Street, Brisbane City.[6] The winning scheme was announced in Brisbane's *Courier Mail* newspaper as the 'House of Tomorrow', a by-line appropriated from media coverage of Robin Boyd's 1949 'House of Tomorrow'. It was illustrated with a perspective drawn by Dalton complete with his characteristic *l'homme architecturale*. Dalton documented the winning design for construction whilst Heathwood was on his honeymoon (Figure 2.1) and it was built at the Exhibition Showgrounds, Newstead, in time for the Royal National Show in August 1957.

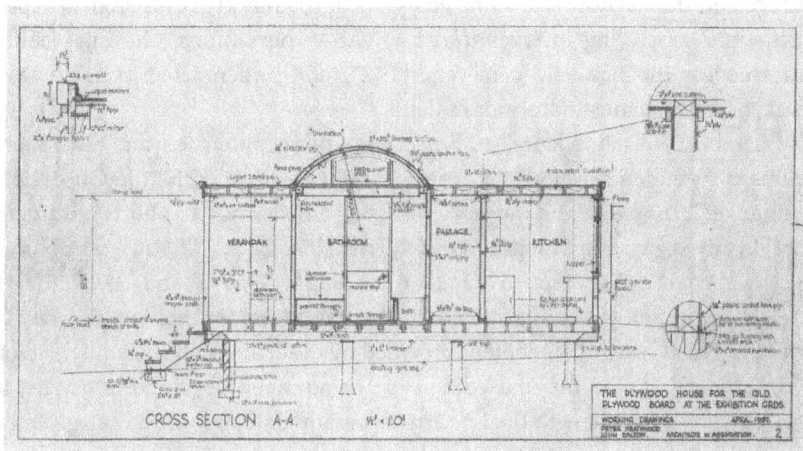

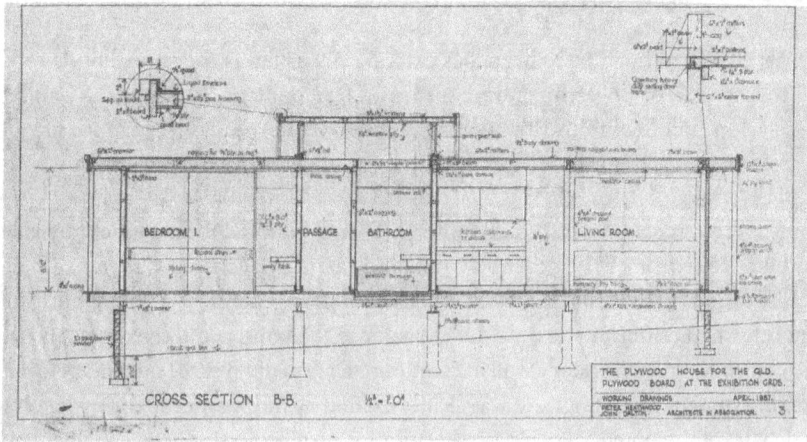

FIGURE 2.1 Plywood Exhibition House, 1957, designed by Peter Heathwood. Sections drawn by John Dalton. Courtesy of Sue Dalton.

DISCOVERING THE IDIOMATIC 39

enable underfloor air flow and the insulation of walls.⁷⁸ A roof-top sprinkler for bush fire protection operated from a cupboard next to the kitchen was a novel feature that turned the flat roof into a playground for Jane and Amanda Dalton in the heat of summer.⁷⁹ In all other aspects, its design reflected the best practice principles of late modernism. It has an economical square plan, lightweight construction and a regular grid, expressed in elevation by cover strips to the fibre cement wall cladding (Figure 2.9). Internal spaces and external courtyards are captured between walls and the horizontal roof extends beyond the building envelope with three-foot overhangs. *Architecture and Arts* chose to illustrate the Dalton House with a plan and section demonstrating sun angles and ventilation, an interior image of open plan living spaces and a view to the house from the north. What was not selected for publication were any one of a number of images demonstrating how interior and exterior spaces were linked through a building envelope that folds open or slides away (Figure 2.10). A photograph demonstrating the most up-to-date cabinet work also draws the bush into close proximity with the kitchen through an opening free of joinery (Figure 2.11). The manner of this photograph is not dissimilar to images taken by Julius Shulman of Neutra's desert houses. It has been noted that Shulman's images, taken under Neutra's direction 'never frame views of the houses, but rather, look through them with dynamic vision'.⁸⁰ Schulman's images capture the experience of interior

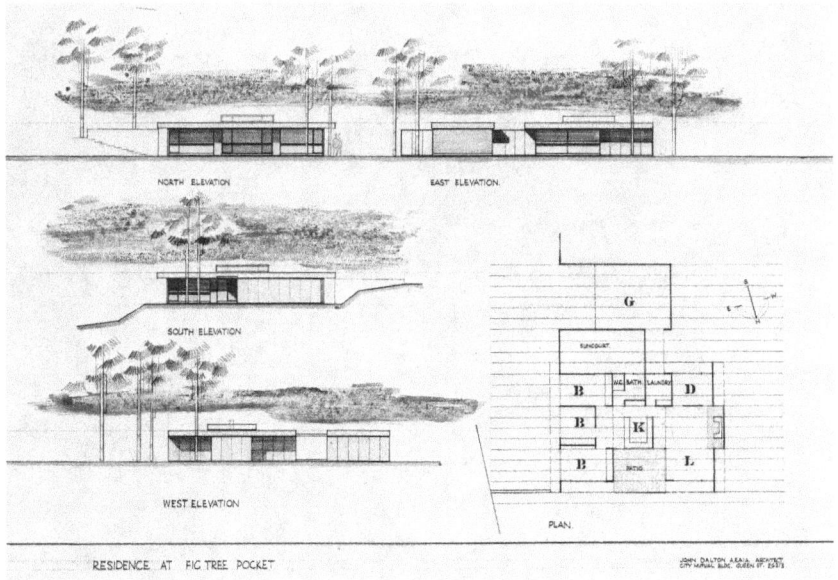

FIGURE 2.9 Design Development. Dalton House, Fig Tree Pocket, 1960. John Dalton Architect and Associates. Courtesy of Sue Dalton.

enable underfloor air flow and the insulation of walls.[78] A roof-top sprinkler for bush fire protection operated from a cupboard next to the kitchen was a novel feature that turned the flat roof into a playground for Jane and Amanda Dalton in the heat of summer.[79] In all other aspects, its design reflected the best practice principles of late modernism. It has an economical square plan, lightweight construction and a regular grid, expressed in elevation by cover strips to the fibre cement wall cladding (Figure 2.9). Internal spaces and external courtyards are captured between walls and the horizontal roof extends beyond the building envelope with three-foot overhangs. *Architecture and Arts* chose to illustrate the Dalton House with a plan and section demonstrating sun angles and ventilation, an interior image of open plan living spaces and a view to the house from the north. What was not selected for publication were any one of a number of images demonstrating how interior and exterior spaces were linked through a building envelope that folds open or slides away (Figure 2.10). A photograph demonstrating the most up-to-date cabinet work also draws the bush into close proximity with the kitchen through an opening free of joinery (Figure 2.11). The manner of this photograph is not dissimilar to images taken by Julius Shulman of Neutra's desert houses. It has been noted that Shulman's images, taken under Neutra's direction 'never frame views of the houses, but rather, look through them with dynamic vision'.[80] Schulman's images capture the experience of interior

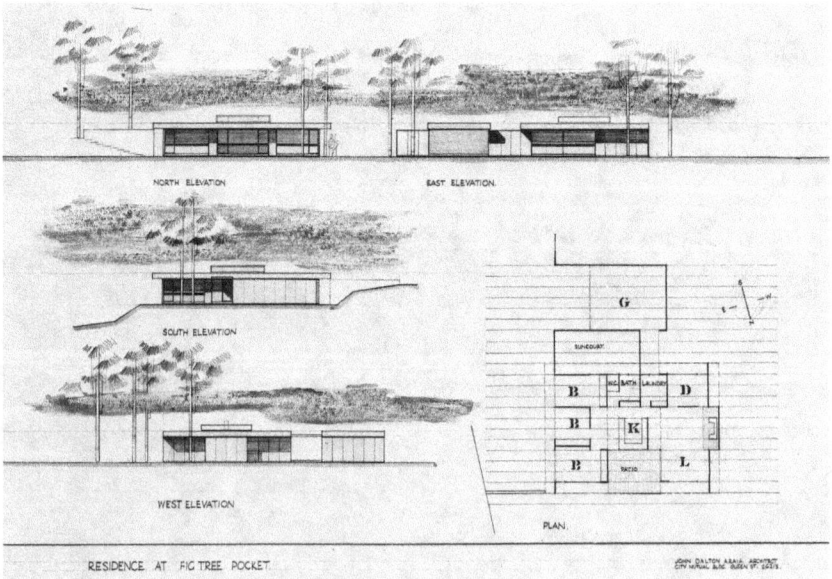

FIGURE 2.9 Design Development. Dalton House, Fig Tree Pocket, 1960. John Dalton Architect and Associates. Courtesy of Sue Dalton.

FIGURE 2.15 'the verandah' as it appeared in *Architecture in Australia* in March 1964.

By this concentration on detail and form, a new respect is developed for the subject and the painter finds a new life in the autonomy of the verandah. The direct immediacy of the post and rail in dark silhouette against the vast Australian landscape gives a startling juxtaposition of volumes. The cool enclosing volume of the verandah is never confining. It always succeeds in reassuring and adjusting the senses to the human scale and provides a gentle variation to the spaces beyond. The psychological comfort of the verandah space is the great certainty in Australian architecture and for this reason is loved and respected.[88]

Initially an investigation of detail, paintings had by 1964 become implicated in authenticating the experience of verandah space, as an essential space and the means by which humans 'adjust their senses' and mediate their relationship with their wider environment. Dalton draws attention to memories evoked by the

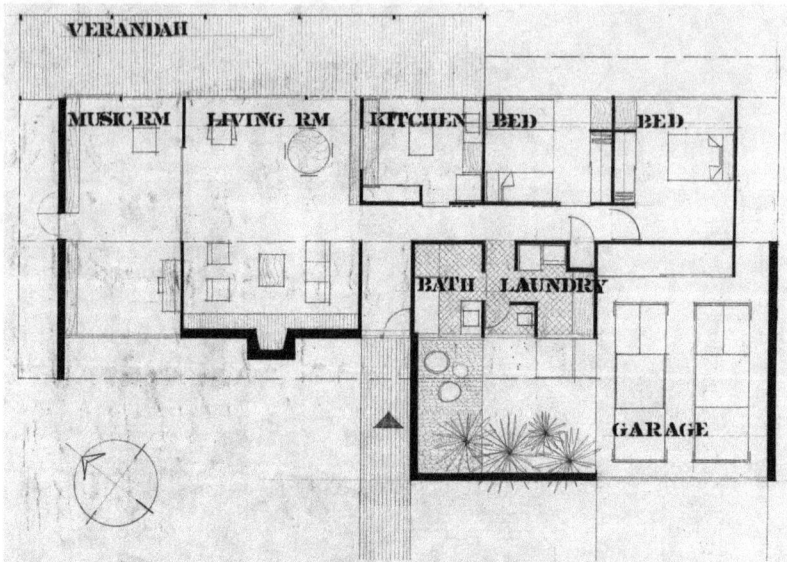

FIGURE 3.4 Plan, Magee House, Woodfield Road, Moggill, 1963. Courtesy of Sue Dalton.

FIGURE 3.5 Magee House, Woodfield Road, Moggill, 1963. View from the street of the south elevation. Photo credit Camera Craft Pty Ltd. Courtesy of Sue Dalton.

the chimney of a fireplace to the living room as a vertical element signifying entry in an otherwise horizontal composition (Figure 3.5). Brick masonry when used was always double skin and increasingly from the mid-1960s, roughly rendered and painted white. Dalton never utilized brick veneer construction and refused to entertain the suggestion if it was raised by potential clients.[22] The role of white walls in reflecting light and heat and mediating indoor temperature cannot be ignored, but they also have significance in a language of modern architecture that distinguishes technology from nature.

FIGURE 3.14 East elevation of the Graham House, Gower Street, Taringa, 1966. Photo credit David Knell. Courtesy Sue Dalton.

courtyard and a low roofed family/service zone (Figures 3.15 and 3.16).[43] The result is not unlike a split gable. In a 1967 letter to the editor of *Architecture and Arts*, Dalton writes:

> This house is an indication of this Architect's return to Australian traditional forms, which incorporates raking roofs over deep verandahs, steeper roofs for airy large volume interiors, lattice and louvred [*sic*] sun screens etc., A return to an 'Australian Domestic Style' seems inevitable and this Architect's design is a significant contribution. The imaginative use of 'Space,' 'Volume,' 'Shape,' 'Form' are the new key words to describe this house ('Colour,' once the darling of the 50's, is now taboo).[44]

Dalton's reference to 'Australian Domestic Style' recalls Robin Boyd's oft repeated assertion that Australian architects had not succeeded in producing an 'Australian style', first articulated in *Australia's Home* and maintained in his 1967 survey 'The State of Australian Architecture'.[45] An elaboration in the Hughes House roof would became another Dalton trademark. In the vernacular, a change in the pitch of a roof is typical over a verandah and results in a crease in the roof plane along the plate line of the wall to the house core – a cripple.[46] Although a cripple crease was not always associated with a verandah in Dalton's Houses, it was used in the Hughes and Rabaa Houses. In the Graham House the change in roof pitch occurs over an internal corridor. In either circumstance it is clear that Dalton intended his 'crippled' roofs to denote verandah spaces.

FIGURE 4.1 A selection of issues of *Broadside* 1966–9.

dirt-sheet for the student mass .... Published every month for kicks (mine) – paid for by Monier [Monier Qld was a manufacturer of roofing tiles].'[39] Initially called *Broadsheet* the change of name to *Broadside* – 'a nearly simultaneous firing of all the guns from one side of a warship', 'a strongly worded critical attack' or the act of 'collide[ing] with the side of (a vehicle)'[40] – confirms an inclination to activism. The anarchist tone of these broadsheets reveals Dalton's frustration with Brisbane's conservative profession and the extent to which Dalton self-identified with students. Whilst concerned to broaden the range of critical literature students were exposed to, Dalton also sought to raise questions relevant to local circumstances.

Publication of *Broadside* ceased in 1969 and was followed immediately by publication of *diametrix* (Figure 4.2).[41] The name of this new broadsheet possibly owes something to Buckminster Fuller's naming of the 1927 'Dymaxion House', a conflation of '*dynamic*', 'maximum' and 'ion'. *diametrix* similarly conflated 'dia' meaning through, 'metric' marking Australian architects' metrication from 1969 and 'trix' denoting straight lines. It was also the name of Dalton's small sailing boat. *diametrix* adopted a similar format and layout to *Broadside* involving a polemical statement prompted or supported by original or borrowed texts and images. The new handbill, punchier in style, was now sponsored by a number of building product companies petitioned by Dalton including Hardboard Australia, Stramit Industries and Walpamur Paints in addition to Monier Qld. Both *Broadside* and *diametrix* are journalistic in tone and material cited is poorly referenced by today's standards, if referenced at all, but reveals what

FIGURE 4.2 A selection of issues of *diametrix* 1969–72.

was then current in debate. The range of topics canvassed was broad in scope and embraced architecture's relationship to environmental, technological and sociological concerns. Dalton's use of collage in these newssheets, an extension of his art practice, was now purposefully deployed in a new search for relevant meanings for architecture.

Texts and images for *Broadside* and *diametrix* were gleaned from student conventions; magazines such as *AD*, Perspecta, *Ecologist, Journal of the Society of Architectural Historians;* books by Ralph Nadar, Serge Chermeyaff, Harold Nicholson and Marshall McLuhan; and the writings of Paul Ritter, Buckminster Fuller, Aldo van Eyck, Colin St John Wilson, Tony Gwilliam, E.R.D Goldsmith and Warren Chalk of Archigram. They provide a record of the eclectic range of issues that captured Dalton's attention and his idiosyncratic take on them. *diametrix* No. 10 in 1971 provided commentary on the state of Indigenous housing, reprinting quotes from the then Leader of the Federal Opposition in the House of Representatives, Gough Whitlam, and a report by Balwant Singh Saini for a 1967 issue of *Architecture in Australia*. It was marked across its banner in capitals 'REPRINT REPRINT REPRINT' as if to encourage its further circulation and was illustrated with a series of images of 'temporary aboriginal shelters' made from found materials seemingly cobbled together. Today, such shelters are understood to be the physical manifestation of complex social and environmental

relationships[42] but in 1971 they only served to underscore the poverty of a dispossessed and marginalised Aboriginal people. From the material available to him on the subject, Dalton first described the problem of housing for Aboriginal and Torres Strait Islander people and then selected a series of pithy statements advocating consultation with First Nations people on their needs rather than between 'experts', a seemingly novel idea at that time. He quoted Topper Carew, Black American activist, architect, lecturer in urban design at Yale and Director of the New Thing Art and Architecture Centre, Washington, on 'whites' definition of the culture of 'Blacks' as 'crude, primitive, crime-infested, dope-infested … but never as being beautiful' and on the innate human need for self-expression. *diametrix* No. 10 1971 may have been intended as a wake-up call to students about their comfortable, 'white' and privileged lives, but it also coincided with the 1971 Australian census, the first census since the 1967 Referendum and the first time Aboriginal and Torres Strait Islander people were included in the census count.

Broadside and *diametrix* did not seek to replace or compete with student initiatives such as magazines *Scarab* and *ASM*, the Architecture Revues, art exhibitions and 'happenings', but added another voice to the groundswell of protest against the authority of establishment institutions and the social and political status quo. Calls for student action and participation in all aspects of disciplinary life were a consistent feature. AASA conventions were advertised and reported on. Students were encouraged to extend the focus of their civil unrest from social renewal to urban renewal.[43] When in 1966, the position of the Chair of Architecture at University of Queensland became vacant at about the same time the Queensland Institute of Technology was appointing its new Head of Department, *Broadside* conducted a ballot of students to identify their preferences.[44] The very notion of a ballot drew attention to the possibilities of a non-hierarchical and collegiate school structure in which students had a say in their own education – notions then emerging in education and society that would excite major students uprisings globally in 1968.

Advocacy: The buzzword was ecology

Dalton returned to two key themes in subtly different ways over time: a pre-occupation with living as the mainspring for an appropriate and 'indigenous' architectural form and ecology, the 'buzzword' of radical students. These two themes provided a scaffold enabling contemporaneous issues or ideas with global significance to be linked to local concerns. Unsettling juxtapositions of text and images drew connections between seemingly unrelated stimuli and rhetorical questions drew readers' attention to dilemmas. Dalton's key themes are raised together in one of the earliest 1966 issues of *Broadside* in which Dalton reports on two speakers at the 1966 AASA *Educreation* Convention in Perth – educationalist, architect and planner Paul Ritter and Dutch architect Aldo van Eyck. The headline 'Ecology has shown that FORM is crystallized life' is followed by a carefully selected quote from Paul Ritter's keynote address:

> ARCHITECTURAL FORM should not serve the function of structure, services or enclosure, in a narrow architectural sense – but rather FORM should serve the function of life [capitalization by Dalton].

An editorial aside – typical of Dalton – supports the central message about form arising from a rational design process: 'Mies, Gropius S.O.M are "out" …. The old form makers (with perhaps the exception of Aalto) have little to say to the new METABOLISTS, BOWELLISTS etc.' The aside indicates that Dalton was clearly struck by the Metabolists – recognizing something about the movement's fundamental concepts enabling growth and change – but he did not analyse too closely its implications for a way of living.

In a separate 1966 *Broadside* Dalton cited from Aldo van Eyck's address at the AASA Perth Conference in which van Eyck advocated that students be immersed in the 'totality of things' from the very beginning of their studies, not introduced to the discipline through a series of separate and rapidly multiplying academic courses. Van Eyck argued that 'enveloping' students, providing them with a 'nest' and enabling them to tackle the difficult questions of 'total environment' in their studio practices will lead to enculturation and to productivity:

> 'education through evocation' [is] necessary …. to open the door … I think you should be introduced to the whole phenomenon of the relationship between human beings and the natural surroundings, and the way they nestle into those surroundings and make their environment, in all forms from house to village and city forms … right from the very first year …. our country is becoming almost uninhabitable as a result of urbanism being considered as one thing and architecture as another. Architecture, urbanism and town planning form a single discipline.[45]

Van Eyck's text establishes the significance to students of an integrated environmental design approach, which is dependent on establishing awareness of architecture's capacity to build relationships.

Dalton's preoccupation with ways of living featured in an interesting and provocative way in a 1968 *Broadside* issue in which he quoted Colin St. John Wilson's 'Letter to an American student'.[46] In his letter, St John Wilson speculated casually on why the Nazis might have closed the Bauhaus. Dalton latched onto this idea and used it as a banner. Under 'why did the Nazis close the Bauhaus?' he posited a response 'Surely it was not on stylistic grounds' and further paraphrasing St John Wilson: 'because "architectural forms" contain dangerous implications of a way of life. Namely that the forms so clearly carry information about their origin, that they may be said to represent a culture. They also enable a society to recognise itself in them'. Rhetorical questions followed: 'How do we as architects enlarge and celebrate the powers of life in our work? What "forms" can we expect to flow from Australian Architecture? What implications of a "way of life" will be found in our activities?' St John Wilson's letter called attention to the significance of ideas and intentions in directing architectural design, but Dalton used his words to support an argument for authentic forms. His rhetorical questions pick up again on his fixation with an architecture corresponding to an Australian way of life and cultural identity.

Identity is first encountered in an earlier 1966 *Broadside* in which Dalton places an image of a [male] settler beside the door to a humble timber structure alongside the words: 'the "myth" weighed against the reality/the "dream" measured against the fact'. Dalton poses another rhetorical question – 'What is your dream?' – which he attributes to philosopher Alfred North Whitehead, whose writing on the interconnectedness of things made him a significant figure in early ecological thinking. Dalton continues: 'It's a fair question as it suggests that the mainspring of action is one's imagination.' The architect works with the 'dreams that are valid for him and the society around him … Wake up in the back there and start dreaming.' Dalton's endorsement of the use of imagination is illustrated with an image embodying the myth of a settler culture. Whilst Dalton appears to insist that an authentic culture arises from the ordinary interactions of humans with their environments and that architecture has a significant role in expressing that culture, it appears he believes that new and appropriate forms – and by extension the identity that attaches to those forms – still have their roots in a settler culture. When read in the light of the earlier polemical texts 'the verandah' and 'Queensland's Pragmatic Poetry' it suggests that for Dalton imagination is limited to the sensory apprehension of the consequences of select form rather than an imaginative engagement with the full realm of architectural ideas that Colin St John was advocating. For Dalton bush mythology was the source of relevant ideas. Dalton's grasp of imagination is further supported by comments made by him as an assessor of the Australian Gas Association-sponsored competition run in association with the 1967 AASA convention in which he encouraged students' 'anticipation': 'Instead we can sniff out the patterns of living that are suitable to Australia so we may structure forms that are amenable to change.'[47]

From the late 1960s the themes of lived-life and identity became subordinated in *diametrix* to the more urgent problem of an environmental crisis. The environmental movement now encompassed a diverse range of approaches from the rational and the scientific to the mystical, with often complex scientific arguments becoming simplified as the movement became more populist.[48] The intersection of these different strands of environmentalism with architecture resulted in a shifting discourse that gathered social, moral and political dimensions. In *diametrix,* Dalton aired a range of positions from the objective to the uncritical new-ageist. Eco-catastrophe was imminent.[49] Pollution levels were rising.[50] Population growth was unsustainable.[51] A wider acceptance of ecological principles was advocated.[52] *diametrix* no 1 1971 featured a picture frame around a white space 'a blank canvas ready to receive pollution' with the following instructions:

> 'right now at Tennyson [Brisbane's coal fired power station] they're stoking the powerhouse to give your canvas an incredible range of tones. The oil refineries at the mouth of the river are working hard on that black streaky overlay effect and throughout the city internal combustion engines are out to give your ECO ART that eerie blue tint'.

diametrix 3, 1971 featured a passage credited to Wayne Davis, predicting eco-catastrophes and pandemics and promoting a holistic view of humans as part of a complex interconnected web with humanity's future dependent on the ecosystem's health. *diametrix* 4, 1971 was a brown paper bag inscribed with the words 'Make ecology your bag' and a quote from E R D Goldsmith identifying capitalist economics as the main driver of the environmental crisis:

> we are trapped in a vicious circle, one of our own making. Perhaps the day will come when we no longer take pride or pleasure in the gew-gaws of our culture, when we realise that fulfilment does not come with trinkets, however sophisticated. It will come the sooner when those already concerned with the quality of our environment refuse to supinely accept the economic dogma and begin to defend and campaign for the wider acceptance of ecological principles.

diametrix 7 1971 introduced the concept of 'Ecotactics,' a term used by the Sierra Club to describe a raft of strategies that might be deployed by environmental activists against 'enemies' of the earth.[53]

In the context of environmental debates, the role of technology in maintaining ecological equilibrium proved a problematic subject. As the root cause of ecological catastrophe, many commentators could not countenance technology being part of the solution. Dalton presented both sides of this argument. Technology provided new ways of enclosing space with less material. Images of Tony Gwillam's 'Nova' dome and a pneumatic rhombicuboctahedron (twelve-sided structure) mega-structure featured in *Broadside* 4, 1968,[54] and closer to home, *diametrix* 1, 1972 featured Howard Choy's low-energy cardboard and duct tape dome eco-structure in the township of Samford to the west of Brisbane. In *diametrix* 6, 1971, Warren Chalk of Archigram was cited in defence of the use of technology to solve the problems of the world: 'But if we are to prevent eco-catastrophe, it can only be done by more sophisticated environmental systems, not by dropping out. Nor the hippy type philosophy ... Apart from being a head in the sand attitude we need to fight technology with technology'.[55]

Reports on technological solutions were balanced with stories from communes and solutions for alternative lifestyles, peppered with references to 'squares' and 'dropping out'.[56] The *diametrix* 9, 1971 issue reported on the AASA Congress '71 in Auckland and was illustrated with an image of a young, bare-chested Sim Van der Ryn, member of the College of Environmental Design [CED] at Berkeley and pioneer of ecologically integrated living design, constructing shelters with students. Both Serge Chermayeff and Sim Van der Ryn were keynote speakers at the 1971 Auckland Congress, which Dalton attended, whilst Chermayeff was also a keynote speaker at the 1971 RAIA National Convention, 'The Consequences of Today' in Sydney. At the student convention Chermayeff identified a condition he described as 'capsule syndrome' as a drawback of 'total environment'. Essential to avoiding 'capsule syndrome' was keeping the capsule's inhabitants human by making them feel at home in their world, an insight which resonated with Dalton's personal belief system.

Dalton's pamphleteering was an individual initiative, outward looking and questioning, but always seeking to locate questions firmly in relation to a locally rooted practice of architecture, and to return debate to what he perceived as architecture's core concerns. Subversively and over time he socialized an awareness of environmental issues in architecture. Analysis of Dalton's own practice indicates that from the 1970s, his view of environmentally tuned architecture was becoming more sophisticated. Dalton had always problematized architecture as harnessing environmental conditions and situating the occupant in relation to their surroundings. Increasingly, solutions did not come from imposing preconceived solutions, but rather from seeking out the order inherent in each particular situation. Implicit in such an approach is an understanding that a built work becomes an integral part of a web of pre-existing relationships.

Change was also occurring in other realms of Dalton's life. In 1972 John Dalton and Sue Stirling married and embarked on a trip to the UK, the first that Dalton had undertaken since emigrating in 1949. The trip provided a circuit breaker. The students Dalton had been associating with had graduated or travelled overseas, the CAS had folded and Dalton's enthusiasm for pamphleteering waned. The last issue of *diametrix* is dated 1972. Dalton and Sue had for some time been travelling to Allora on the Darling Downs to visit Sue's sister and in 1974, they purchased 'Lambtail Cottage'[57] which quickly became a second home; somewhere the couple could indulge in a healthy, green and 'authentic' lifestyle.

Proto-environmentalism in practice

Whilst pamphleteering Dalton continued his editorial work for *Cross-Section* and *Architecture in Australia*, his part-time lecturer position at The University of Queensland and his executive roles on the Council for the Queensland Art Gallery, the CAS Queensland Branch and the RAIA Queensland Chapter Council. His busy practice was now attracting commissions for larger and more complex houses. He selected the site and completed the Los Nidos Resort (1972, demolished) in Hastings Street, Noosa for Frenchman, Mr D.D. Couche. It was also during this time that the Queensland Department of Public Works engaged John Dalton Architect and Associates to undertake several very specific institutional commissions.

Dalton's domestic work from the late 1960s and early 1970s reveals increasing attention given to the house in its setting. The problem of form became subservient to positioning the occupant in relation to the sun and breeze, to details creating shade and shadow, to constructing short views within and long views to the landscape. Dalton's materials palette remained limited in the number of elements – white masonry walls, dark stained timber structures, awnings of asbestos cement sheet, Trimdeck profile or tile roofs, red quarry tiles and the continued use of strong horizontal datum lines broken only by a chimney element. Over time Dalton developed a strategy involving narrative to order the elements of his preferred architectural language, but the language itself remained largely unchanged.

One important commission – the Smith House (1966) – is an anomaly in work dating from this time and reveals a tension between the will to form on one hand and Dalton's interest in indoor-outdoor spatial relationships on the other. The Smith House, located on an open site in the peri-urban suburb of Brookfield, was commissioned by clients who were returning to Australia after spending time in Papua New Guinea and who expressly asked for an airy Queensland house.[58] Unlike other houses in Dalton's practice from this period, the cultural references in the Smith House are unambiguous (Figure 4.3). That Dalton remained conscious of links to bush mythology is evident from commentary accompanying its publication:

> Stilts, verandahs, screens and a dominant roof form relating to the four sides of the house – not only two – are the prime elements of this character developed by the pioneers to symbolise their struggle against the environment.[59]

The house, with eight-foot-wide verandahs on its north, 'appears to sit above the site and landscaping in a personal defiant attitude as if it had mastered the environment'. Its determinate form is similar to the Queensland house precedent it seeks to emulate. Consequently, pergolas used to 'create a very strong link between the site, landscaping, outdoor living area and the ground floor of the

FIGURE 4.3 View to Smith House, Brookfield Road, Brookfield, 1966. Photo Geoff Dauth. Courtesy of Sue Dalton.

house' do not do so convincingly.[60] The Smith House resonated with Robin Boyd, chair of the panel who selected it for display at Expo '67 in Montreal Canada. One of five Australian houses and the only Queensland house, it was exhibited alongside the Lockhead House (1965) by Keith Cottier of Allen, Jack & Cottier, Palm Beach House (1963) by Ross Thorne Architect, Woolley House (1962) by Ken Woolley, Ancher, Mortlock, Murray & Woolley and Muller House (1963) by Harry Seidler, all of which were located in NSW. In explaining his selection, Boyd writes that they '… represent its best domestic architecture and show the development of a style with regional character. This is characteristically of natural brick and rugged timber built in a direct and uncomplicated way – but freely, not packaged into a rigid box.'[61] Of the Smith House Robin Boyd would write in correspondence to Dalton, referring to one of Australia's oldest domestic constructions: 'I've not seen anything looking more Australian since Experiment Farm. Congratulations.'[62]

More typically Dalton's larger commissions from this time involved courtyard strategies. Two different strategies for forming courtyards were deployed – through the addition of volumes to enclose an external space or through the erosion of a volume to make external space. Early courtyards in the Day Residence (1955), which Dalton worked on with Robin Gibson whilst in the office of Theo Thynne and Associates, and the Brennan House (1959), from the partnership of Dalton and Heathwood are formed by eroding a form – to enable cross-ventilation and winter sun. The strategy of erosion of form reappears in later domestic work, the Covalevich (1975), McGuckan (1976) and Chick Houses (1977), and coincides with Dalton's explorations in larger institutional commissions. The first strategy for making courtyard space – enclosing or partly enclosing space using a building's wings – is more frequently used during the late 1960s and early 1970s.

Courtyard houses: Additive processes

Organizing the programme for living into discrete wings, such as a living wing and a bedroom wing, and orientating them to take advantage of climate and the specific circumstances of site, provided flexibility in siting and planning. The strategy, first exhibited in 'Morocco' for the Wippell family, was also used for the Hughes, Cameron (1969), Vice-Chancellor's (1972), Peden (1975), Musgrave (1973), Louis (1973), MacFarlane (1975) and Ibbotson (1977) houses. In photographs commissioned by Dalton many of these projects appear not unlike the collection of buildings that might comprise a rural homestead. Most would be complemented with gardens designed by landscape architects Arne Fink or Beth Wilson. The courtyard plan became a useful strategy on steep sites, leading to the introduction of a half-level. The Cameron, Musgrave, MacFarlane and Ibbotson houses deployed this strategy. Whereas earlier house forms, such as the Dalton, Leverington and Wilson houses hover over or sit on their flattened sites, later houses are carefully situated to create private territory adjacent to the house and are oriented in relation to the specifics of topography and view, in addition to light and prevailing breezes. The Hughes House at Brookfield, one of the earliest courtyard houses, comprises a formal living wing and a bedroom wing with family living spaces between to create an H-shaped footprint capturing space on the northeast and southwest sides of the house (Figures 3.15 and 4.4). A generous screened porch occurs between the two wings on the north-east and an entry courtyard is located on the south-west.

FIGURE 4.4 Interior of Hughes House, Brookfield Road, Brookfield, 1966. Photo Geoff Dauth. Courtesy of Sue Dalton.

Dalton's thinking process is evident in preliminary design drawings prepared for discussions with clients. The very few of these drawings still extant are in poor condition. Design drawing plans are not dissimilar to the clean line drawings that Dalton prepared for publications of his work except that they also include information about sun, breezes and the direction of desirable views. Interior and exterior spaces are defined by open and closed boundary conditions. Solid walls order the sequencing of movement and space and define desired environmental relationships. All spaces open to north light and views. When the solid walls in these sketch drawings are understood to be double skin masonry, rendered and painted white and the glazed boundary conditions are understood to be fringed with pergolas of stained timber – it is possible to apprehend the transactional nature of the spaces Dalton imagined at the edges of building form. In Dalton's process, plans ordering programme and environmental relationships came first. Formal composition of spatial volumes and their elevational treatment followed.[63]

The choreographing of a sequence of spaces is most evident in the Vice-Chancellor's Residence (1972 demolished) at the University of Queensland. After taking advice from Robin Boyd, the newly appointed Vice-Chancellor of the University of Queensland, Professor Zelman Cowen (1919–2011) negotiated with University Chancellor, Sir Alan Mansfield for John Dalton Architect and Associates to be commissioned to design a residence – a home for the Vice-Chancellor's family and a venue for entertaining official University guests.[64] Boyd had previously designed a family home for Anna Cowen (1925–) in Studley Park Kew in 1958 where the family lived until 1966 and was a greatly admired personal friend of the Cowens. Sir Zelman's idea to commission a residence on the University campus was prompted by his experience as Vice-Chancellor of the University of New England where he resided in a stately home on the University grounds, 'Trevenna' (1892) designed by John Horbury Hunt (1838–1904). The experience confirmed his belief that a Vice-Chancellor should identify with and live on the campus to be accessible to students and staff.[65] He maintained this view despite several student incursions into his private spaces, on one occasion leaving a noose in a toilet.[66] During difficult years marked by student occupation of the JD Storey Administration building and protests against the Vietnam War and the Springbok tour, Sir Zelman negotiated outcomes between students and the University and on behalf of students with the Queensland Police Force and the suspicious and highly interventionist Premier.[67]

The Vice-Chancellor's Residence was located on an open greenfield site in Walcott Street on the western edge of the St Lucia Campus. A former tip with falls to the north and west, it was not the first choice of site. A location near the river was not approved by the Senate. After Dalton received a preliminary estimate for work from Lockwood, a strict budget of $80,000 was agreed by the deputy Vice-Chancellor on behalf of the University and the State Treasurer. A complex programme for family living and university entertaining was organized by Dalton across three levels with courtyards maximizing morning sun and breeze to spaces adjacent (Figure 4.5). The house was situated so that all major rooms had a northern or eastern aspect. Upper level rooms facing north had verandahs with lattice screens closing their east and west ends. The plan arrangement enabled living spaces to be open to outside but private and protected whilst sections were manipulated to maximize cross-ventilation. The courtyard had now developed into a spatial type responding to zoning for different uses: formal versus informal living, ceremonial versus family.

The Vice-Chancellor's Residence was approached diagonally across an open lawn (Figure 4.6). A pathway following a contour line along the slope of the site led to an entrance recessed between white walls and marked by a prominent chimney. Beyond was another double height threshold, from which the visitor could move down two steps into the formal reception rooms on the right, straight ahead to a double height formal dining space, left into the double height family living wing or climb upstairs to take a mezzanine walkway to private family areas, which stretched along the contours in an east west direction, at a higher level in the landscape. Private family spaces and formal reception spaces were separated by a wing of service spaces comprising kitchen, laundry and maid's quarters and the 'atrium', an indoor-outdoor room that recalls the intermediate space described by Aalto in his essay 'From Doorstep to Living Room'. The atrium was a double height space opening into a courtyard, lit by a full height wall of glazing and crossed at the upper level by the mezzanine walkway connecting private and public realms (Figure 4.7). Its use was not specified but could best be

FIGURE 4.5 Design Development drawings for Vice-Chancellor's Residence, University of Queensland, St Lucia, 1972. Courtesy of Sue Dalton.

FIGURE 4.6 View to entry, Vice-Chancellor's Residence, University of Queensland, St Lucia, 1972. Photo credit Richard Stringer. Copyright Richard Stringer.

FIGURE 4.7 'Atrium', Vice-Chancellor's Residence with stair climbing to bridge, University of Queensland, St Lucia, 1972. Photo credit Richard Stringer. Copyright Richard Stringer.

described as an anteroom – a place in which to wait before being received into either public or private domain.

Sequence in the Vice-Chancellor's Residence is reinforced by a rational strategy for structure/construction. The plan is ordered by parallel walls in cavity brickwork, bagged and painted white, running east west across the site. Space captured between these walls was either internal or external. Walls took the form of retaining walls, garden walls or interior walls depending on the circumstances of their situation and the spatial relationships they defined. The north south promenade that ran counter to the east west alignment of these walls facilitated movement from the most public reception rooms to the most private family rooms and out into the landscape at the upper level. Changes in grade were exploited to vary room volumes. From this set of careful strategic moves arose an array of experiences. It was possible on each level, to step out of interior spaces onto a verandah or into a courtyard with northern aspect. Diagonal views were available from the upper level into reception rooms and across the adjacent verandahs, or through family spaces across private courtyards and into the suburban landscape beyond (Figure 4.8). The diagram enabled occupants to orient themselves in relation to site, prevailing breezes and the passage of the sun.

Formally, the house was roofed by skillions at a range of angles. The major circulation spine was roofed with a skillion at 35 degrees and balanced compositionally by an opposing skillion at a similar angle over the guest bedroom at the highest point in the site. The reception room and bedroom wings were roofed by skillions at 15 degrees, verandahs at 25 and 35 degrees and sunhoods over pivoting wall vents at 60 degrees. Trimdeck roof sheeting was pulled to a consistent eaves line delivering the sense of a unified composition despite this variety of roof pitches. The appearance of a 'broken profile' of roofs in the Vice-Chancellor's Residence and the Peden Residence which followed was not unlike a clustering of farmhouse roofs denoting territory within a wider landscape (Figure 4.9). The Peden House demonstrates how, on a peri-urban

FIGURE 4.8 View from entry to reception rooms, Vice-Chancellor's Residence, University of Queensland, St Lucia, 1972. Photo credit Richard Stringer. Copyright Richard Stringer.

FIGURE 4.9 View to Peden Residence, 'Merindah', Glenhurst Street, Pinjarra Hills, 1975. Photo credit Richard Stringer. Copyright Richard Stringer.

site overlooking the Brisbane River, courtyards became the means of creating protected living spaces linked visually and spatially to farmland and to the riverscape beyond (Figure 4.10). Dalton is known at this time to have referred to the historic Wolston House, a collection of farm structures built in 1852 at Oxley, to describe his design intentions to clients.[68] Yet Dalton's houses from this period did not 'look' like Wolston House, confirming that his interest in historical building forms as precedent for an 'indigenous Australian' architecture was indirect, concerned with spatial relationships and their experience. Jennifer Taylor makes this distinction most succinctly in her essay in *Old Continent: New Building* (1983) in which she draws a distinction between the characteristic elements of Dalton's forms and their spatial consequences:

> Dalton's buildings at first seem to have little in common with the Queensland vernacular. The lessons are hidden in the subtle ways he uses breeze, shade and sun to bring comfort and delight to semi-tropical architecture.[69]

The Vice-Chancellor's Residence ceased to a home after Sir Zelman Cowen's successor, Emeritus Professor Brian Wilson relinquished the Vice-Chancellor role. Wilson's successor Professor John Hay lived in the house for a very brief time after his appointment in 1996. After a period, during which it was used as offices by Examinations during the refurbishment of UQ's administration building, Elizabeth Watson-Brown Architects was engaged to undertake a report with a view to its repurposing and Robert Riddel was commissioned to prepare drawings

FIGURE 4.10 Courtyard, Peden Residence at Pinjarra Hills. Photo credit Richard Stringer. Copyright Richard Stringer.

for its possible reuse. The EWB Architects report notes that on inspection in 1996 the house was in good condition, but that when inspected on 7 June 1999 it was in a state of disrepair including termite infestation, rot, vermin infestation [with both dead rats and evidence of live activity], roof leakages, clogged gutters, and that the swimming pool had not been emptied and was choked with algae and the garden neglected.[70] In 2000 as discussions were underway regarding its listing on the State Heritage Register the house was demolished by the University. Demolition freed a building site that was quickly identified for student housing. At the time of this writing the site is still vacant. EWB Architects statement of significance included the following passage:

> The house is associated with the highest levels of intellectual and cultural achievements of its period and reflects the preoccupations of historically significant figures such as Zelman Cowen, Robin Boyd and John Dalton.[71]

In 1979 in an address to the NSW Chapter of the RAIA on its fiftieth anniversary, delivered at the Sydney Opera House, Sir Zelman recounted his experiences with architects and architecture. He described bumping into his friend Robin Boyd shortly before his death and telling him of how much enjoyment he had in the house in St Lucia: 'It was a beautiful house, authentic in its design and line and splendidly attuned to the environment in which it was built.'[72] That it was unceremoniously and suddenly demolished under cover of darkness is a measure of the protection afforded modern and contemporary architecture in Queensland.

Courtyard houses: Erosion of a volume

The second strategy for courtyards – erosion of a volume – involved ordering a sequence of spaces rising up (as in the Covalevich [1975] and McGuckan [1976] Houses) or down (as in the Chick House [1977]) a slope and sheltering them under a continuous skillion or low gable roof. It is a strategy that recalls Peter Johnson's house at Chatswood, Sydney. More significantly, this strategy appears in Dalton's domestic work after the completion of campus buildings exploring mat-building typology, which are discussed in the following chapter. 'Incorporating nature into buildings' through the ordering of building envelope became an increasingly important element of this strategy.[73] Such an approach implicitly eschews the notion of house as a grand statement in favour of house as a collection of settings. The courtyard becomes one such setting, deployed as an external space adjacent to internal living space or as an interval in a sequence of movement. The idea of the architectural 'whole' as a 'cluster' of small places and spaces recalls the writings of Team 10, the Smithsons and Archigram all of whom Dalton borrowed text from for his student handbills.[74]

The Covalevich and Chick Houses are instances of this second courtyard strategy. The Covalevich House for a family who were relocating to Cairns deployed a mat plan in which bedrooms and a family living wing are separated by an open living space and punctuated by three triangular courtyards. These courtyards set up a 45-degree geometry in the plan enabling views to the ocean in the less favourable southeast direction, whilst maintaining a northern aspect. Images of the Covalevich House and the Peden Residence were used to illustrate an article in *Australian House and Garden* by Anne Leonhard titled 'Cool Houses for Hot-House Climates' in which she reports on research by Bal Saini:

> The triangular shapes in the roof house glass prisms full of plants so the rain can get to them and the owners can enjoy the sight and sound of rain and the exotic leaf patters, virtually in the living rooms.[75]

Programmatically, the Chick House comprises three zones – a parent's wing, a children's wing and a shared open planned living wing – conceived as a series of linked platforms under a single roof following the fall of the site (Figure 4.11). It has three courtyards, each with a particular role in articulating pathways and territories and a different character. One courtyard provided the main entrance to the house. Another, a pebbled garden lined with white fibre-board sheeting and dark timber cover strips and containing a tropical birch and a contemporary sculpture, had a Japanese air. It provided light to the living room and kitchen and separated a service corridor from the main living wing. A courtyard 'void' belonged to the service zone. It was a double height space wrapped by a timber drying deck at the upper level, allowing light and views into a workshop level below and enabling kitchen and workshop occupants to maintain contact with each other. The house

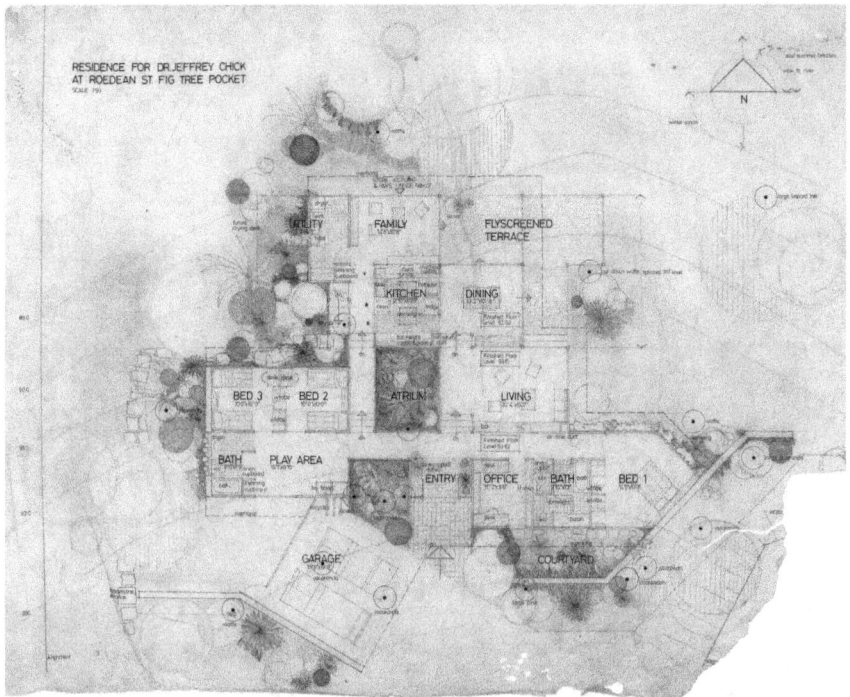

FIGURE 4.11 Design development plan drawn by John Dalton, Chick House, Roedean Street, Fig Tree Pocket, 1977. John Dalton Papers, UQFL499, Tube 5, Fryer Library, University of Queensland.

was experienced as a sequence of spaces linked to nature; a descent from street level through the house to a flyscreened 'lanai', a verandah-like room very similar to the Wilson House atrium, perched above the garden on the north-east corner, and offering views into a ravine of remnant rainforest views and along a reach of the Brisbane River (Figure 4.12). From the lanai the promenade continues onto a walled patio perched above the garden and down a series of garden terraces to the bottom of the site (Figure 4.13).

The changing nature of the courtyard in these houses mirrors an increasingly sophisticated environmental response in Dalton's practice. Initially a device for supplying sunlight and ventilation to all rooms in a deep plan, the courtyards in Dalton's houses developed into a device for linking the house to the site, for bringing inhabitants into closer proximity to nature and for orienting the occupant in relation to context near and far. In his institutional buildings the courtyard also served as an expression of community and a new social order.

The notion of architecture as being in a co-productive relationship with its environment, now understood as all-encompassing, comprising the physical and the atmospheric and as having political, social and cultural dimensions, has been largely normalized in architectural discourse and practice. In Dalton's work, we can

FIGURE 4.12 View to garden from 'lanai', Chick House, Roedean Street, Fig Tree Pocket, 1977. Photo Dianna Snape. Copyright Dianna Snape.

FIGURE 4.13 View of the Chick House with garden terraces, Chick House, Roedean Street, Fig Tree Pocket, 1977. Photo Dianna Snape. Copyright Dianna Snape.

see the trajectory whereby such a view of architecture came into focus. Through his writing between 1965 and 1972 we can trace the threads of disciplinary theory and general press that Dalton pulled together in consolidating his position on architecture. In the houses from this period – particularly the Vice-Chancellor's, Peden and Chick Residences – we can see how and the extent to which this position informed his architectural practice.

An environmentalist approach is now evident in a design process that sought to uncover the order inherent in a situation, to gear occupants in relation to environment and to the patterns of a life lived in the sun. In this context authenticity – understood as a straightforwardness or a lack of pretence or affectation – presupposes awareness of the particularities of a situation and a belief in the value of living in harmony with the surrounding milieu. It allows buildings to take on a third level of experience as a work that relates to the site and which becomes part of the site, rather than a building on the site, and in Dalton's practise it resulted in work that was compositionally and spatially richer through integration with environment.

5 ECOLOGIES IN PRACTICE: STRUCTURING THE INTERACTIONS OF INDIVIDUAL AND COMMUNITY

The four university campus buildings completed by John Dalton Architect and Associates between 1971 and 1977, three in association with the Queensland Department of Public Works, demonstrate how Dalton extended his architectural preoccupations to the structuring of communities of people and of relations between individuals, communities and their physical environments. They demonstrate Dalton working with ideas and strategies borrowed from the social sciences and urbanism. Significantly all four projects were predominantly passively conditioned. Allocated budgets dictated the extent of HVAC systems in some projects, nevertheless Dalton used planning and passive design techniques to provide both comfortable conditions and a pleasing spatial experience. Like Neutra and Frank Lloyd Wright, Dalton believed the key to achieving pleasure in buildings was a connectedness between inside and outside spaces. The resulting solutions sit in contrast with the modern orthodoxy that informed most of Brisbane's institutional and commercial buildings at this time.

All four campus projects were commissioned as a direct consequence of changes in Australia's education sector; rapid economic growth and the post-war baby boom demanded the expansion and restructuring of tertiary and vocational education. Planning for and implementation of the necessary change was greatly influenced by processes already underway in UK's tertiary education sector as a result of the Robbins Report (1963).[1] The implementation of recommendations in the UK resulted in entire new campuses and new and hybrid building types, and their progress, documented in *The Architectural Review,* was followed by Australian architects. In Australia, a similar set of changes was triggered by the Murray Report (1958). Over the following decades, Federal and State governments enacted legislation that initiated the planning of new university campuses, elevated existing colleges to tertiary level status and created new institutions offering new types of programmes.[2]

Coincident with this urgent need for growth was the challenge to universities to rethink their traditional academic organization to enable a more flexible structure capable of supporting new and interdisciplinary fields of knowledge and research. Progressive forces campaigned for new pedagogies to extend the intellectual powers and social capacity of students rather than simply transfer knowledge and technical skills, and the students themselves agitated for a greater say in their own education, leading to experimentation with flatter academic structures. The pressure for change was amplified by student uprisings across the globe in 1968. The uptake of innovation in the Australian education sector was uneven and reflected the culture and politics of individual state jurisdictions, in particular the receptivity of the respective states' education departments to new ideas. Queensland at this time was notable for its conservatism.

It was against this background that John Dalton Architect and Associates undertook four projects: the Art and Music Building at the Darling Downs Institute of Advanced Education [DDIAE] (1974) completed in association with Queensland Department of Public Works;[3] University House (1974) at Griffith University; the Hall of Residence, Kelvin Grove (1977, partially demolished 2002) at the Kelvin Grove College of Advanced Education (CAE) in association with Queensland Department of Public Works;[4] and the Bardon Professional Development Centre (1976, demolished 2014) also in association with Queensland Department of Public Works.[5] All four commissions were for educational buildings for which no precedent existed in Queensland, on new campuses or campuses in transition. Three of the four commissions came to Dalton's office through the Director of Public Works, Peter Prystupa, who recognized that unusual client or contextual issues required a fresh approach.[6] For his part Dalton was familiar with debates around education through his participation in AASA and QASA activities[7] and his role as a sessional lecturer and member of the Faculty Board of Architecture at UQ.[8] In two early projects, the Arts Theatre Petrie Terrace (1962) and his unbuilt competition winning scheme for the Anglican Church, Kenmore (1964) he had explored the dynamic of people coming together to meet and mingle. He had declared his position with respect to urban planning and architecture in a 1967 issue of *Broadside* in which he rejected the modernist planning principles of the 'old guard'. He was alert to the potential of ecology as a metaphor for an architecture of open-ended structures providing for growth and change and grasped the opportunity to test such ideas in educational settings.[9] From 1970 as John Dalton Architect and Associates expanded to address a growing amount of work, Dalton and Charles Ham were joined by Tim Macrossan, Peter Chiltern and Hedley Kidd. Although the principal driver of design, Dalton preferred to work in a collaborative way, allowing his employees room to develop ideas.

Structuring interdisciplinarity: Art and Music Building

The Art and Music Building (1974) or 'A' Block at the Darling Downs Institute of Advanced Education (DDIAE) in Toowoomba, the least well-known of Dalton's buildings, unequivocally reflects notions of community as an ecology. It was contentious from the beginning; as a project for the creative arts, it did not fit neatly with the Queensland Department of Education's agenda, at that time directed at addressing shortages of technologists (professional) and technicians (tradespersons).[10] The DDIAE itself came into existence through community pressure. Toowoomba, an inland regional city perched on the edge of the Great Dividing Range, was already an education hub attracting children from across rural Queensland to its many boarding schools. Its citizens had agitated for a separate tertiary education facility, one that reflected their needs and identity. From the outset they understood that the creative arts, in particular the performing arts, not technology and science, were intrinsic to this identity.[11] In response, the Darling Downs Institute of Advanced Education (DDIAE) came into existence, elevated from its previous status as a satellite campus of the Queensland Institute of Technology and granted autonomy in 1971, with a new campus on the outskirts of Toowoomba overlooking the fertile farmland of the Darling Downs.[12] John Dalton Architect & Associates was commissioned to design the Art, Craft and Music Teaching Building on a highly visible site adjacent the DDIAE's ceremonial approach.

Tensions between conservative forces within the Education Department and the progressive community on the Darling Downs around what was to be the focus of the project surfaced almost immediately, delaying progress. Toowoomba citizens understood this facility would provide a venue for experimental theatre, opera recitals and exhibitions of contemporary art; an important link binding DDIAE to its community. An impasse was eventually resolved by separating out the vocationally oriented teacher training required by the Department of Education into a separate School of Education, leaving a school dedicated to studies in the performing and creative arts. Construction finally commenced on the Art and Music Building or 'A' Block as it came to be known, in 1973.

In a manner reminiscent of the University Grants Committee process in the UK, Dalton worked in close collaboration with the Director of DDIAE, Lindsay Barker, a Toowoomba local who supported the community's vision for an arts school, and the newly appointed Head of Creative Arts, Robert Gist, an American actor and film director.[13] He also conducted his own research, seeking advice from painters, musicians and dramatists on practical matters pertaining to 'the type of environment' required by each discipline. He gave the pottery wing to Charles Ham to develop.[14] The preferred organizational strategy, agreed with Barker, was to contain all teaching and performance spaces, classrooms and offices for each of the various discipline areas in one building, thereby giving expression to a pedagogical philosophy that encouraged interaction between different disciplines (Figure 5.1).[15]

Tactically each discipline's studios and support spaces were collected by a dedicated courtyard to create a 'framework' for incidental and programmed activities. Dalton's design report lists five courtyards – an entry courtyard and one each for pottery, craft, sculpture and painting. Ultimately the wing with dedicated pottery studio was not built, resulting in a reduced pottery courtyard. The largest volume and major space in the complex, the 250-seat theatre, is equivalent to a courtyard in the way it gathers ancillary spaces to itself, and a service yard, sunken below the level of the surrounding landscape out of view of approaching vehicles, might also be considered a courtyard. The resulting plan diagram, a series of interlocking cells, recalls contemporaneous schemes by Shadrach, Josic and Woods, such as their 1963 competition winning submission for the Freie Universitat, Berlin in which they adopted a strategy of 'web'.[16] It is also similar to the approach adopted by Alison and Peter Smithson in their 1970 Kuwait Urban Study and 'mat-building' project.[17]

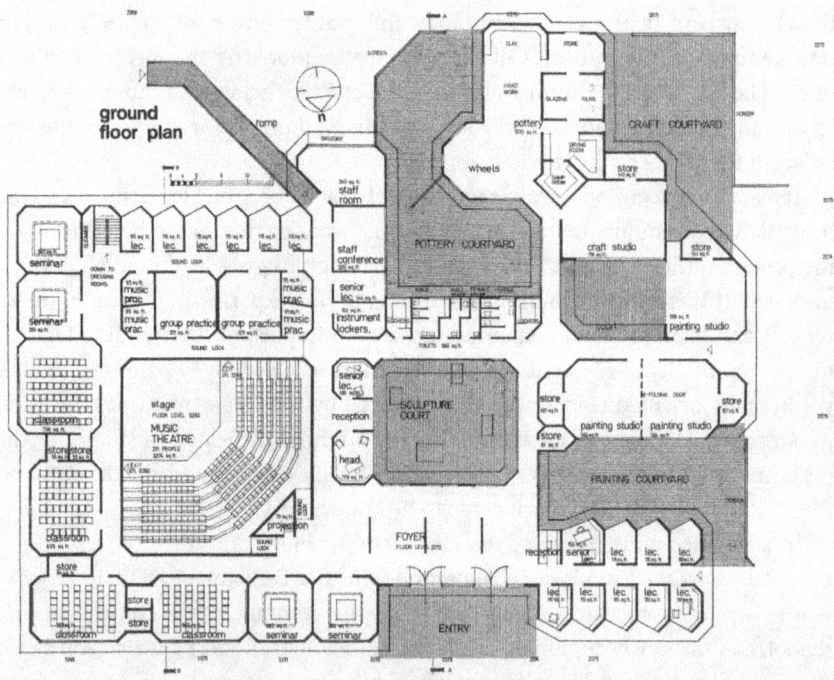

FIGURE 5.1 Plan of the Art and Music Building, Darling Downs Institute of Advanced Education, Toowoomba, 1974, reproduced in *Design Report: Department of Works Queensland Institute of Technology Arts Crafts and Music Teaching Building* prepared by John Dalton Architect and Associates with assistance from Richard Stringer c1971.

The mat strategy supported Dalton's design 'conviction' – set out in the project's design report – for 'a strong and organic building … suited to the programme'.[18] That the use of a 'mat' strategy was intentional is given further weight by the treatment of courtyards which are not formed through the positioning of a series of blocks to enclose space.[19] Rather, courtyards register as open rooms in a matrix of other rooms and perform a range of functions. They provide light and natural ventilation to studio spaces; the only HVAC conditioned spaces in 'A' Block were the theatre and music and group practice rooms – internalized rooms with no external wall – and the staff conference room. Courtyards are alternatively exhibition spaces and outdoor teaching spaces protected from the harsh winter winds that blow across the Darling Downs and containing the messiness associated with creativity in a building that is prominent in the campus landscape. In 'A' Block courtyards are not symbolic or emblematic of an educational typology with origins in the monastery cloister – the classical reference for courtyards in campus settings – but spatial figures expressing the needs of a community of people coming together for the express purpose of learning; an ecology.

Noteworthy too, is the treatment of rooms. Right angles and cube volumes are avoided, corners are truncated or dissolved to create a 'matrix of irregular spaces' to 'reflect' the creative spirit of the building's occupants.[20] Studios and teaching spaces are centred with no dead corner spaces. The 45-degree geometry establishes a diagonal which is exploited at the scale of the individual; each office has a bay window projection into the landscape that also enables registration of the individual in the expression of the architectural whole. Corridors are given additional width at intersections, creating bays for incidental gathering and eliminating problems arising from lack of visibility around corners.

In 'A' Block Dalton experimented with a Brutalist aesthetic. Construction is primarily of off-form concrete. The corrugated treatment to external walls imparts a 'robust' and 'expressive' character seen as reflecting 'craft methods'. Pre-cast concrete hoods over doors to the theatre at the lower level are integral with the walls and also corrugated. Consistent with Dalton's viewpoint that the practical needs of students should take priority over the expression of the architecture, concrete was painted white internally, and is without 'precious and refined' finishes allowing students to fix materials and equipment to walls directly without restriction.[21]

'A' Block's external expression is a consequence of strategizing architecture as an organic 'framework' and a straightforward construction process. In effect it presents a non-elevation quite unlike Dalton's earlier carefully composed modernist houses. Again, this lack of emphasis on elevational treatment is characteristic of the mat plan typology. The strategy matched the DDIAE's desired pedagogical approach – a dynamic, hothouse situation leading to new and hybrid practices in the arts and underpinned by a democratic, non-hierarchical and cross-disciplinary approach to curriculum. The life of the building was described on the fortieth anniversary of its opening: 'the visual artists overheard music practice and drama students had to occasionally shout to be heard above students playing the piano …. Life in the building was always a lot of fun.'[22]

Dalton's intentions for 'A' Block extended to building relationships between occupants and the wider setting. There is sufficient evidence to suggest that 'A' Block was conceived as a landscape building.[23] On approach and from various vantage points in the campus – in particular from within the central quadrangle courtyard – 'A' Block appears to emerge out of the ground. Early photographs depict it in relation to the wider Darling Downs landscape, then still free of suburban development (Figure 5.2).[24] The roof-scape is predominantly flat, punctuated by skylights over larger studio and theatre volumes. Even the theatre volume – which as the largest volume would usually be given some sort of architectural treatment – is pressed into the ground and opens through a lower ground level into a large service yard well below the natural ground line of the surrounding landscape. A consistent horizontal datum mirroring the Downs landscape is ensured through the use of a V-shaped precast concrete gutter edge treatment that hides roof falls. 'A' Block does not dominate the landscape through verticality – appropriately, the University Executive Building by James Birrell, on axis with the main entry drive is the dominant element in this grouping of campus buildings – and theatre back-of-house spaces are hidden from view.

Correspondence between Dalton and Head of Visual Arts Robert McGowan reveals the flat concrete roof was initially proposed as a green roof to be 'frolicked'

FIGURE 5.2 View from central quadrangle across Art and Music Building roofscape to Darling Downs landscape taken on completion of project in 1974. Photo Richard Stringer. Copyright Richard Stringer.

on.[25] Dalton had envisaged a daisy covered roofscape with ivy-covered walls; he perceived such detail as critical to conveying the building's landscape intentions. Risk-adverse public servants in the Department of Public Works did not share Dalton's enthusiasm. A folder amongst Dalton's papers contains transparencies of earth-roofed precedent projects together with an undated collage demonstrating his intention for 'A' Bock, whereas the Design Report includes a series of elevational studies recalling the work of Kevin Roach John Dinkaloo and Associates in particular the Oakland Museum of California (1969) or the Behavioural Sciences Centre at the University of Illinois by Walter Netsch of Skidmore Owings and Merrill (1969). It was after a visit to the campus in 1979 that Dalton wrote to Robert McGowan drawing attention to the awkward and unkempt appearance of 'A' Block without some sort of vegetal covering. McGowan responded by pointing to the building's presence as a strong force in student's lives and constantly 'humming' with student activity.[26]

Landscape has always been an important reference point for Australian architects. Melbourne architect and academic, Paul Walker has noted how in the 1980s, campus architecture was routinely presented as representational of or analogous to landscape and that this strategy was deployed to support arguments for a national identity.[27] Similarly, Jennifer Taylor draws attention to a reciprocity between the horizontality of the Cameron Offices (1976) by John Andrews and Associates or the Benjamin Offices (1979) by McConnel Smith and Johnson and the wider Australian landscape.[28] In this instance and unlike his houses from this time, which did reference the vernacular, Dalton is not concerned in a self-conscious way with registration of an Australian identity but with how building form is experienced as integrated with its landscape setting.

'A' Block represented a new dimension to the practice demonstrating attention to the specific needs of a community of artists, a willingness to experiment with materials and form, and the use of ideas and strategies to consciously gear a building to its environment. However, Dalton's peers, when reflecting on this era, argued that this campus project didn't have the qualities that made him influential.[29] Dalton's radicalness is revealed when 'A' Block is compared with other contemporaneous work. The Resource Material Centre at DDIAE by James Birrell in association with Department of Public Works and 'A' Block were both recognized with citations of Meritorious Architecture by the RAIA Queensland Chapter in 1976. But the higher award, the Bronze Medallion was awarded to two buildings – the Library, Arts, Crafts, Music and Students Union complex at Mt Gravatt CAE designed by Robin Gibson and Partners also in association with Works Department (1969–76) and the Chemical Engineering Building (1974) at The University of Queensland by John Andrews International with John Simpson as project architect. Robin Gibson's Library, Arts, Crafts, Music and Students Union complex at Mt Gravatt CAE, with its similar programme, provides a point of comparison for 'A' Block at DDIAE. Because it was primarily for vocational teacher training, Gibson's complex at Mt Gravatt CAE avoided the ambitious creative arts agenda of 'A' Block at DDIAE and although it housed the campus's student services facilities, it was not complicated by aspirations to foster links with the broader community. Completed in stages over a number of years, the different programmatic functions are housed in a series of concrete-framed buildings in the functional modernism favoured by institutions.[30] At this time John Andrews International was renowned internationally for projects in North America that utilized urban planning strategies at the scale of building. The Chemical Engineering building's plan and stepped corrugated concrete form is generated from an existing campus axis. A functional plan is married with a rational construction system. Both the Chemical Engineering building and the Mt Gravatt CAE campus buildings were designed to be air-conditioned and as a result neither engaged occupants with their immediate setting in a direct way.

Structuring non-hierarchical relations: University House

Two other campus buildings by John Dalton Architect and Associates also make use of mat-building strategies to different degrees. University House (1974) was one of four foundation buildings commissioned in 1971 by the newly founded Griffith University for their campus at Nathan, a remnant bushland site on the edge of Toohey Forest Park. The Bardon Professional Development Centre (1976) was a stand-alone facility for the post-graduate retraining of teachers for the new 'chalk-and-talk' era such that they might 'become skilled in a more fluid and personalized educational philosophy' and in the integration of 'new equipment' such as radio and television into their teaching practices, and was sited on the suburban fringe adjacent Mt Coot-tha Forest Park.[31] Unlike 'A' Block, an experiment in the use of brutalist concrete, the characteristic elements of Dalton's domestic projects are present to some extent in both these buildings. White masonry walls anchor each project to a landscape site whilst timber pergolas cast patterns of shade. Projecting vertical slit windows in white masonry walls, also used in the Vice-Chancellor's and Peden Houses, amplify the heavy groundedness of walls. The Bardon Professional Development Centre registered as a series of skillion roofs in a bush landscape in a manner that recalls Dalton's domestic work whereas University House's form was constrained by the provisions of a master plan devised by architect and planner Roger Johnson, which was directed at achieving an overall unity in campus form.[32] Consequently, University House adopted a deep horizontal fascia to conceal roof falls, a detail corresponding to the functionalist modernism preferred by Queensland's Department of Public Works.

The four foundation buildings initially commissioned for the Griffith University campus were the Library and School of Humanities Building from Robin Gibson and Partners (two buildings), the School of Science and Lecture Theatre from

Blair Wilson and Associates and the Community Services Building, comprising University House and a Commercial Centre from John Dalton Architect and Associates. Of the two buildings completed by Dalton's practice, University House is the more interesting. A second stage of the Commercial Centre, including an experimental theatre, did not proceed. A short time after the completion of these four projects John Andrews International was commissioned to design the Australian Environmental Studies Building (1977) for the first undergraduate degree programme in Environmental Studies in Australia, whilst Blair Wilson undertook phase two of Science (1978).

In his preface to Roger Johnson's 1973 campus master plan design report, Griffith University's inaugural Vice-Chancellor Professor F. J. Willett confirmed the University's commitment to exploring alternative pedagogies and identified as influential, principles pioneered at the University of Sussex, amongst the earliest of Britain's New Universities.[33] Johnson's master plan was conditioned by the University's desire for a flat organizational structure and interdisciplinary schools as distinct from the conventional disciplinary 'silo' structure of the established sandstone universities. From the outset it was appreciated that a striking campus would reinforce a distinctive institutional identity and that the bush landscape of the Nathan Campus site was key to an identity as a progressive institution; buildings and landscape were to be in a harmonious relationship with each other.[34]

Johnson's master plan introduced a central axis running north south, bisecting an existing ring road, the remnant of an earlier 1965 master plan by James Birrell. Communal facilities were located along this 'spine' with the new inter-disciplinary schools stretched along the cross-axes enabling, east-west orientation and narrow floor plates to maximize cross-ventilation. Initially, very few buildings were to be air-conditioned. Consistent with the idea of a 'bush setting' this grid was penetrated by fingers of bush, whilst emerald green lawns were carefully inserted at key locations according to a plan devised by landscape architect, Barbara van den Broek.[35]

The proposal for a University House, in which staff and students could 'intermingle', was a radical departure from the tradition on established campuses of a separate students' union and staff house. The Vice-Chancellor, given his remarks in Johnson's report, was probably inspired by College House, later known as Falmer House, by Sir Basil Spence at the University of Sussex.[36] Like its predecessor at Sussex, University House at Griffith was also intended to be a common meeting place for staff and students. Its pivotal location on a spur of land at the northern end of the central spine also meant that like Falmer House, University House was to be the first building encountered by pedestrians approaching the campus from bus and car parking, at that time proposed for the ring road to the north. Dalton's commercial centre, a more straightforward two-storey arcaded building addressing the spine on the east and concealing a service yard to the west, sits behind University House and between it and the Library and School of

Humanities. The commercial building is linked by an arcade to University House, which steps down the site opening in a series of decks overlooking the bush landscape and a proposed lake to be formed by the damming of a creek, and which did not proceed on environmental grounds (Figures 5.3 and 5.4).[37]

Developed design plans for University House reveal an open grid with social spaces over two levels defined by columns or by white blockwork walls into interior space, decks or courtyards covered by pergolas. This strategy provided a range of

FIGURE 5.3 University House and Community Services Building, Griffith University, Nathan, 1974. Photo Richard Stringer. Copyright Richard Stringer.

FIGURE 5.4 View to University House taken on approach from the north. Photo Richard Stringer. Copyright Richard Stringer.

non-hierarchical spaces for small and large groups to meet and mingle casually. Courtyards and decks are open and transparent allowing exchanges between individuals and groups and between people and the wider environment. Light, breezes and the landscape context are drawn deep into the building's non-air-conditioned spaces. One of the most fondly remembered features of this project was the bar with its mechanical punkah above the bar counter.

In *Australian Architecture since 1960*, University House is discussed alongside the Humanities, Library and Administration Building by Robin Gibson.[38] Gibson's building is described as 'typical of Gibson's mature work',[39] whereas Dalton's University House 'with its horizontal lines, provides a reciprocal, co-ordinated partner with Gibson's more dominant group' with 'a relaxed mood with inner courts and sheltered verandahs ....'[40] Robin Gibson's 'dominant' air-conditioned Humanities, Library and Administration buildings adopt a more generic plan arrangement than University House and were built, to a far more generous budget, in precast and off-form concrete. Large open areas for the library and office spaces double-banked around a central corridor deliver a deep plan that necessitated the use of air conditioning from the outset, whilst the design of an efficient air-tight building envelope meant interior spaces were disconnected from the surrounding bushland. It is illustrative of Gibson's work (Figure 5.5). In comparison, University House is a hybrid adapting domestic modes of construction to an institutional context and remaining open to its surroundings. It is indicative of Dalton's reputation that it was a building intended to house the social life of a community. Functional modernism was the preferred language of Queensland Government, commerce and tertiary institutions, sustained by the work of establishment firms such as Conrad and Gargett and Bligh Jessop Bretnall but executed to the highest standards in Brisbane by Robin Gibson.

Ultimately, the construction of the lake did not proceed and the terminus for buses was located at the top of slope drawing the campus hub to the other end of

FIGURE 5.5 Robin Gibson, Humanities Library and Administration Building, Griffith University, Nathan, 1973. Photo Richard Stringer. Copyright Richard Stringer.

the central spine. The potential for University House to become the entrance to the campus was not realized. The 'flat' organizational structure of Griffith University quickly evaporated as the student body increased in size, older notions about the role of authority in the institution re-emerged and neo-liberal policies were adopted by the tertiary sector.[41] A place for the social mingling of students and academics became obsolete; the punkah was dismantled and the open spaces of University House, divided into smaller offices for the increased range of academic services needed by students.

Planning for the incidental: The Bardon Professional Development Centre

The Bardon Professional Development Centre, a teachers' in-service training centre, was also located in a bushland setting, this time in the foothills of Mount Coot-tha to the west of Brisbane city. A residential block for remote teachers to be built adjacent was designed and documented but not built. Dalton's design report proposes a 'Scholars Village' and cites the idea of an Italian hill town as a precedent. However, it is clear that the plan diagram was informed by a strategy involving a repeated and open-ended structure and not the close fit of a circulation route to site, typical of hill-towns. The strategy did enable the project to meet one aim identified in the project design report: 'to preserve the semi-rural urban character and avoid a large-scale complex that would disrupt the existing pattern of the area'.[42] During the early stages of the Bardon Professional Development Centre project Dalton became ill and required hospitalization followed by a six-week convalescence at home. Charles Ham took the project lead, visiting Dalton each day with new drawings to progress the work.[43]

The Centre was situated on an east west ridge running along the southern boundary of the site. Its programme, stretched out and stepped down the north-east facing slope, was open to cool north-east breezes and winter sun angles (Figure 5.6). The analytical brief provided by the Department of Education was augmented with outdoor areas for open-air instruction and an extended circulation system offering opportunities for incidental meetings. Air conditioning was specified for the theatre which also operated as a film studio, the main southern foyer and the library spaces only. The enlarged programme was accommodated through a tartan grid positioned diagonally across the slope; in an echo of the structuralist work of Jaap Bakema, Aldo van Eyck or even John Andrews in the South Residences at Guelph University Canada (1965–8).[44] The circulation system is the dominant element in the figure of the plan, a series of deep walkways expressed as loggias or arcades stepping diagonally across the slope and offering the visitor a variety of views and experiences as they amble between venues. Interior spaces captured by this diagonal arrangement were able to make use of the slope for raked floors to auditoria and lecture rooms

FIGURE 5.6 View to Bardon Professional Development Centre, Simpsons Road, Bardon, 1976 (demolished 2014). David McCarthy Photography. Courtesy of Sue Dalton.

(Figure 5.7). The strategy also gave rise to two distinctive interior-exterior spatial relationships; a series of pergola covered decks for social activities on the northern edge of the Centre looked across an open field to Enoggera Creek (Figure 5.8) and a series of internalized and sloping courtyard spaces captured within the plan became amphitheaters (Figure 5.9). Practically, these courtyards accommodated changes of level and planting and ensured provision of sunlight and breeze to adjacent internal spaces. Envisaged as external spaces for programmed activities, they also operated as quieter spaces for incidental meetings and exchange of ideas.[45] There is evidence of a concern to provide a balance between spaces to 'stimulate group learning and activity' and those for 'essential retreats and quietude for the individual', and as always in Dalton's work an emphasis on providing a 'correct human scale'. One consequence of the Centre's *parti*, in which the echo of the traditional university quadrangle can be discerned, is that once again, the building elevation is concealed behind walkways and pergolas laden with creepers. The relaxed and unforced approach to expression of form is consistent with Dalton's humanist approach and his 'abhorrence of large scale and "brut" unrelieved surfaces'.[46] A concern with the experience of the individual as a social being in a mutually dependent relationship with their environment is also indicative of an ecological approach to making architecture. Dalton's insistence on the inside-outside connectivity of teaching spaces made the use of air conditioning unnecessary and indeed problematic. His passive environmental response now placed him at odds with practices working within Brisbane's commercial sector which had embraced air conditioning, deep plans requiring fluorescent lighting and sealed building envelopes.

On opening, the Centre was described in local press as a 'large Spanish-modern building', possibly because its white walls and heavy dark stained timbers delivered a fashionable Mediterranean air.[47] Yet in a 'personality profile' in the Institute of Architects *Chapter News*, it was a promoted as a 'contemporary expression of

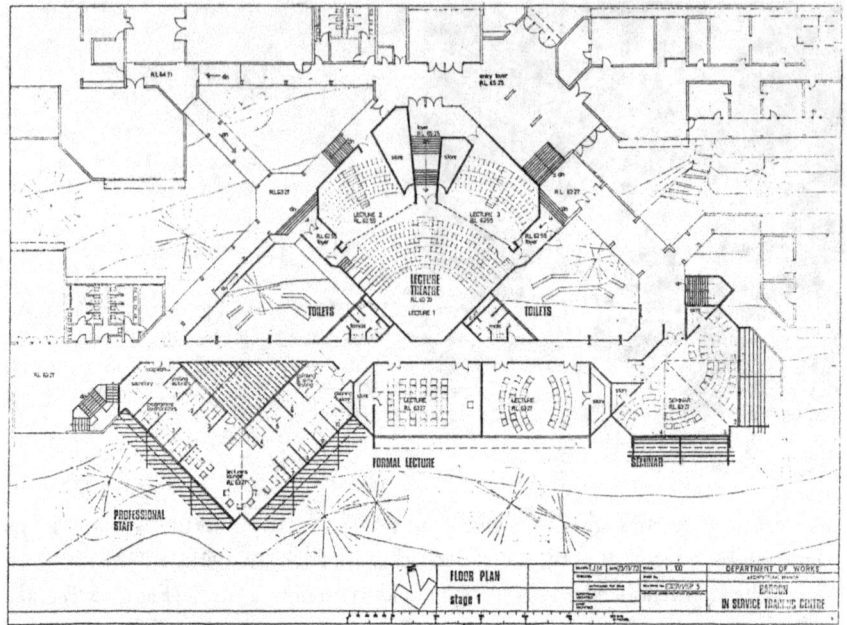

FIGURE 5.7 Part plan of the Bardon Professional Development Centre, Simpsons Road, Bardon as reproduced in *Design Report: In Service Training Centre, Bardon, Department of Works* prepared by John Dalton Architect and Associates.

FIGURE 5.8 Dining terrace overlooking Ithaca Creek, Bardon Professional Development Centre. David McCarthy Photography. Courtesy of Sue Dalton.

FIGURE 5.9 Courtyard, Bardon Professional Development Centre. David McCarthy Photography. Courtesy of Sue Dalton.

the Queensland Vernacular'.[48] Both descriptions suggest it was associated in the public imagination with domestic architecture rather than civic architecture. Its potential however was recognized by Queensland planner and UQ academic Phil Heywood, who when it was threatened with demolition in 1993 described the Bardon Professional Development Centre as a model offering clues to a timeless public/civic architecture ideal for Queensland.[49]

The Bardon Professional Development Centre was awarded a citation for meritorious architecture in 1977 and the RAIA Queensland Chapter Bronze Medal in 1978[50] but was sold by the Queensland Education Department in the late 1990s at a time when new technologies were again challenging the sector. It was demolished in 2014 to make way for a medium-density housing development.

Individual and community: Hall of Residence, Kelvin Grove

The fourth project discussed here, the Hall of Residence, Kelvin Grove (HRKG), coincides with the Bardon in-service training centre but adopts a cluster planning strategy rather than the mat strategy characteristic of other educational projects. The Hall of Residence provided accommodation for young apprentices travelling to Brisbane from remote rural areas to complete their training. It was a response to the newly identified need to standardize and regulate the education of technicians and tradespeople state-wide. The built scheme was the second scheme provided by John Dalton Architect and Associates; the first scheme which contained the programme in a single building at the top of the steeply sloping site was deemed by the Queensland Department of Public Works to not meet their expectations for a non-institutional expression. Dalton and his associates responded with the archetypal village or hill-town model, as a means of avoiding 'the "harsh" design of the educational institute' and enabling young apprentices – many of whom were leaving remote and rural locations to travel to the city for the first time in their lives – feel 'at home'. The HRKG was recognized through RAIA Queensland Chapter awards and was selected by the Australian Design Council's Architecture and Design Committee to represent Australian architecture in an exhibition, *Contemporary Australian Architecture: Old Continent: New Building,* in London, Paris, New York and Los Angeles. It was partially demolished in 2001.[51]

The project site was a steeply sloping remnant bush reserve on what was then the fringe of the CAE campus in Kelvin Grove, an inner-city working class suburb undergoing change.[52] Again, no provision was made for air-conditioning and Dalton's design report calls attention to the fundamentals of climate-responsive design:

> The Northern and Eastern orientation of all residential units exposes them to cool North-eastern summer breezes, winter sun and protects them from cold winter Southerly and Westerly winds, as well as providing each unit with a generous view of the bush. The whole could be described as a village within the urban environment, which should stimulate social activities as well as providing the essential retreats for the individual.[53]

The strategy adopted at HRKG for achieving a 'village' is different to that deployed in the Bardon Professional Development Centre; the site strategy is not structured by an imposed circulation system; pathways follow or climb contours as required. Nor does HRKG involve the close fit of programme to contour, the process adopted by William Turnbull and Charles Moore, at Kresge College, University of California Santa Cruz (1971), and by Harry Seidler in his later project, Hillside Housing at Kooralbyn (1979–82), a rural resort south of Brisbane. The HRKG achieves a 'calculated informality' through the simple repetition of a cluster of maisonette units on a slope.[54] In this regard it is more like student residences by John Andrews International at the Australian National University, Canberra in its structuring of relationships between part and whole, individual and community.[55]

The HRKG complex comprised five clusters of maisonettes and a community building (Figure 5.10). The idea of a village gains a local resonance through the use of the limited palette of materials and idiomatic detail characteristic of Dalton's domestic work; bagged brick walls painted white and punctured by vertical slit windows, on which timber lattice, post, rail and pergola cast shadows, deep roof overhangs to 'protect against the subtropical sun and the heavy rain in the wet season'.[56] The white walls with their dark timber-framed verandah boxes and skillion roofs set up repetitive patterns that reflect the verandahs of generic working-class cottages. But they are also the elements of a utilitarian domestic architecture already familiar to the young apprentice travelling to the city from remote and rural Queensland. Each housing cluster represented a social unit, and consisted of five maisonettes and a tutorial room around a shared courtyard.

FIGURE 5.10 Site Model, Hall of Residence, Kelvin Grove, constructed by John Dalton Architect and Associates. Photographed by Knell & Chester. Courtesy of Sue Dalton.

A section, demonstrating Dalton's environmental response, depicts a maisonette comprised of bedrooms and shared facilities for four apprentices, with each bedroom opening onto a private patio or verandah (Figure 5.11). This pattern was repeated on the falling site. The effect was to achieve the sense of townscape very similar to the stepping of worker's cottages along the hilly streets of Kelvin Grove.

The decision to organize the groupings diagonally across the fall of the slope meant each courtyard was at a different level in the landscape. Paths climbed steeply around and between double-height white brickwork walls, across grassy knolls punctuated by remnant eucalypts and upwards to the recreation dining room, with its chimney the tallest element on the site (Figure 5.12). Pergolas marked pause points at thresholds: Dalton believed that 'plants and the spaces between are as important as the building themselves'.[57] The experience arising from this careful ordering of elements reflects Dalton's interest in harnessing narratives of experience and more particularly here the experience of interstitial spaces in urban environments.

In writing about this project at the time Dalton speaks of the desire to 'avoid the "dumb" character of the educational institute'. He also calls attention to the role of architecture in mediating the experience of the individual within a community:

> Maintaining the individual's identity within the larger community is the aim of this planning, so the buildings rely on the familiar and commonplace for obvious reasons.
>
> A resort for learning ? ….perhaps.
>
> A holiday camp with tutors? … maybe.[58]

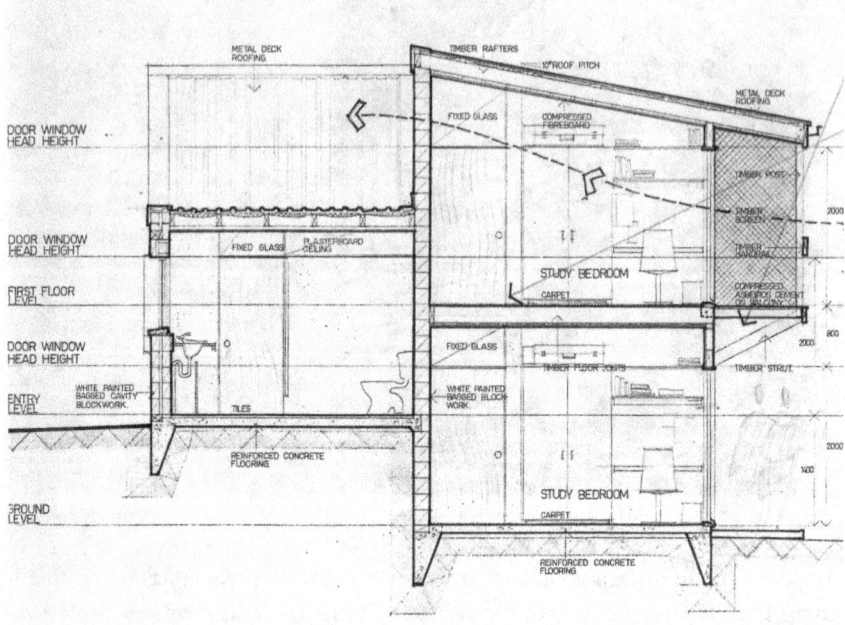

FIGURE 5.11 Section of four-person Maisonette annotated with sun angles and breezes by Dalton. Annotations were made for reproduction in 'Detailing, National Identity and a Sense of Place in Australian Architecture', *International Architect* 4, 1984.

FIGURE 5.12 View of Hall of Residence taken from north-east. The chimney to a fireplace in the Community Centre is in the centre of this view. Photo Knell & Chester. Courtesy of Sue Dalton.

In later commentary for *International Architect: Detailing, National Identity and a sense of Place in Australian Architecture* (1984) Dalton links the HRKG to themes of high density and cluster housing, community and sense of place but also to his ongoing concern for Australian idiom. As a jury chair for the Queensland Chapters' Civic Design awards, Dalton had been critical of Harry Seidler's Kooralbyn project, describing it as 'Grecian Cycladic'.[59] At Kooralbyn Seidler deployed a language of white brickwork with red tiled roofs, but no overhangs. Dalton considered that the project did not sufficiently acknowledge local building traditions or weather and that it was too accepting of the popular 'neo-romantic fashion' or 'Mediterranean style' which Dalton attributed to a fascination with postmodernism. Ironically Seidler was also a critic of postmodern thinking. In his appraisal of the HRKG for *International Architect*, Haig Beck aligns Dalton with Sydney architect Ken Woolley, a contemporary of Dalton's and one of the leaders of the Sydney School. Beck references the Australian Archives, Canberra 1983 and Police Headquarters, Canberra 1984 both by Anchor Mortloch & Woolley in association with National Capital Development Commission: 'Woolley has since become preoccupied with Beaux-Arts formalism and semantic issues. Dalton, as this project demonstrates, has remained constant to his earliest formation of the "Australian" House'.[60]

After its acquisition by University of Queensland Technology (QUT) in 1993, the HRKG remained as student housing until 2000, at which time the site became part of a redevelopment plan. The complex was listed on the Queensland Heritage Register in May 2001, but demolition of three clusters was approved by the Heritage Council in 2002.

Environmental paradigms at work in the institutional project

Dalton did not complete many larger projects; he had no family or old-school-tie networks in Brisbane to draw on and such was his reputation as a domestic architect that commercial and institutional commissions were rarely offered him. The four campus buildings discussed here are very different from each other indicating that each was initiated afresh from a carefully deliberated position encompassing social behaviours and environmental circumstances in addition to the functional brief. Air conditioning if used at all, was limited to a few interiorized spaces. Instead, every effort was made to link interior and exterior space. The courtyard, a spatial figure recurring in each project, offered not only the means of tuning adjacent interior spaces, but of responding to the explicit and implicit needs of users including the incidental or unexpected. Courtyards anticipated possible patterns of behaviour and were not emblematic of a monastic or campus type.

With the exception of the Art and Music Building at DDIAE, time has not been kind to these campus projects. Architectural historian Stefan Methusius, citing German architect and university planner Peter Jokusch writes, 'Functional obsolescence usually predates physical obsolescence'.[61] Such is the case for three of Dalton's campus projects, which have been partially or fully demolished or unsympathetically refurbished in response to shifts in educational policy or the failure of the social and pedagogical philosophies underpinning the projects' inception in the first place. It is ironic that 'A' Block, the campus building that attracted fewer accolades and awards from Dalton's peers, continues to accommodate the School of Creative Arts at the University of Southern Queensland. Its refurbishment in 2011 which included installing air-conditioning throughout did not involve the reconfiguration of spaces and spatial relationships indicating the enduring nature of the building's strategies, their fit with intended purpose and responsiveness to pedagogical change.

In a report on the architecture profession in Australia, published in the *RIBA Journal* to mark the centenary of the RAIA in 1971, Boyd reaffirmed his long-held opinion on the inability of Australian architects to uncover a distinctive 'Australian style', which he attributed to their fascination with imported fashions and a facility in working with them.[62] His description of the style currently in vogue, clinker bricks, undressed timber stained brown, off-form concrete and fragmented forms, is illustrated with work by a small 'proportion of men in the creative class, who build with spirit, intellect and a love of architecture'[63] including Graeme Gunn in Melbourne, Dickson & Platten in Adelaide and Dalton, whose Bucknell House (1968) was included. Boyd noted this style was mostly confined to domestic architecture, with only an 'echo' evident in public buildings and university campuses, and expressed his alarm that the same intellect and creativity had not informed larger works of architecture. Dalton's practice is consistent and there is a clear correlation between his campus buildings and houses from the 1970s. An 'echo' is evident in the language of form, organizational strategies incorporating environment and the consistent use of a human-centred design process. The inventiveness of these larger commissions has been overlooked by critics and historians perhaps because – with the exception of DDIAE 'A' Block – they utilized the same palette of materials that Dalton had refined through his domestic architecture and which many felt had become predictably consistent in Dalton's oeuvre – 'John Brown and Dalton Straw'.

Interestingly, the style of architecture that Boyd described in 1971 as 'anti-progressive and highly romantic in sprit', Graham Jahn would categorize in 1994 as 'an approach that was largely anti-art, anti-style and anti-establishment; squarely aimed at issues of life-quality, justifiable use of land materials and energy resources' and 'a quiet, low maintenance ideology of social responsibility'.⁶⁴ Jahn identified a most comprehensive order of environmental thinking in the work of architects practicing in the 1970s. However, environmental thinking as an approach to making architecture would be challenged in Australia during the 1980s by postmodernism which was gaining traction particularly in cities in the southern states and by changes in the profession as it responded to an increasingly commercial world. Dalton remained hostile to the alignment of the profession with commercial interests and to the ingress of postmodernism and kept faith with his humanist ideals.

6 SYNTHESIZING ENVIRONMENTAL AND ARCHITECTURAL PERSPECTIVES

In an episode of the Australian Broadcasting Commission's (ABC) *The Australian Artist* television series for secondary and technical school students Dalton again reiterates climate as central to his practice. Aired in 1978 and titled 'John Dalton: Sunlight Shade and Shadow', it depicts Dalton explaining that climate 'demands careful analysis of every aspect of building' and that in addressing climate a building will always express the local 'vernacular' and be 'related to the Australian style'.[1] He is filmed in one sequence demonstrating his process of incorporating environmental considerations in plan and section, and in another he descends through the space of the Vice-Chancellor's reception rooms whilst describing how spatial volume enables the evacuation of hot air. There are sequences of him working with associates Charles Ham and Peter Brown in the Queen Street office, and with architecture students in a studio discussing design project work intended to demonstrate methods for energy conservation. There is also footage of two-time client and Queensland's contributing editor to *Vogue Living*, Pamela Dunlop entering her Fig Tree Pocket house (Figure 3.18) from a bush garden and ascending through light-filled spaces, and of the populated and sunlit loggias at Griffith University, Bardon Professional Development Centre and Hall of Residence at Kelvin Grove to demonstrate a human-centred architecture in which interior spaces are linked to their environment through an articulated and layered building edge. Dalton identifies the practice's preoccupation at the time of filming as about introducing nature into buildings, 'not as in a flowerpot' but by 'bringing the landscape inside'. He advocates 'covering buildings with vegetation' especially the large areas of untreated concrete found in new city buildings, which he considered 'unsympathetic to the human spirit'.² Filming concludes with an observation that whilst most people agree that climate is important in design very few people think of sun, shade and shadow. Attention to climate is the means for creating delight in the reception and experience of architecture and nature working together and the means for humanizing buildings.

This ABC documentary was produced shortly before Dalton closed his Queen Street practice and announced Allora as his primary residence. Considering how engaged he had been with discourse during the 1970s, Dalton now appeared more circumspect about changes in the profession and the social and cultural landscape of the nation. During the 1980s rapid increases in migration and urbanization, the advent of free tertiary education, advances in women's rights and the gradual awakening to decolonization processes had shifted debate away from its focus on establishment interests and changed the way Australians viewed themselves. National values such as mateship, once the province of larrikins and workers, were now embraced by the well-educated and affluent – the 'cosmopolitans' – generating a new nonconformist national character for the global stage.³ Traditional anti-authoritarian heroes such as bushranger Ned Kelly and poets Banjo Patterson and Henry Lawson were replaced by a different sort of larrikin in the national consciousness, possibly best personified by former Sydney Harbour Bridge rigger, Paul Hogan, who shot to prominence through his hugely successful television series *The Paul Hogan Show* (1973–84) and as the star of the highest-grossing Australian film ever, *Crocodile Dundee* (1986). The new larrikin figure gained legitimacy through the work of Barry Humphries, the comedian whose many alter-egos include Dame Edna Everage and Sir Les Patterson, and who with Philip Adams and Bruce Beresford created the iconic film *The Adventures of Barry McKenzie* (1972), which followed the antics of a 'yobbo' in London. A new image of Australia was exported globally with the emigration to the UK of notable intellectuals and libertarians including Germaine Greer, Robert Hughes and Clive James, but also Richard Neville, Richard Walsh and Martin Sharp, the co-founders of *Oz* magazine. The larrikin persona suddenly became mainstream and was appropriated by captains of industry, members of the fourth estate and political leaders including Bob Hawke who served as Prime Minister between 1983 and 1991 and media baron Kerry Packer.⁴ Dalton continued to espouse characteristically Aussie phrases and slang in his still unmistakeably English voice and self-identified as 'the proud Australian, an immigrant'.⁵ Already a Fellow of both the RIBA and RAIA he was in 1982 elevated to Life Fellow of the RAIA. Although now a senior member of the Australian profession, he continued to be regarded by some as an 'English gentleman architect'.⁶

The postmodern/modern divide and the pleasures of architecture

In footage from the ABC's *The Australian Artist* television series, Dalton also denounces influences 'coming in from overseas' – his way of referencing postmodernism. His opposition to postmodernist thinking, which he claimed had no relationship to Australian living or the Australian climate, was as always underpinned by reading. His library contained books on and by Charles Moore, Peter Cook, a copy of Charles Jencks's *Modern Movements in Architecture* (1973) which was commissioned by his former indentured student Haig Beck when he was editor at *AD* and *Late Modern Architecture and other essays* (1980).[7] He continued to subscribe to journals from France, Italy, UK and the United States and his files contain annotated copies of articles on postmodernism with marginalia.[8] Dalton identified with some criticisms of orthodox modernism; including for instance, commentary by Ernesto Rogers in *Cassabella* on continuity and the role of history in architectural design and the 'Townscape' campaign in *Architectural Review* directed towards a more human urbanism and prosecuted by Ian Nairn, Gordon Cullen – whose drawings Robin Gibson once compared Dalton's student work to – and others. Dalton also admired the work of many architects who came to be associated with postmodernism, such as Charles Moore; there are echoes of the Sea Ranch (1963) section in several of Dalton's later houses including the McGucken (1976) and Chick Houses (1977). Compatible ideas from the likes of Colin St John Wilson and Aldo Rossi and imagery by Nairn and others found a place in Dalton's pamphlets. He had long held the view that functionalism and structural rationalism were not enough to determine architectural form – 'too sterile' – and whilst he continued to advocate for magic in architecture it was now a 'messy magic', one that prioritized a 'sense of place' and 'an Australian presence that is familiar and friendly'.[9] Nevertheless many postmodern ideas were insupportable. Dalton believed an architecture that conveyed meaning symbolically or semantically was ideological and formalist. Dalton referred to the rhetoric used to justify different theoretical positions as 'flummery': 'Where's the real stuff?' he would ask Charles Ham.[10] Writing about the Hall of Residence Kelvin Grove, Haig Beck observed that Dalton did not undergo a 'conversion' of the sort he attributed to architects in southern states, describing the shift from Sydney School aesthetic to classical formalism in work completed by Ancher Mortlock and Woolley in Canberra as 'something akin to a spiritual conversion'.[11]

Much of Dalton's criticism of postmodernism related to his observation that Australian architects were appropriating a reductive classical language of architecture without recourse to complexity or contradiction. Small or no roof overhangs, small windows without shading, cornices and architraves – were characteristics that Dalton associated with a Mediterranean 'style' and considered inappropriate for Queensland's climate.[12] In comparison Dalton considered the White Residence, a timber framed, gable roofed structure with encircling verandahs by architects Lindsay Clare and Ian Mitchell to be a very fine project. It corroborated his understanding of what an Australian architecture might be. The house described by Clare as 'a direct response to climate and environment' won the RAIA Queensland Chapter House of the Year Award in 1982.[13]

Dalton had a powerful ally in his condemnation of postmodern architecture; Australia's pre-eminent modern architect Harry Seidler shared his views. Seidler was provoked into a fervent debate by events surrounding the RAIA Conference 'Pleasures of Architecture' held in Sydney in June 1980.[14] In order to stimulate conversation at the conference, which brought Rem Koolhaas, Michael Graves and George Baird to Australia as keynote speakers, convenors launched a competition for the completion of 'Engehurst' a set of colonial buildings by architect and builder John Verge dating from the 1830s.[15] Competition entries were solicited from Australia's leading architecture practices. Publication in *Architecture Australia* revealed a range of approaches.[16] A number of entries were clearly derivative in their approach – Ken Woolley's approach has been described as evoking interventions by Frank Gehry at his Santa Monica House (1987), Philip Cox's as emulating Charles Moore's Piazza d'Italia in New Orleans (1978) and Daryl Jackson's neo-classical pile as suggestive of Michael Graves[17] – whilst Glenn Murcutt worked in a modernist idiom and Maggie Edmond and Peter Corrigan's entry tapped the new Aussie larrikin zeitgeist in a collaged submission featuring references to beer, cricket and the Sydney Opera House, and leaving no doubt that they believed the Australian culture was not high-brow and that it resided in the suburbs.[18] Initially no Queensland architects were included in the list of invitees, a situation that was rectified after appeal to competition organizers. The Queensland entries however, received a lukewarm response from the three international judges and were entirely omitted from discussion in *Architecture Australia*.[19] More controversially, the list of invitees published in *Architecture Australia* clearly spelt out that Seidler had declined the invitation to be involved.[20] At a subsequent RAIA conference hosted off-shore in Singapore in 1982 Seidler delivered his scathing assessment; Postmodernism was a 'style' and like style movements before it, it would be quickly forgotten. Dalton concurred and his last published article for *Vogue Living* in May 1982 appears to take aim at debates around the completion of Engehurst competition. In 'Messy Magic', a reference to his 1960 article 'Sun + Life + Useful Form = Architectural Magic', he dismisses both '"post-modern" antics' and 'critical regionalism,' the 'new theory of the mandarins of architectural criticism', declaring: 'The desire for a "depth of field" interest, "layered facades" and interlocking "visual codes" is just highbrow jargon for a rich palette of forms and spaces that are never austere and boring'.[21]

The presence of Graves, Koolhaas and Baird provided an opportunity for reflection on Australian architecture's relationship to the discipline globally. Asked to comment in an interview for the Royal Melbourne Institute of Technology (RMIT) journal *Transition*, Baird described competition entries as 'heterogeneous' whilst Koolhaas drew attention to two things that he had observed about Australian architecture during his travels from Adelaide to Brisbane along the east coast. Firstly, Koolhaas noted an architecture of transpositions in which 'similar or universal or international issues [were] inserted into different contexts'.[22] Secondly he observed the significance of local circumstances to architecture; 'the natural environment is so strong and the conditions are so obvious ....'. For Koolhass it was the fact of its being situated in a particular location that made a work identifiably 'Australian' and that far from being a problem, in 'an architecture of fresh transplantations' relationship to environment should be considered 'the source of its excitement'.[23]

If Australia was considered peripheral to centres of discourse in Europe and the United States, Queensland was at the periphery of the periphery. The uptake of postmodernism by Queensland architects was limited in stark contrast to the uptake of postmodernism by architects in southern states, particularly in Melbourne where Peter Corrigan, Darryl Jackson and others returning from overseas were quick to implement the theories of Robert Venturi, Michael Graves and others. Instead of a modern/postmodern divide, the profession in Queensland became organized along slightly different lines; an old guard with modernist allegiances, who chose to largely ignore a younger group of architects who would in time come to be associated with Critical Regionalism.

Brisbane comes of age

In 1981, bored with the limitations of his self-imposed exile in Allora and in need of the 'nudge of young men's (sic) ideas', John Dalton returned to sessional teaching, this time at QIT.[24] He also began accepting new house commissions. By 1980 Brisbane was transitioning from an over-grown country town into a global city with strong economic links to Asia. Air travel was becoming more affordable. The hosting of the 1982 Commonwealth Games proved to be a coming-of-age event and was followed in 1988 by World Expo 88, a specialized expo to coincide with the nation's bicentennial celebrations addressing the theme 'Leisure in the Age of Technology'. State and local government policy settings favoured development, perceived as key to the transformation of the Queensland economy by Premier Bjelke-Petersen. Much of the local profession maintained a disinterest in disciplinary discourse and instead organized itself along business lines with strong connections through its Chapter Council and newsletter to the Brisbane Development Association (BDA), the Building Owners and Managers Association (BOMA) and other organizations, whilst young women graduates formed Women in Architecture. Intellectual life was limited to cohorts within the two schools of architecture and divided itself according to its allegiance to one or other – UQ and QIT (which in 1988 achieved university status and became the University of Queensland Technology QUT).[25] Differences between the two schools arose from the distinct structure of their offerings – UQ was full-time whilst QIT offered both part-time and full-time streams. Both institutions had reinvigorated the life of their architecture departments by making new appointments from overseas and interstate. In 1978 following on from a short contract in 1977, the Department of Architecture at UQ under the leadership of Professor Balwant Singh Saini (1930–) appointed Norwegian born and trained architect Brit Andresen (1945–) who had studied with John Harbraken at Eindoven Technical University, the Netherlands and had experience teaching at Cambridge and the AA. UNSW and Liverpool-educated Steven Vajk Szokolay (1927–) and AA-educated Michael Keniger (1947–) were also appointed at this time. The degree programme at QIT under the leadership of first Edwin Codd (1939–) and then Tom Heath (1931–98) gathered an entourage of its own alumni to teach in its programme, including Daniel Callaghan, who had qualifications from University College London where he worked under Bill Hillier, and Robert Riddel (1945–) a graduate of CTC and the Royal College of Art.

Two initiatives from this time are revealing of Brisbane's architectural milieu. In 1983, *Chapter News* announced the formation of the Brisbane Architect's Group (BAG) initially under the leadership of young QIT graduates Peter Smith and Frank Spork.[26] Targeting 25–35-year-olds, BAG sought to build networks for young architects aspiring to work in the highly lucrative commercial sector by encouraging them to promote their 'architectural services' based on 'competence and professionalism'.[27] Its popularity pointed to the enthusiasm with which young architects responded to the reorganization of their profession along business lines. The other initiative, a lecture series 'Architecture is a Community Art' was instigated by Donald Watson (1945–), a part-time lecturer at UQ. After piloting the programme in 1982 the series began officially in April 1983 at the Community Arts Centre in Edward Street, Brisbane City and quickly became a popular, fortnightly event featuring a rich variety of notable local and international architects. International speakers to Sydney and Melbourne lured north by the promise of sun included Ingrid Morris (in 1982), Peter Cook and Peter and Alison Smithson (in 1983), Will Alsop (1984), Andrea Oppenheimer Dean (1984), Jack Zunz (1984) and Peter Davey (June 1985). The inaugural talk by local architect, Russell Hall (1947–), titled 'Bananas and Mangoes' was heralded at QIT in an editorial in their architecture students' magazine *Proscenium,* which also encapsulated the Queensland professions' problem with self-perception;

Brisbane has become painfully aware of her perocial (sic) status amongst her southern counterparts in recent years. Obviously regarded as a detour on the newly born Australian Academic Lecture circuit we've seen many Architectural 'heavyweights' such as Charles Moore pass irritatingly close without actually crossing the forbidden border.

Concerned not to be isolated in an era of critical thinking and tired of not having dedicated 24-access studio space, part-time students at QIT leased John Mills Himself, an inner-city property comprising two three-story brick buildings with basement carparking and located a short walking distance from QIT. They formed a consortium, Entrepôt (free port of call) and by renting studio space to students and sub-letting their basement carpark set about generating an architectural culture of their own; renovating and reconfiguring interior spaces by cutting openings in floors and reconstructing timber staircases they created a lively venue for work and for hosting lectures and exhibitions.[28] Dalton participated in events and contributed to exhibitions at Entrepôt when invited, but as a senior professional rather than the radical activist of his earlier days.

Dalton's students at QIT recall his studios as a 'lively exchange of ideas between as many of the class as possible'. He habitually provoked 'heated debates' and was prone to spontaneous outbursts on 'proudly Australian design'.[29] For a bio in the student magazine Dalton articulated his 'design theory' as 'about LIFE …. not just the styles', in a pointed critique of postmodernism.

> It should not be – but often is … the photogenic image, and the seductive graphic presentation; coupled with the whizz-bang of advertising hyperbole … Meanwhile the environment continues to deteriorate.
>
> If we could argue instead … for a mix of CULTURE AND ENVIRONMENT AND CLIMATE – then perhaps the life process could be enhanced …[30]

Dalton encouraged students to seek clues for architecture in the 'human/animal/plant ecology' of a situation, arguing that whilst 'manifesto architecture (pinched third hand from the latest glossy magazine)' might contribute to interesting debates, it did not address the most important design issues.

When in 1984 the Queensland Chapter of the Institute undertook to host the 1984 RAIA Convention in Brisbane, the organizational workload fell to a small group of QIT academics on the convention committee that included Callaghan and Spencer Jamieson who were team teaching fifth and sixth year design at QIT. Together they devised the convention theme, title and logo, and through their colleague Dalton's association with Haig Beck, secured international key note speakers Ralph Erskine, Henri Ciriani, Uttman Jain, Hervin Romney of Arquitectonica and Ian Athfield of New Zealand. The choice of convention title 'Functions of Architecture', appropriated from the 1980 Sydney conference title 'Pleasure of Architecture', gave a deliberate nod to Louis Sullivan's reading of function as incorporating architecture's pleasures and flagged organizers affinity with modernist values.[31] The conference also included a symposium titled 'Queensland's Culture of Flimsiness' chaired by UQ academic Michael Keniger with architects Rex Addison (1947–), Russell Hall and Gabriel Poole discussing their work. Keniger's selection of speakers favoured architects of lightweight constructions elevated above the topography – Addison and Hall working with the traditional timber frame and its geometry and Poole working in an exploratory and inventive way with steel. At this conference the division in Brisbane between proponents of modern architecture and regionalism became very clear. Robin Gibson, architect of the Queensland Art Gallery, the most anticipated new building in Brisbane, and members of his generation remained faithful to modernism, whilst young regionalists gathered around Russell Hall, Rex Addison, Bruce Goodsir, Graham Davis and Helen Josephson. Interest in regionalism had gained considerable traction during the 1970s through initiatives of the National Trust of Queensland, formed in 1963. Donald Watson was engaged by the Trust in 1974 to undertake a study of the Queensland house and in 1976, Max Bannah and Kent Chadwick completed their colour film *Timber and Tin* for the Trust. Bannah and Chadwick were commissioned to document the story of Queensland architecture but focused on its domestic buildings and their use of timber and corrugated iron.[32] A raft of other publications followed.[33] A changing of the guard was well underway. Dalton was still having his houses published regularly in local newspapers and popular magazines but was no longer at the centre of local disciplinary debate.

Last houses

After his retreat to Allora, Dalton's investigation of an 'indigenous' Australian architecture was sustained through a period of sole practice in a series of larger houses located in Brisbane; the second Dunlop House (1980) Clayfield, the Morahan House (1981) at Manly and some years later the Hendry (1986) and Bythe (1987) Houses in Bardon and Indooroopilly respectively. There were also commissions for projects on the Darling Downs. In these projects Dalton worked with extant building stock, and they demonstrate the wit and playful invention usually associated with postmodernist thinking. None of these later projects were documented by professional photographers, or published in journals, but unlike many earlier houses, drawings survive. There is evidence that Dalton did attempt to progress design problems by experimenting with new processes. In developing the Morahan House for a site overlooking Moreton Bay, Dalton made a series of collages including three-dimensional tableaux of loosely drawn elevations and plans overlaid with photos and magazine images, materials, proposed colour schemes in a process possibly inspired by his reading of Charles Moore and Michael Graves.

These collages do not operate as a mode of abstraction or transformation in the way his earlier 'verandah series' paintings did, to unlock new languages and ideas. Instead, they are more like bricolage; direct and unmediated they are not dissimilar to the collages Dalton used to convey content in his broadsheet newsletters.

Projects located on the Darling Downs are of interest because they involved working with existing building fabric – something that as an architect of modernist houses he had not been confronted with before. His restoration of the house in Allora, 'Lambtail Cottage' (1975–81) would be considered unexceptional today but at the dawn of the 1980s it was unusual for someone of his generation to place any value on such a small and undistinguished structure – a generic worker's cottage (Figure 6.1). Queensland, with a pro-development culture, lagged behind other states in implementing mechanisms for protecting heritage or recognizing character. Indeed, during the 1980s larger practices often relied on the demolition of significant colonial era building stock for commissions to proceed.[34] At 'Lambtail Cottage', Dalton stripped away accretions of material to reveal the original fabric. The back verandah was converted into kitchen and bathroom. The lean-to laundry and outhouses in the garden were retained, but stabilized and made functional. Such projects are never complete but Dalton's objective to evidence a county life as if lived over time was achieved and 'Lambtail' was awarded the inaugural Heritage Award at the 1981 Queensland RAIA Awards. When in 1976, the Methodist church, diagonally across Herbert Street from 'Lambtail Cottage', was placed on the market Dalton and Sue bought it by tender, fearing it might otherwise be demolished.[35] From the 1990s, Dalton made a series of idiosyncratic adjustments and alterations to this church and Sunday School. A large deck floating 600mm above the ground was added on the north side of the church. The Sunday School was converted to include a galley kitchen with dining and sitting areas, a large bathroom and a sleeping loft for sleepovers by

FIGURE 6.1 'Lambtail Cottage', Herbert Street, Allora, 1975–81. Photographer unknown. Courtesy of Sue Dalton.

numerous grandchildren. The work is internalized and not visible externally except for a small turret to enable a spiral stair to the sleeping loft and the large deck. There is a playful amplification of elements such as stair newel posts and the placing of hatches opened with weighted pulleys to gain secret views to outside. The purchase of a back-bar with mirror from a cafe being demolished in Allora and its installation as an over-scaled bathroom vanity was a theatrical move with echoes of Charles Moore.

The O'Dywer Homestead, 'Mt Manning', for a pastoral holding at the junction of the Condamine and Balonne Rivers west of Allora was a much larger project. A survey drawing of the original buildings completed in September 1980 shows the original homestead with a gabled kitchen wing separated from the main house by a hall and one small bathroom located on a side verandah. The completed project involved locating a second cottage onto the site at 90 degrees to the existing homestead, with a gap between the two structures just wide enough for Andrew O'Dwyer to squeeze through. The gabled kitchen wing was extended to the east to create a new guest and family room with the two stacks of the existing chimney located symmetrically on either side of the ridge (Figure 6.2). A 3.3-metre-wide verandah extends the length of the north elevation – a move that recalls the earlier homestead 'Morocco'. A new northeast courtyard zone is captured between the existing cottage and its verandah and the relocated cottage. The new family room is located partially under the gable and partially under the verandah setting up two distinct zones for occupation. Conscious of the daily rituals of rural life Dalton

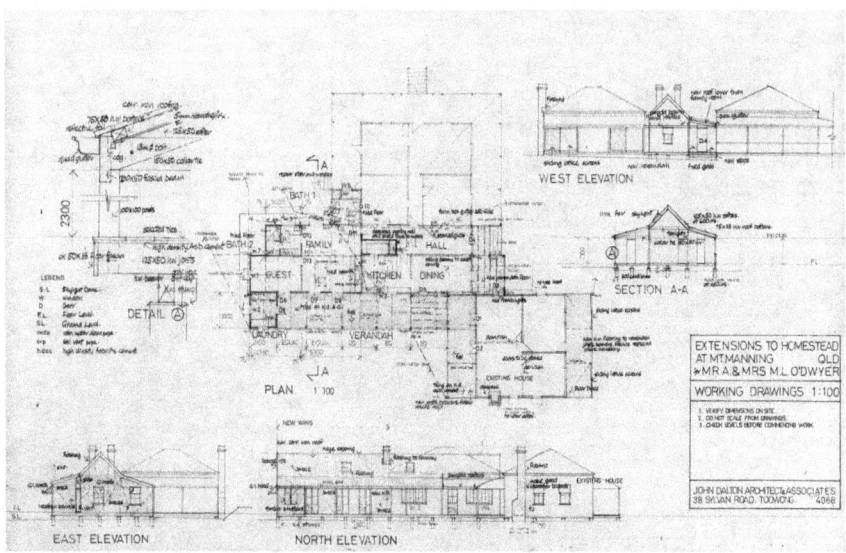

FIGURE 6.2 Working Drawings, Extensions to existing O'Dwyer Homestead, 'Mt Manning' Condamine, 1981. Drawn by John Dalton. John Dalton Papers, UQFL499, Tube 10, Fryer Library, University of Queensland.

maintained the hall as an important node and transition point in coming and going from farm to house and provided a set of broad steps for pulling on and taking off boots. Formally, the O'Dwyer House is composed of a collection of small structures and different elements knitted together – gable and pyramid roofs, bullnose and skillion verandah lines – and a variety of forms and ridge and plate heights. Unity is achieved through a consistent datum this time established by verandah plates and pergola beams. There are instances of wit and play in the articulation of detail and the creation of nooks and crannies.

Around this time Dalton also completed a set of drawings for a new house, the Coughlan House (1981), allegedly in exchange for a bottle of wine.[36] The Coughlan House, a tiny 8 × 8 metre square timber-framed structure with a steep 45-degree pyramid roof, was built on an allotment on the rural fringe of Allora and is known to locals as the 'pizza hut' (Figures 6.3 and 6.4). Organized on a two-metre grid, with open plan, a sleeping platform under the roof apex and a two-metre-wide flat roofed verandah on four sides, its striking appearance in

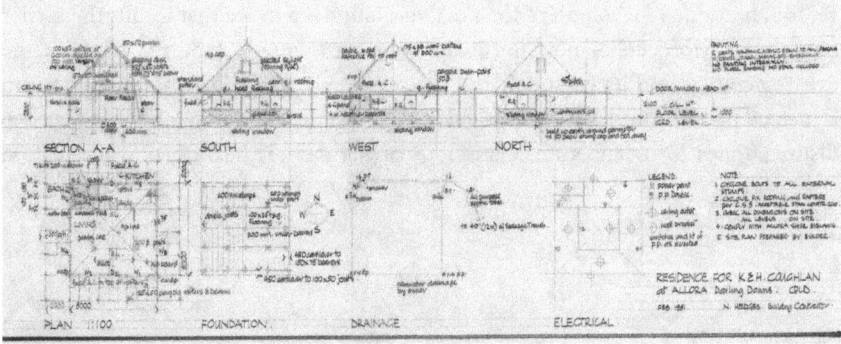

FIGURE 6.3 Working Drawings, Coughlan House, Allora, 1981. John Dalton Papers, UQFL499, Tube 14, Fryer Library, University of Queensland.

FIGURE 6.4 View to the Coughlan House, Allora. Photo credit John Dalton. Courtesy of Sue Dalton.

the open plains landscape recalls the small fly-screened structures used to keep produce cool in outback Australia. It is a structurally rational, materially efficient and economically planned project, in which a key characteristic of the Dalton House is still evident; strong datum lines, one separating the pyramid roof and house volume and another at sill height, recall early houses. Most importantly this project shows Dalton thinking about the Coughlan House – not as a sequence of linked spaces, his preferred modus operandi – but as a spatially, structurally and formally integrated system.

In the last houses that he completed, the Hendry and Bythe Houses, Dalton attempts to find a new formal syntax by marrying the hipped and gabled roof forms typical of large interwar Queensland houses to his modernism-inspired language of white masonry walls with dark timber framework using a first principles design process. The Hendry and Bythe Houses both had extensive programmes to be accommodated and are organized to maximize orientation to the north on steep or narrow sites. Dalton drew on his established process of confirming a workable and environmentally sound planning arrangement before considering volumes and forms. In the deep plans that result, light to large interior spaces comes from the manipulation of the roofline to introduce hips and gables and dormer lights. The horizontal datum line established by the plate line is maintained despite the complex roof forms (Figure 6.5). Whilst the interior spaces of the Hendry and Bythe Houses are delightful – sunlit and airy – they are without doubt the spaces of a 'Dalton House'. A pool house for the Hendry family, completed a year after the Bythe House, is officially Dalton's last work and provided him with an opportunity

FIGURE 6.5 North elevation, Hendry House, 'Burrandool', Carwoola Street, Bardon, 1986. Photographer unknown. Courtesy Sue Dalton.

to play with spatial, structural and formal integration in a symmetrically ordered, Federation style pavilion.

The 1980s was a time of great change culturally in Australia. The city of Brisbane transformed from a large country town with strong links to its rural heartland into a city with aspirations to be more outwardly engaged. Faster and cheaper travel resulted in increased links to metropolitan centres in the southern states but also to the UK and the financial hubs of Asia. The discipline of architecture in Australia was also changing. A fixation on uncovering an appropriate architecture for Australia still persisted into the 1980s in some sectors of the profession but a plurality was becoming increaslingly evident.[37] An influx of new academics and architects from overseas and interstate further broadened debate and ushered in an inevitable changing of the guard, in which Dalton's call for an Australian idiom now seemed anachronistic.

CONCLUSION: LEGACIES OF 'SUNLIGHT SHADE AND SHADOW'

John Dalton is best remembered for a set of distinctive modernist houses for subtropical Brisbane and for his promotion of 'sunlight, shade and shadow' – phenomena attached to environmental conditions – as the source of delight in Queensland architecture. He is associated with a distinctive idiom developed over time in response to climate design principles. Whilst his preferred language of dark stained timbers and white masonry changed little, analysis reveals his work is underpinned by intentions responding to a wide range of interests and motivations. What place does Dalton and his output have now, both in the historiography of environmental architecture in the subtropics and in relation to contemporary practice today?

It has been possible to trace in Dalton's practice a shift from an early emphasis on the efficient transferable house solution of modern architecture to the idea of the house as situated in and constructed on its site. Correspondingly, his early preoccupation with the notion of architecture as an art was supplemented in mid-career by a concern for human, ecological and environmental considerations. Through his activism – agitating students and practitioners to engage with current themes in ways appropriate to local circumstances – he helped shift local debate.

Through his teaching Dalton reached several generations of students. The students he encountered as a practitioner and part-time studio teacher at UQ between 1963 and 1971 engaged with Dalton the stylish, young architect and passionate advocate for architecture, art and design. Students from Dalton's second period of teaching in the 1980s – this time at QIT – encountered the figure of a respected and experienced professional, proud of his elevation to Fellow of both the RIBA and RAIA. This cohort recalls Dalton's enthusiasm for debate and the emphasis he gave to site, climate, engaging nature and the search for an appropriate Australian architecture. They recall an esteemed but no longer charismatic figure.

It is typical of a changing-of-the-guard scenario that serious-minded interest in Dalton and his work skipped a generation to a group of architects, many of whom graduated from the Queensland University of Technology (QUT, formerly QIT) at the turn of the twentieth century. Now with their own practices these architects are at the vanguard of a new urgency to address architecture's relationship to environment and have consciously sought out the lessons of a post-war, climate responsive and materially efficient modernism.

A style for the Australian subtropics

From the moment of its distillation, the maxim 'sunlight, shade and shadow' remained Dalton's touchstone. Its impact on the work of others more generally can be observed as operating at two distinct levels. Firstly, there is the impact that Dalton's distinctive idiom of dark timber, white masonry and split skillion roofs had on the evolution of a subtropical 'style' of architecture. Secondly, Dalton's insistence on sunlight shade and shadow as the mainspring of delight in the experience of architecture did have consequences for the practice of architecture by drawing attention to the characteristics of Queensland's subtropical environment and the potential for its engagement in architecture. Although, discussions around 'style' and the commodification of lifestyle were irritating to Dalton – he did not wish to be remembered as a 'stylist' – his impact at this level cannot be ignored.

Dalton's early houses gained local and national prominence through awards and publication in professional journals and popular magazines. With their emphatically flat roofs or very low-pitched gables and horizontal bands of windows these early houses have much in common with the European modernism-inspired work of Sydney-based architect, Sydney Ancher, and houses resulting from the Californian Case Study House programme. Works by Queensland contemporaries Robin Gibson, Maurice Hurst, Donald Spencer, Geoffrey Pie and Steve Trotter also attracted awards and were published, but Dalton's houses received a greater share of attention.

Over time the 'Dalton House' evolved and became its own special category of modernist house. By the 1970s its formal characteristics were confirmed – a distinctive roof form and section known as the 'Dalton section',[1] the use of a distinctive roof tile edge detail,[2] sill line datum,[3] stained timber, white bagged brickwork or blockwork walls and quarry tiled floors. The persistence of this limited palette does indeed suggest a style.

The language of white masonry and dark timber floors resonates strongly with the humanist architecture of Alvar Aalto and the work of Aalto acolytes working in other regions of the world, most notably in Peter Aldington's three village houses at Turn End in Buckinghamshire UK (1964–8) which are highly regarded for their integration of landscape with architecture. Just as Peter Aldington had transposed the language of white walls, quarry tiles and dark timber to re-envision a twentieth-century English rural village, Dalton transposed a similar language of materials into the suburbs of Brisbane, Queensland to create a distinctive verandah form that was both modern and familiar. White walls are read against leafy subtropical or bush gardens with bright sunlight casting sharp shadows across light surfaces and throwing recesses into deep shade. At the (now-demolished) Los Nidos resort in Noosa, the same language used in the context of a sandy foreshore and casuarinas evoked suggestions of more exotic locations – Spain or Mexico (Figure 7.1). A language of white walls was also deployed by Don Gazzard of Clarke Gazzard and Partners in the Wentworth Memorial Church (1965), Sydney which through scale, careful siting and composition elicits comparisons with Greek acropolises.[4] Without a doubt, white walls and dark stained timbers belong to a transferable language system, used by many modernist architects. In each situation it is the architect's capacity to use this language in response to ideas, site and environmental conditions that makes work distinctive.

In Brisbane, builders of project homes and architects alike made use of the architectural language associated with the Dalton 'style'. Even highly regarded architecture practices produced houses redolent of Dalton's work. There are striking congruences between Dalton's Stoneham (1964) and Leitch (1967) houses and the white walls, low gable and exposed timbers of the Penfold House (1969) at Brookfield by Robin Gibson Architect.[5] Fergus Johnston acknowledges a likeness to Dalton's work in speculative house projects at Chapel Hill completed early in his career. Johnston, who commenced his architecture studies at UQ in

FIGURE 7.1 'Los Nidos' Resort, Hastings Street, Noosa, 1972 (demolished c. 1985). Photo Richard Stringer. Copyright Richard Stringer.

1963 along with Don Watson and Rex Addison recalls Dalton as an excellent teacher. After completing his studies Johnston completed a block of five units in Durham Street, St Lucia (1972–3) that step in plan and section down a steep north facing site between white masonry walls in a manner that resembles The Penthouses (1967) apartments in Darling Point, Sydney by Ancher Mortlock Woolley which were widely published at the time.[6] Dark tiled roofs follow the topography with interior spaces opening into each other and onto quarry tiled patios and gardens in a manner redolent of Dalton's mid-career work. A group of four houses on another steep site in Ironside Street, St Lucia followed, again with skillion roofs, dark timber, and the use of white masonry, its plan carefully stepping around existing mature eucalypts (Figures 7.2 and 7.3). This

FIGURE 7.2 Four houses in Ironside Street, St Lucia, 1979, designed by Fergus Johnston Architect. Copyright Fergus Johnston.

FIGURE 7.3 Interior, Ironside Street houses, St Lucia, 1979, designed by Fergus Johnston Architect. Copyright Fergus Johnston.

project, comprising two houses for family members and two speculative houses, was awarded the RAIA House of the Year in 1979, in recognition of its fit with the natural topography and existing landscape elements and for generating a sensitive streetscape.[7] However, despite being emulated widely, the language for which Dalton is most remembered would eventually be an encumbrance to him, with the distinctive mission brown timber stain and white walls caricatured by students as 'John Brown and Dalton Straw'.[8]

In recent times there has been a rediscovery of modernist architecture and interiors. A fascination with modern furniture and furnishings, joinery items and household appliances has flourished with features in journals, websites and blogs casting an often-nostalgic view onto life during the optimistic boom years following the Second World War. Aficionados of mid-century modernism rank Dalton's work highly with 'Dalton Houses' in the western suburbs of Brisbane sought after as real estate regardless of unsympathetic remodelling. Much of this attention is narrowly focused on Dalton's stylist achievements and obscures his intentions regarding architecture's relationship to environment.

Praxis: Architecture engaging sunlight, shade and shadow

Dalton's fixation early in his career on form's correct orientation had its origins in scientific principles of climate design and a concern to address the physiological and psychological comfort of occupants. Matters of budget and buildability meant minimizing the material impact of a project on its site, whilst maintaining connections to the ground enabled the 'indoor-outdoor' living considered essential to the 1960s Australian lifestyle. Dalton was also aware that an architecture in dialogue with its landscaped setting gives rise to a distinctly Australian form. In the last years of Dalton's practice, a desire to engage nature into the experience of his architecture is linked to a renewed concern for the physical and mental well-being of occupants. Dalton's developing environmental awareness mirrored the work of interstate architects; houses by Ian McKay, Peter Johnson and Ken Woolley and other architects associated with the Sydney School of architecture in Sydney and Kevin Borland and Graeme Gunn in Melbourne demonstrate similar sets of preoccupations.

A changing of the guard was well underway when in 1985 the Design Arts Board of the Australia Council included works by Glenn Murcutt, John Andrews, Ian McKay, Christine Vadasz, Greg Burgess,[9] with Gabriel Poole and Rex Addison but not Dalton from Queensland, in a photographic exhibition and catalogue, *Australia Built: A Photographic Exhibition of Recent Australian Architecture* which toured internationally. Work cataloged under headings such as 'Living with the Land' and 'Under the Sun' was described as concerned with 'impact on the quality of environment',[10] whilst the search for 'a national identity' was proclaimed to be both 'parochial and absurd'.[11] Environment was now firmly on the disciplinary agenda but interestingly commentary around work in *Australia Built* focused on the image of architecture responding to its context; fit with context was perceived to be largely a problem of form.

Despite his omission from the *Australia Built* exhibition, Dalton had been amongst the first in Queensland to engage with and to promote environmental perspectives. Furthermore, from the early 1960s he linked environmental thinking to experiential outcomes. Environmental perspectives have remained a strong force in Queensland architecture, playing out in different ways and in line with individual architects' personal preoccupations and interests. Following on from Dalton were, on the one hand, modernist sympathizers such as Gabriel Poole, who established his practice on the Sunshine Coast north of Brisbane, Patrick Moroney who on the advice of Dalton studied sculpture in Melbourne whilst working for Grounds and Boyd and in Barcelona, before returning to establish a successful practice in Brisbane, and Peter O'Gorman, who continued to practice architecture after being appointed a lecturer at UQ in 1968. On the other hand were Rex Addison and Russell Hall, who rejected modernism and were more interested in the tectonic capacity of the traditional timber frame. Addison, Hall and their peers did not distinguish between the Miesian-inspired modernism of Gibson or the Aaltoesque humanism of Dalton. For Addison and Hall, both represented a disruption to what they understood to be a continuing tradition of Queensland architecture. Their opposition was generational as much as it was ideological. It is interesting then that although Poole and Addison operated from very different positions, their work was aligned in *Australia Built* and other contemporaneous accounts as sharing the characteristics associated with a distinctly Queensland architecture; a lightweight, permeable architecture, tuned to site and climate.[12] What connects the work of the modernist-sympathizer and the regionalist in these accounts is the identification of a shared interest in architecture engaging its surroundings.[13] Such accounts support the premise that environmental thinking can be harnessed by a range of different paradigms and finds its expression in different forms.

Gabriel Poole is best known for a series of lightweight steel framed houses on the Sunshine Coast north of Brisbane, remarkable for their exploratory attitude to materials, structure and construction, in particular their use of fabrication and assembly systems. The first of these, the Dobie House (1972), a steel framed house perched above its steeply sloping slip prone site, is very different to the Schubert House, which was an anomaly in Poole's oeuvre. Built for a client who explicitly requested a Queensland house, the Schubert House solution was inspired by conversations with Dalton about ways of addressing the problem of light and air in the dark inner rooms of the traditional bungalow. Significantly, the Dobie House predates Glenn Murcutt's Kempsey Farmhouse also known as the Marie Short House (1975) which is frequently cited by historians as a pivotal moment in the development of a truly modern Australian architecture free from nostalgia and romantic associations.[14]

Most of Poole's practice involved experiments in steel and were directed by his search for a 'better house and better lifestyle' and 'better ways of living than those now available to us'.[15] Rational, materially efficient and rigorously detailed, his lightweight houses embodied the notion of minimal shelter, open to their surroundings but able to address weather through the tuning of their building envelopes. They provided relaxed settings for living in the subtropics. Like Dalton, Poole believed that revolution in architecture should involve the way people lived and was not a matter of style.

In comparison Rex Addison and Russell Hall worked with the vernacular timber frame and its geometry, thereby contributing to its development as a construction technique and an idea. In his Taringa House (1975 and 1981), Addison bisected the traditional bungalow revealing the section in elevation and placing the typically dark interior spaces of the Queensland house at the edge of building form. In speaking about this house Addison acknowledges his debt to an unbuilt beach house by Robert Venturi (1959).[16] Over the years Addison produced a series of works that privilege the roof and its geometry in a manner that recalls Kenneth Frampton's notions of 'consciously bounded territories', leading theorists and critics to identify his work with Critical Regionalism.[17] In *Homegame*, a print commissioned by *Architecture Australia* to celebrate seventy-five years of publication, Rex Addison included images of his own O'Rorke-Graham House (2004) together with houses by Robin Dods, Beatrice Hutton, Eddie Oribin and Russell Hall to précis his understanding of the trajectory of Queensland architecture across the twentieth century. In these houses pitched roof forms predominate – not flat or low gable roof forms – and in text accompanying publication and at a subsequent symposium, Addison argued that mid-century modernism in Queensland constituted a dislocation in the otherwise seamless development of a distinct regional architecture.[18] In his own work Addison engages with specific environmental conditions through a knowing calibration of the geometries of the traditional framing system and the detailing of building envelope. For Addison and others, the specific characteristics and phenomenon of place are lodged in vernacular forms and their tectonic.

The work of Andresen O'Gorman represents a different engagement with environment. Peter O'Gorman, appointed as a senior tutor in 1967 and lecturer in 1968 at UQ, had been a frequent visitor to Dalton's unit at 'Burrawood' in Toowong, where with other students and members of the CAS he deliberated on life and architecture. In 1965, with Dalton's studio teaching partner Bill Carr, O'Gorman was awarded first place in a competition run by the RAIA Queensland

Chapter and sponsored by the *Brisbane Telegraph* newspaper for the design of cluster housing.[19] O'Gorman and Carr's scheme, a mat plan comprising sixteen units, was a demonstration of best climate design practice. By 1977 O'Gorman had completed a number of houses that experimented with timber construction, and enjoyed the rhythms and proportioning systems made possible by the timber frame. The tectonic potential of hardwood continued to be a focus of O'Gorman's research by design, after the formation of Andresen O'Gorman in 1977, whilst Brit Andresen's interests extended to the spatial and formal properties of archetypes and their potency for engaging surrounding landscape settings in architecture. Their practice together is a distillation of shared interests. After the principles of Critical Regionalism were codified, theorists identified Gabriel Poole, Rex Addison, Lindsay and Kerry Clare and Andresen O'Gorman as adherents, alongside architects working elsewhere in Australia including Glenn Murcutt, Rick Leplastrier, and Adrian Welke and Phil Harris of Troppo: architects already engaged with the contextual precepts underpinning this new movement. Critical Regionalism marked a point when the principles of an aesthetic theory aligned with the consolidation of environmental thinking in architecture.

By the end of the twentieth century, a concern with environment had been identified as a particular feature of Queensland architecture.[20] As a preoccupation environment gathered new dimensions over time and with the arrival of new people from interstate and overseas, but without a doubt, the trajectory of its development passes through Dalton who had from 1960s appealed to architects to be aware of the potential of the environment for generating an architecture of delight.

Dalton in the twenty-first century

At the end of the twentieth century the work of Dalton and his peers came to the attention of a younger generation of architects via different means. Many of these architects were students at QUT where they encountered architect and historian Professor Jennifer Taylor, newly appointed from the University of Sydney and the author of such key texts as *An Australian Identity: Houses for Sydney 1953–63* (1972) and *Australian Architecture Since 1960* (1986).[21] Other QUT students undertaking part-time study had access to drawings and images of key modernist buildings from the 1950s and 1960s completed by the established practices in which they worked.[22] At the end of the twentieth century many of these buildings were in need of maintenance or refurbishment to bring them into line with updated building codes. Interest in the Queensland's Post-Second World War architecture led to two significant exhibitions. 'Cool: the 60s Brisbane House' in 2004, an exhibition and accompanying catalogue curated by Peta Dennis, together with Tracey Avery and Paula Whitman, levered research undertaken by Peta Dennis for a dissertation supervised by Jennifer Taylor.[23] Work by John Dalton featured prominently in this exhibition. The 'Cool' exhibition followed an earlier exhibition in 2002, *Hayes and Scott: Post-war Houses* curated by Andrew Wilson at The University of Queensland Art Museum. These exhibitions represent the first time that modernist houses by Brisbane architects were celebrated as historical artefacts. Their timing coincided with a growing fascination with mid-century modernism in art, interior architecture, joinery, furnishings and furniture design.[24] Much of this fascination was focused in separating out innovators from followers but a group of young architecture graduates was more interested in the 'legitimate' and 'authentic' realization of abstract and transferable ideas 'in *our* setting'.[25] Put simply they were intensely interested in how material and spatial outcomes were achieved.

As a QUT student Jason Haigh's studies were reinforced by his experiences working as a student at Fulton Gilmore Trotter Moss, an established form with a body of exemplary work from the 1960s. In particular, the experience of working on International House (1964) a residential hall at the University of Queensland designed by Stephen Trotter seeded an interest in climate responsive modernism. Of most interest to him in the modernist houses of Hayes and Scott, Dalton and others is the relation of structural and material ordering systems to occupiable space. Haigh recognizes in the articulation of beams and trims and the use of datums and tonal contrasts to generate space and sub-spaces within space, the key to making a small house feel larger. It is a tactic he deploys in his practice with Charissa McCaughey.[26]

Dalton's later skillion roofed houses are of greater interest to Stuart Vokes and Aaron Peters, whose mostly domestic practice, Vokes and Peters, is noted for the correlation of interior and exterior space. Vokes and Peters see in Dalton's skillion roofed houses the marriage of a timber tradition with a masonry tradition – a hybrid architecture. In discussing the Graham House, they identify masonry elements supporting timber framing with the masonry 'grounding the building' and 'anchoring the composition' and the 'lightweight timber cantilevered off a masonry backbone' (Figure 3.14).[27]

Vokes and Peters' interest in modern architecture was seeded in different ways. Vokes grew up in the western suburbs of Brisbane and became inculcated into the modern aesthetic through visits to the homes of his school friends. Undertaking research for an undergraduate dissertation on mid-century modernism meant that he reengaged with houses observed during his adolescent years but in a more scholarly way.[28] Peters first became aware of Dalton through the 'Cool – 60s Houses in Brisbane' exhibition. Both admire the seemingly effortless yet elegant way that the composition of elements in Dalton's work is productive formally whilst also establishing territory for occupation. They observe that the use of masonry is sensible for termite management in Queensland but when used in 'benching' and 'remaking the site' also facilitates living at ground level and on the threshold between inside and outside. They describe the use of masonry in the Chick House as extending into the landscape 'remaking site as ideal' and 'uniting garden and house' (Figure 4.13)[29] and identify similar strategies at play in the T2 House, Taringa (2004) by Timothy Hill of Donovan Hill.[30] Vokes and Peters Indooroopilly House (2007) uses natural brick rather than white masonry to anchor, suspend and orient timber-framed living spaces above a bush landscape (Figure 7.4). Similarly, the Newmarket (2004) and Chapel Hill (2005) Houses completed by Owen, Vokes and Peters demonstrates strong parallels with Dalton's houses in the making of outdoor rooms and their orientation to garden landscapes. In a series of recent projects – the Block Modular Houses – Vokes and Peters maintain a similar set of strategies. These projects comprise lightweight structures prefabricated off-site and masonry walls retaining platforms and creating territory for garden spaces. Postwar modernist house plans were examined for lessons about spatial efficiency and economy of means that could be applied to modular unit design, and to identify the potential of various unit designs for modularization and variety in configuration.

Whilst Vokes and Peters are not the only contemporary architects in Brisbane using masonry elements and timber framing to fit buildings to site and to articulate settings linking interior and exterior space, and they are certainly influenced by other contemporaneous work, they clearly articulate the role that analysis of Dalton's work plays in their practise. Haigh and McCaughey, Vokes and Peters recognize that the globalization of architecture with its quest for novelty and newness has resulted in a loss of local cultural knowledge and that the work of the early practitioners of subtropical modernist architecture still holds lessons for today. One of the lessons they believe needs recovering urgently is the capacity to persist with a particular line of enquiry in architecture. To this end they are absorbed in exploring the role of architecture in mapping out relationships between occupants and their situation to reflect new patterns of living in the twenty-first century in Brisbane, Queensland.

FIGURE 7.4 Indooroopilly House by Vokes and Peters, 2007. Photo Jon Linkins. Copyright Jon Linkins.

The environmental response

This narrative returns to a time when environment was emerging as a disciplinary concern, to draw out environmental perspectives in the practice of one architect, John Dalton. It traces over a period of architectural history usually framed, first through reference to climate-responsive design and then as a regionally inspired modernism, offering not a re-conceptualizing of historical accounts of this period, but a different lens on practice. In this study environment operates as a physical construct with cultural and social dimensions to which an architect must respond through design but also as an attitude or mindset that interacts with other disciplinary theories and practices in an architect's personal hierarchy of concerns.[31]

During the 1960s the discipline's engagement with environment broadened from a focus primarily on climate and functional systems to embrace an understanding of the environment/architecture entanglement as co-dependent, interrelated and as having social, cultural and political consequences. A focus on the individual and their comfort was augmented by a conception of the individual as part of an ecosystem, an awareness evidenced in actions that worked to limit architecture's impact on the natural world but also to bring humans into closer association with each other and their world.

Whilst analysis of Dalton's work reveals he was very conscious of the broadened scope of architecture's interest in environment, he was and is remembered primarily as an architect of houses. Dalton's early houses are pragmatic, efficiently planned for climate but also carefully detailed to achieve a modern aesthetic. His many houses in the western suburbs of Brisbane provided a template for modern living in subtropical Brisbane. It was Dalton's awareness, realized through painting, that the edge of building form is where decisions about space and its experience intersect with the articulation of form. The edge is where principles of design to limit solar gain and glare and to maximize ventilation intersect with processes for tuning the house container to its setting; where the use of roof overhangs, screens and blinds also gives rise to the patterns of sunlight, shade and shadow that accompany and enhance life in the subtropics. The edge is where the archetypal space – the verandah – is to be found. The careful calibration of its space and form in response to the specific environmental circumstances of site and climate offered the potential to enrich life by engaging the senses.

In Dalton's process the making of architectural experience begins with a set of decisions about how a building form is situated and oriented to engage the environment; how it positions the occupant in their daily life in relation to the sun, the breeze and the natural world. He believed that such decisions would support patterns of living that were 'indigenous' – by which he meant patterns natural to a particular place. In declaring that an architecture so initiated was unequivocally Australian, he also kept faith with Robin Boyd's quest for an Australian architecture. Dalton's preoccupation with environmental considerations did not change with the onset of postmodernism in the antipodes – if anything he became more vocal in his call for an identifiable Australian architecture.

The demolition of significant buildings completed by John Dalton Architect and Associates is demonstrative of issues related to building in timber in a subtropical climate with termite activity, humidity and a high annual rainfall; of the densification pressures of a growing city on what were once outer suburbs in bushland; and of being the architect of choice for a mobile population of musicians, artists and university academics for whom Brisbane was a stepping stone to somewhere more significant. But demolition of work also points to problems with the status of an architecture that arises from an environmentalist approach. Innovation in relation to engaging environment experientially is not readily identifiable in photographs of work and the environmental dimensions of work are not what has interested scholarship of mid-century modern architecture to date. If anything, historiography is challenged to recognize and value relational thinking in built work.

In Dalton's process, the focus on relationships set up in and by work often comes at the expense of achieving a coherent architectural whole. This 'shortcoming' is most evident in the DDIAE Art and Music School and the Bardon Professional Development Centre. Neither delivered an iconic architectural image but each was commended at the time for the experience of its teaching spaces. The reception of these works by colleagues at the time suggests that an identifiable image was a non-negotiable expectation of the profession, and the lack of a civic building with an identifiable image is offered by some today as one reason why Dalton slipped into obscurity by the end of the twentieth century.[32] Instead Dalton's body of work has been conflated into a single image – that of the 'Dalton House', a subtropical house addressing climate – an oversimplification.

Dalton's concern with an environmentally tuned architecture also has unexpected consequences. The straightforward articulation of territory in Dalton's domestic architecture led to a set of robust, linked spaces – inside and outside – correctly oriented and scaled for human comfort, which has contributed to a flexibility in the work. Very few Dalton houses survive in the manner they were originally designed but many have been successfully adapted for the lifestyle demands of another generation. Spaces have been reassigned programmatically, reorganized and remodelled in response to new patterns of living. Houses are accommodating of ways of living in relation to sun, breeze and views rather than overly deterministic of a particular lifestyle at a particular point of time.

This study acknowledges that environmentalist thinking is not a theory of aesthetics or of architecture. Rather it is a mindset, a way of working through a design problem strategically in an ethical and socially and materially responsible and responsive way; of seeking out the order in each project's particular circumstances. It offers a lesson with currency, for the discipline in Australia is presently working to appreciate and absorb a new dimension of environmental thinking. Australia's professional and accrediting bodies have made a commitment to acknowledge and embed First Nations approaches to country into the practice of architecture and planning. First Nations knowledge of and respect for country constitute a 'mindset' with implications for processes, again not linked to the discipline's established theoretical constructs. Environment continues to disrupt the discipline of architecture in Australia.

Subtropical architecture is characterized by its permeability[33] achieved through the application of shutters, louvres, screens, and blinds; material fabric at the edge of building form that breathes, slides away, rolls up or drops down and that relies on detail to circumscribe the operation of building envelope and to establish connections between the occupant and their environment. The 1960s and 1970s were critical to the development of ways of thinking about architecture in relation to environment, for late modernism brought into disciplinary focus in new ways, a first principles interest in orientation, siting, the linking of interior and exterior space, and the filtering of light, shadow and breeze at the edge of building form. In Australia's subtropics such concerns resonated and were absorbed into a local culture of practice to be addressed by environmentally aware architects in increasingly sophisticated and nuanced ways. In the work of thoughtful architects, environment is not an abstract backdrop but a framework integral to thinking and action. John Dalton acquired the habits of environmentalist thinking and by actively promoting such an approach locally and nationally, he positioned himself as a significant figure in Australian architecture's turn to environment.

NOTES

Introduction

1. See John Maxwell Freeland, *Architecture in Australia: A History* (Ringwood Victoria: Penguin, 1968), 277; 'Ten Years of Architecture and Arts', *Architecture and Arts* 10, no. 1 (January 1962): 20.
2. 'Four Houses by Dalton & Heathwood Architects', *Architecture and Arts* (September 1959): 58; John Dalton, 'Flats at Toowong, Brisbane: Extract from address to Queensland Architecture Students Association', *Architecture and Arts* (August 1961): 46.
3. Dalton's preferred spellings have been adopted for this text; hence verandah is used instead of the now more frequent verandah.
4. Robin Boyd, 'California & Victoria, Architectural Twins', *Age*, 9 October 1948; Philip Goad, 'Constructing Pedigree: Robin Boyd's "California-Victoria-New empiricism" Axis', *Fabrications* 22, no. 1: 4–29, DOI: 10.1080/10331867.2012.685633.
5. Royston Landau, 'British Architecture. The Culture of Architecture: A Historiography of the Current Discourse', *International Architect* 5 (1984): 6–9. Landau describes the formation of an architect's personal position.
6. Emel, Jody (1994), 'Ecology', in Johnston, R. J., et al., *The Dictionary of Human Geography* (1994): 145–7.
7. Ian Bentley et al., *Responsive Environments: A Manual for Designers* (Amsterdam; Boston: Elsevier/Architectural Press, 1985), 9.
8. Jiat-Hwee Chang and Tim Winter, 'Thermal Modernity and Architecture', *The Journal of Architecture* 20, no. 1 (February 2015): 92–121. DOI: 10.1080/13602365.2015.1010095. Chang et al. describe the introduction of international modernism to the tropics, made possible by air-conditioning, as homogenizing.
9. Isabelle Doucet 'Hesitant (Hi)stories: Whose Environment? Which (Architectural) Imaginations?' in Sophie Hochhäusl and Torten Lange eds., 'Field Notes: Architecture and the Environment', *Architectural Histories* 6, no. 1 (2018): 5; Esther da Costa Meyer, 'Architectural History in the Anthropocene: Towards Methodology', *The Journal of Architecture* 21, no. 8 (2016): 1206. DOI: 10.1080/13602365.2016.1254270.
10. da Costa Meyer, 'Towards Methodology', 1217.
11. Ginger Nolan and Alla Vronskaya, 'Building the Ineffable: Human-ness and the Reification of Environmentality' in S. Hochhäusl and T. Lange et al., 'Field Notes: Architecture and the Environment', *Architectural Histories* 6, no. 1 (2018): 20, 9.

12 Hochhäusl and Lange et al., 'Field Notes: Architecture and the Environment', 1.
13 Daniel A. Barber 'The Environmentalization of Architectural History', in Sophie Hochhäusl and Torten Lange, 'Field Notes: Architecture and the Environment', *Architectural Histories* 6, no. 1 (2018): 4/13.
14 Daniel A. Barber, *Modern Architecture and Climate: Design before Air Conditioning* (New Jersey: Princeton University Press, 2020).
15 David Leatherbarrow, *Uncommon Ground: Architecture, Technology, and Topography* (Cambridge MA; London: The MIT Press, 2002). Also, Leatherbarrow, *Architecture Oriented Otherwise* (New York: Princeton Architectural Press, 2009).
16 Royston Landau, *New Directions in British Architecture* (London: Studio Vista, 1968), 14; Landau, 'British Architecture. The Culture of Architecture', 6-9.
17 The significance of the individual architect is also argued by Julie Willis and Philip Goad, 'A Bigger Picture: Reframing Australian Architectural History', in *Fabrications* 18, no. 1 (2008): 7.
18 In an undated transcript, 'Talks to students of Brisbane Girls' Secondary School', Dalton refers to a 'strange body of men known as ARCHITECTS' and encourages this audience, as 'mothers and partners' to engage architects rather than buy project homes. Source: Dalton's Papers. Courtesy Sue Dalton.
19 da Costa Meyer, 'Towards Methodology', 1217.

Chapter 1

1 Heinz Jacobsohn, *Digital Archive of Queensland Architecture* https://qldarch.net/architect/summary?archetId+4337.
2 David Malouf, *Johnno* (Ringwood, Vic.: Penguin Books, Aust, 1976), 84.
3 Unless otherwise stated in footnotes and references, information relating to Dalton's extended family and early life is contained in letters to John Dalton from his sisters Helen Pratley and Sallie Cook.
4 Letter from Helen Pratley to John Dalton dated 13 October 1994.
5 Interview with Sue Dalton at Allora, 21 May 2012.
6 Conversation with Amanda Turner at Brisbane City Hall, 6 September 2022.
7 Letter from Helen Pratley dated 26 May, 1998. Letter from Helen Pratley dated 15 June 1997.
8 Letter to John Dalton from Sallie Cook dated 3 March 1995.
9 Activities recounted in childhood newsletter included in Correspondence Files. Dalton's papers. Courtesy of Sue Dalton.
10 Architect and friend Dan Callaghan recalls a conversation in which Dalton spoke of attending a match in which a series of records were broken by Australian batsmen. In the 1934 Ashes Test at Leeds, a Ponsford and Bradman (304) partnership resulted in 388 runs – then a world record. In 1934 Dalton would have been six years old. Interview with Dan Callaghan at Mount Tambourine, 13 January 2017.
11 Photocopy of newsletter included in Correspondence Files. Dalton's papers. Courtesy of Sue Dalton.
12 Confirmed by Sue Dalton. In an early (but undated) typed curriculum vitae Dalton states he attended St Chad's Church of England Primary School between 1932 and 1940. In later bibliographies he refers to being 'educated at Adel', which is a nearby suburb.

13　National Diploma in Building Transcript of Studies issued by The Institute of Builders in conjunction with The Ministry of Education on 7 February 1947. Courtesy of Sue Dalton.
14　Photocopy of letter written by Dalton dated 16 April 2004 which begins 'Hi Bruce'. It included photocopied pages from a 'kids' newspaper, *The Headingly Herald* dated Sept. (1941).
15　Hand-written notes in Dalton's files. Courtesy of Sue Dalton.
16　Letter confirming discharge dated 1 June 1950. Forwarded to Dalton's address at 271 Bowen Terrace, New Farm, Brisbane. Courtesy of Sue Dalton.
17　Letter dated 5 July 1949 at termination of employment. Courtesy of Sue Dalton.
18　Commonwealth of Australia, Ministry of Labour and National Service Overseas Settlement Application Form, National Archives of Australia, NAA: BP23/1, 6156. Item ID 5040470. Dalton lists Protheroe and McNab Ltd. Leeds as his employer.
19　Interview with Sue Dalton at Allora, 21 May 2012.
20　Letter from Commonwealth of Australia. Dalton's papers. Courtesy of Sue Dalton.
21　Migration record, National Archives of Australia, NAA: BP23/1, 6156. Item ID 5040470.
22　RAF discharge papers dated 1 June 1950 addressed to 271 Bowen Terrace New Farm. Courtesy of Sue Dalton.
23　Scott Chasling, 'Frank Costello: City Architect 1941–1952 City Planner 1946–1952' (B.Arch diss., The University of Queensland, 1997), 18.
24　Chasling, 'Frank Costello', 19. Robert Freestone and Darryl Low Choy, 'Enriching the Community: The Life and Times of Frank Costello (1903–1987)', in *Australian Planner* 50, no. 1: 56.
25　Chasling, 'Frank Costello', 199.
26　Alice Hampson, 'The Fifties in Queensland Why Not? Why!?' (B. Arch diss., Depart. of Architecture, University of Queensland, 1987), 4.
27　Reference from Frank Gibson Costello dated 13 November 1952. Courtesy of Sue Dalton.
28　Ibid.
29　Brisbane City Council Archive. BBC drawings viewed on 17 December 2014.
30　Sue Dalton interview with Elizabeth Musgrave at Allora, 21 May 2012.
31　Don Watson and Fiona Gardiner, 'Bend Like Bamboo: Always Bounce Back', in *Karl Langer: Modern and Migrant Architect in the Tropics*, edited by Deborah Van Der Plaat and John Macarthur (London: Bloomsbury, 2022), 79–81.
32　Jacobsohn, *Digital Archive of Queensland Architecture*, https://qldarch.net/architect/summary?archetld+4337.
33　Ian and June Cameron interview with Elizabeth Musgrave at Bycroft Street, Pullenvale on 20 March 2014.
34　The group included Ian Cameron a consultant engineer, his wife June and June's best friend Shelia Harvey. Betty Kelly and her husband, Bryan a musician, were also jazz enthusiasts. The Camerons, Leveringtons and Kellys, all bushwalkers, would commission Dalton to design houses.
35　Sue Dalton interview with Elizabeth Musgrave at Allora, 21 May 2012.
36　Amanda Turner, Email correspondence dated 22 October 2022. A severe teacher shortage after WWII meant that teacher training was only twelve months long.
37　Andrew Saniga, *Making Landscape Architecture in Australia* (Sydney: New South Publishing, 2012), 17–18, 70–1.

38 The Queensland Art Gallery was known as the National Art Gallery, Queensland until 1959 when the Queensland Art Gallery Act 1959 led to a change of name.
39 Helen Fridemanis, 'Artists and aspects of the Contemporary Art Society (Queensland Branch)' (M.Arts diss. The University of Queensland, 1989), 3.
40 Dalton was introduced to Jazz by Betty and Bryan Kelly and became a jazz follower. The Kelly, Magee, Farbach and MacFarlane commissions were houses for jazz musicians.
41 John Dalton interview with Peta Dennis in Brisbane, 21 April 1999. 'Architectural Practice in Postwar Queensland (1945–1975): Building and Interpreting an Oral History Archive', Fryer Library at the University of Queensland.
42 Conversation with Amanda Turner at Brisbane City Hall, 6 September 2022.
43 Letter from Clifford Chew dated 6 April 1951. Chew, Principal of Leeds Technical College, confirmed 'the standard of entry to this course is that of School certificate and the standard of Mathematics, Physics and Chemistry attained in the course is comparable to the Matriculation examination in these subjects'.
44 Certificate for Senior Public Examination issued by the University of Queensland dated 23 December 1952. This was followed by a letter dated 30 April 1953 and signed by Lange Powell, Principal of the BCTC advising Dalton that he is now admitted to the Diploma Course in Architecture and apologizing for any inconvenience caused.
45 John Dalton interview with Peta Dennis in Brisbane, 21 April 1999.
46 Peter Heathwood interview with Peta Dennis in Brisbane, 11 February 1999.
47 Robin Gibson, Obituary, Funeral of John Dalton, 1 June 2007. CD Rom Courtesy of Sue Dalton.
48 Commonwealth Department of Works Certificate of Service dated 21 April 1954 indicates Dalton was employed between 13 July 1953 and 30 April 1954. Courtesy of Sue Dalton.
49 John Dalton interview with Peta Dennis in Brisbane, 21 April 1999.
50 Ibid.
51 Bruce Walker, *Gabriel Poole: A Space in Which the Soul Can Play* (Noosa, QLD.: Visionary Press, 1998), 28.
52 Steven Trotter, *Cities in the Sun* (Enoggera, Brisbane: Crusade Press, 1964).
53 Musgrave, Elizabeth, 'The Plywood Exhibition House – An Investigation of Local Idiom', *ADDITIONS to Architectural History XIXth Papers of the Annual Conference of SAHANZ* (2002).
54 Peter Heathwood interview with Peta Dennis, 11 February 1999.
55 Ibid.
56 Copy of letter to Peter Heathwood from John Dalton dated 12 December 1960. John Dalton interview with Peta Dennis in Brisbane, 21 April 1999. For further detail refer also to Peter Heathwood interview with Peta Dennis, 11 February 1999.
57 'Projects Completed 1956–1972', Dalton's papers.
58 Haig Beck interview, *Digital Archive of Queensland Architecture* http://qldarch.net/architect/summary?architectId=273.
59 Charles Ham interview with Elizabeth Musgrave at Caloundra on 25 September 2015.
60 Charles Ham conversation with Elizabeth Musgrave, February 2022.
61 Lech Blaine, 'Top Blokes: The Larrikin Myth, Class and Power', *Quarterly Essay* 83 (2021): 13–15.
62 Ibid.

63 John Dalton interview with Peta Dennis in Brisbane, 21 April 1999.
64 Charles Ham conversation with Elizabeth Musgrave, February 2022.
65 Ibid.; 'Annual Awards 1978', *Queensland Chapter News,* December 1978, 1. Edition also included a profile of the office illustrated with an image of Peter Brown, Charles Ham, Stanley Witchell and John Dalton. 'Personality Profile: John Dalton', *Queensland Chapter News,* December 1978, 7.
66 Ibid.
67 Ibid.
68 Ibid.
69 Haig Beck and Jackie Cooper conversation with Elizabeth Musgrave, March 2022.
70 Charles Ham conversation with Elizabeth Musgrave, February 2022.
71 Sue Dalton conversation with Elizabeth Musgrave at Allora, 18 February 2022.
72 Ibid.
73 Amanda Turner conversation with Elizabeth Musgrave at Brisbane City Hall, 6 September 2022.
74 Peta Dennis, 'Innovative Architecture for Living: Brisbane Architect-designed Houses of the 1960s' (B.Arch diss., University of Queensland Technology, School of Architecture Interior and Industrial Design, 1999), 4. Dalton's work was published on nineteen occasions during this period; the next most published architect was Graham Bligh whose work was published five times.
75 Paul Hogben, '*Architecture and Arts* and the Mediation of American Architecture in Post-war Australia', *Fabrications* 22, no. 1 (2012): 53.
76 'Ten Years of Architecture and Arts', *Architecture and Arts* 10, no. 1 (January 1962): 20.
77 This initiative was banned by the Head of Architecture Gareth Roberts after neighbours complained about noise and bad behaviour. Letter from Dalton to Bill Carr in London, 26 February 1969.
78 Peter Brown interview with Elizabeth Musgrave, 8 September 2022.
79 Ibid.
80 Dalton cited by Jennifer Taylor in *Australian Architecture since 1960* (Sydney: The Law Book Company, 1986), 122.
81 Peter Brown interviewed by Elizabeth Musgrave, 6 September 2022.
82 Charles Ham conversation with Elizabeth Musgrave, February 2022.
83 John Dalton is linked with Peter Heathwood and Hayes and Scott as informed by climatic design principles in Graham de Gruchy (1988), Balwant Singh Saini (1970), Haig Beck (1984), Jennifer Taylor (1986) and Graham Jahn (1994).
84 Donald Leslie Johnson did not substantially address Queensland architecture in *Australian Architecture 1901-51: Sources of Modernism* (1980). Robin Boyd did not refer to architecture from Queensland in *The Walls around Us* (1962), *The New Architecture* (1963) or in his landmark essay, 'The State of Australian Architecture' (1967).
85 Robin Boyd, *Australia's Home: Its Origins, Builders, and Occupiers* (Melbourne: Melbourne University Press, 1952); Taylor, *Australian Architecture since 1960.*
86 Philip Goad, 'Homes in the Sun: Climate and the Modern Australian House 1945-1965', in *Celebration: Proceedings of the XXII Annual Conference of the Society of Architectural Historians Australia and New Zealand,* Napier New Zealand (September, 2005): 133.
87 Deborah van der Platt, Andrew Wilson and Elizabeth Musgrave, 'Twentieth-Century (Sub)-Tropical Housing: Framing Climate Culture and Civilisation in

Post-War Queensland', in John Macarthur, Deborah Van der Plaat, Janina Gosseye and Andrew Wilson eds., *Hot Modernism: Queensland Architecture 1945-1975* (London: Artifice, 2015), 76-81.

88 Commonwealth Housing Commission, *Final Report: 25th August 1944* (Sydney: Government Printer, 1944): National Archives of Australia: A9816, 1944/244.

89 Daniel Ryan, 'Settling the Thermal Frontier: The Tropical House in Northern Queensland from Federation to the Second World War' (PhD diss., The University of Sydney, NSW, School of Architecture Design and Planning, 2017), 208, 234-5. Ryan notes the unpublished QTHC 'Report on Tropical Housing' (1943) was strongly influenced by the medical interests of Sir Raphael Cilento, the Director General of Health in Queensland and an expert in tropical health, and the development focus of economist and Director of Bureau of Industry, Colin Clark.

90 Walter R. Bunning, *Homes in the Sun: The Past, Present and Future of Australian Housing* (Sydney: Nesbit, 1945).

91 Karl Langer, *Subtropical Housing* (Brisbane: The University of Queensland, 1944), 2, 6 and 8; Douglas Neale, 'The "Essentials" of the Subtropical House: An Exegesis of the "Modernistic" Town Planning Principles', *Limits: Proceedings from the twenty-first SAHANZ conference* 2 (2004): 349.

92 David Malouf, *12 Edmonstone Street* (Ringwood Vic.: Penguin Books, 1985).

93 Robin Boyd and Peter Newell, 'St Lucia: A Housing Revolution Is Taking Place', *Architecture* (July 1950): 106.

94 Boyd and Newell, 'St Lucia', 106.

95 Boyd, *Australia's Home*, 211, 213.

96 Goad, 'Homes in the Sun', 134, 136; Stuart King, 'A Climate of Confusion: The Significance of Climatic Adaptation in 19th Century Queensland Architecture', in *Panorama to Paradise: Proceedings of the 24th Annual Conference of Architectural Historians of Australia and New Zealand*, Adelaide (21-24 September 2007): 1; Graham de Gruchy, 'Architecture in Queensland', *Art & Architecture* 6, no. 4 (March 1969): 297-302.

97 E. J. A. Weller, *Buildings of Queensland* (Brisbane: Jacaranda Press, 1959), 27.

98 Ibid., 27.

99 Ibid., 28.

100 John Maxwell Freeland, *Architecture in Australia: A History* (Ringwood Victoria: Penguin, 1968), 277; Richard Apperly, Robert Irving and Peter Reynolds, *A Pictorial Guide to Identifying Australian Architecture: Styles and Terms from 1788 to the Present* (North Ryde, N.S.W.: Angus & Robertson, 1989), 222-3; Peter Cuffley, *Australian Houses of the Forties and Fifties* (Knoxfield, Vic.: Five Mile Press, 1993), 109. Also Graham de Gruchy (1988), Balwant Singh Saini (1970), Haig Beck (1984), Jennifer Taylor (1986) and Graham Jahn (1994).

101 Taylor, *Australian Architecture since 1960*, 118.

102 Michael Keniger, Judy Vulker and Mark Roehrs, *Australian Architects: Rex Addison, Lindsay Clare and Russell Hall* (Manuka, A.C.T.: Royal Australian Institute of Architects, 1990), 4.

103 Graham Jahn, *Contemporary Australian Architecture* (East Roseville, NSW: Gordon and Breach Arts International, 1994), 7.

104 Jahn, *Contemporary Australian Architecture*, 7.

105 Julie McGlone, *HEAT: Queensland's New Wave of Environmental Architects* (Brisbane: Creative Industries Unit, Department of Tourism, Regional Development and Industry, 2008), 7.

106 Peter Hay, *Main Currents in Western Environmental Thought* (Sydney: University of New South Wales Press, 2002), 1.
107 Ibid., 3 and 16.
108 Ibid., 16.
109 Joel A. Tarr in Frank Uekoetter ed., *The Turning Points of Environmental History* (Pittsburgh, PA: University of Pittsburgh Press, 2010), 84.
110 Ibid., 16, 2; Victor Papanek, *Design for the Real World* (London: Thames and Hudson, 1972), 212–16; Hay, *Main Currents in Western Environmental Thought*, 174; David Arnold, *The Problem of Nature: Environment, Culture and European Expansion* (Oxford: Blackwell Publishers Inc., 1996), 1; Jens Ivo Engels, 'Modern Environmentalism' in Uekoetter, *The Turning Points of Environmental History*, 119–25.
111 Ross Fitzgerald, *A History of Queensland from Dreaming to 1915, Vol. 1* (St Lucia: UQ Press, Prologue, 1986); Also, Ross Fitzgerald, *A History of Queensland 1915 to the 1980s* (St Lucia: UQ Press, 1985).
112 Susan Holden, 'Parallel Narratives of Disciplinary Disruption: The Bush Campus as Design and Pedagogical Concept', in Elke Couchez and Rajesh Heynickx eds., *Architectural Education through Materiality: Pedagogies of 20th Century Design* (London: Routledge, 2022), 183.
113 Ian Bentley et al., *Responsive Environments: A Manual for Designers* (London: Architectural Press, 1985), 9.
114 'School Description' accompanying letter to Dalton dated 25 November 1977 from MJ Toohey, Personnel Officer QIT. The proposed curriculum for a Faculty of Environmental Design at The University of Queensland was to include Regional and Town Planning, Landscape, Civic Design Industrial Design and Building Science.
115 Meeting notes prepared by Professor Gareth E. Roberts for the Faculty of Architecture Sub-Committee reporting on the proposed new Faculty of Environmental Design at The University of Queensland dated 13 October 1970.
116 Richard Neutra, *Survival through Design* (New York: Oxford University Press, 1954), 4.
117 Paul Walker and Karen Burns, 'Constructing Australian Architecture for International Audiences: Regionalism. Postmodernism, and the Design Arts Board', *Fabrications* 28, no. 1 (2018): 25–46, 36.
118 Jeannie Sim ed., *Thematic Study of the Cultural Landscape of Queensland: Investigating Queensland's Cultural Landscapes: Contested Terrain Series Report 2* (Brisbane: Cultural Landscape Research Unit, University of Queensland Technology, 2001), 86.
119 Tom Griffiths and Libby Robin eds., *Ecology & Empire: Environmental History of Settler Societies* (Seattle: University of Washington Press, 1997); Richard H. Grove, *Green Imperialism: Colonial Expansion, Tropical Island Edens and Origins of Environmentalism 1600-1860* (Cambridge; New York: Cambridge University Press, 1995), 95–125.
120 'Post War Domestic Architecture', *Architecture and Arts* VIII, no. 92 (June 1961): 37–51, 43.
121 Walker and Burns, 'Constructing Australian Architecture', 25–46.
122 Daryl Jackson, 'From Edge to Centre: Sense and Stylism in Current Australian Architecture', *International Architect* 4 (1984): 4–5.
123 Walker and Burns, 'Constructing Australian Architecture', 30, 42.

124   Rachel Perkins, *The Australian Wars,* Blackfella Films; SBS, 2022. Earlier groundbreaking work includes: Henry Reynolds ed., *Race Relations in North Queensland* (Townsville, Qld.: Department of History and Politics, James Cook University, 1993); Bill Gammage, *The Biggest Estate on Earth: How Aborigines Made Australia* (Crows Nest, NSW: Allen & Unwin, 2011); Griffiths and Robin eds., *Ecology & Empire.*

125   Saniga, *Making Landscape Architecture,* 17–18, 70–1.

126   An instance in Queensland is Bernard O'Reilly, *Green Mountains,* originally published in 1940, an account of O'Reilly's search for the survivors of a plane crash in the dense rainforest of the Lamington National Park.

Chapter 2

1   'Four Houses by Dalton & Heathwood Architects', *Architecture and Arts,* no. 71 (September 1959): 58.

2   John Dalton, 'Flats at Toowong, Brisbane: Extract from address to Queensland Architecture Students Association', *Architecture and Arts* VIII, no. 94 (August 1961): 46.

3   Robin Boyd, *Australia's Home: Its Origins, Builders, and Occupiers* (Melbourne: Melbourne University Press, 1952), 213.

4   Dalton's files include a large format negative of an axonometric of Case Study 4 House (1954) by Ralph Rapson.

5   Alice Hampson, 'The Fifties in Queensland', Vol 2 Catalogue no. 08/1958/06. Confirmed in conversations with Peter Heathwood and Dalton at the time of writing 'Plywood Exhibition House', 2002.

6   Elizabeth Musgrave, 'The Plywood Exhibition House – An Investigation of Local Idiom', ADDITIONS to Architectural History Papers of the XIXth Annual Conference of SAHANZ, Brisbane, 4–7 October, 2002.

7   Elizabeth Smith ed., *Blueprints for Modern Living: History and Legacy of the Case Study Houses* (Los Angeles: The Museum of Contemporary Art, 1989), 94. Also Peter Blake, *Marcel Breuer: Architect and Designer* (New York: Architectural Record in association with The Museum of Modern Art, 1949), 89.

8   'A New Glamour for a Standard Material', *Australian House and Garden* 19, no. 2 (January 1958): 38, 92; Charles Pickett, *The Fibro Frontier: A Different History of Australian Architecture* (Sydney: Museum of Applied Arts and Sciences Powerhouse Museum, 1997), 97.

9   Shirley Gott, '"House of To-morrow" at Show', *Courier Mail,* 8 August 1957, 11. 'Queensland Builds a Plywood House', *Australian House and Garden* 19, no. 4 (March 1958): 56.

10   'In 10 Best for Home', *Courier Mail,* Thursday 27 November 1958, 10.

11   In 1963, it was purchased by Heathwood's brother-in-law and sister, Don and Patricia Marshall, and moved to its current location at The Gap. Musgrave, 'Plywood Exhibition House', 9.

12   *Architecture and Arts* (February 1958): 20.

13   Dalton consistently spelt verandah with an 'h' as in 'verandah'. The OED indicates both spellings are acceptable today. verandah is in common usage in contemporary texts. http://www.oed.com.ezproxy.library.uq.edu.au/view/ Entry/222348?redirectedFrom=veranda#eid accessed 11 March 2019 at 09:30.

14 'Queensland Builds a Plywood House', 56.
15 Interview with Gabriel Poole, at Tim Bennetton Architect, West End, Brisbane on 02 November 2015.
16 Hampson, 'The Fifties in Queensland', Vol 2.
17 Dalton and Heathwood, 'Four Houses', 58.
18 Lewis Mumford, 'An Address to Architectural Students in Rome', *Architecture and Arts* VII, no. 82 (August 1960): 29–31. Dalton's library contained three books by Lewis Mumford, *The Transformations of Man* (London: George Allen and Unwin Ltd., 1957), *The City in History: Its Origins, Its Transformations and Its Prospects* (London: Secker and Warburg, 1961) and *The Condition of Man* (London: Mercury Books, 1963 ed., *The Condition of Man* was first published in 1944).
19 W. Boesiger, 'Foreword by the Editors'', in W. Boesiger et al., eds., *Richard Neutra: 1950-60: Buildings and Projects* (Zurich: Editions Girsberger, 1959), 7.
20 Silvia Micheli and Andrew Wilson, 'International Influences in Post-War Queensland: Protagonists, Destinations and Models', in John Macarthur et al., eds., *Hot Modernism: Queensland Architecture 1945–1975* (London: Artifice, 2015), 119–20.
21 Richard J. Neutra, 'The New and the Old in Architecture', *Richard Neutra: 1950–60*, 8.
22 Richard J. Neutra, *Survival through Design* (New York: Oxford University Press, 1954), 21.
23 Dalton and Heathwood, 'Four Houses', 58–64.
24 The Speare House is attributed to Heathwood, but Dalton has claimed that it was his suggestion to make the clerestory of the Speare House ventilating. The Cullen House (1954) and Burnie Board Administration Building by Dalton at Theo Thynne and Associates both deployed roof lanterns.
25 Dalton and Heathwood, 'Four Houses', 61.
26 Letter to Messrs. Dalton and Heathwood at 55 Moordale Street, Indooroopilly from A.C.Wood, Director of Trade Publicity, Commonwealth Department of Trade, dated 14th April 1960.
27 Robin Boyd and Peter Newell, 'St Lucia: A Housing Revolution Is Taking Place', *Architecture* 38, no. 3 (July 1950): 106. Also Boyd, *Australia's Home,* 213.
28 Letter from Dalton to Peter Heathwood dated 12 December 1960 indicates that Peter Heathwood vacated the office in the City Mutual Building Queen Street between 25 December 1960 and 16 January 1961.
29 'Post War Domestic Architecture', *Architecture and Arts* VIII, no. 92 (June 1961): 37–51.
30 Ibid., 43.
31 Ibid., 39.
32 Ibid., 43.
33 Philip Goad, 'Constructing Pedigree: Robin Boyd's "California-Victoria-New Empiricism" Axis', *Fabrications* 22, no. 1 (2012): 10.
34 'Port Phillip Idiom: Recent Houses in the Melbourne Region', *Architectural Review* 112, no. 671 (November 1952): 310.
35 Wilson, 'Simple Dignity in Ranch', *The Australian Home Beautiful* (June 1963), 8–11.
36 *Sunday Mail Magazine,* 25 October 1964, 14.
37 Glenn R. Cooke, *A Time Remembered: Art in Brisbane 1950–1975* (South Brisbane: Queensland Art Gallery, 1995), 37.
38 Helen D. Fridemanis, 'Contemporary Art Society Queensland Branch, 1961–1973: A Study of the Post-War Emergence and Dissemination of Aesthetic Modernism in Brisbane' (Master of Arts Diss., The University of Queensland, 1989), 14.

39 Fridemanis, 'Contemporary Art Society', ii; Cooke, *A Time Remembered*, 74.
40 CAS Papers Fryer Library, The University of Queensland, Box FGF120; Cooke, *A Time Remembered*, 73. The inaugural president of CAS Queensland Chapter was Bernard Schaffer, Senior Lecture in Public Administration (later known as Political Science) at the University of Queensland. Cooke, *A Time Remembered*, 74–5.
41 CAS Papers Fryer Library, The University of Queensland, Box FGF120; Cooke, *A Time Remembered*, 73–81.
42 Betty Churcher, *Molvig: The Lost Antipodean* (Ringwood, Vic: Penguin Books Australia Ltd, 1984), 43, 2.
43 Fridemanis, 'Contemporary Art Society', i, 3.
44 Louise Martin-Chew, '"Like Topsy": The Johnstone Gallery 1950–1972' (Master of Creative Arts Diss. Townsville: James Cook University, 2001), 33.
45 Cooke, *A Time Remembered*, 48. The original Marodian Gallery operated behind Hugh Hale's interior decorating shop in Spring Hill.
46 Ibid., 36.
47 Betty Cameron travelled to London in 1953 to study at the Royal College of Art on the inaugural Younger Artists' Group Scholarship, a travelling scholarship. She and Roy Churcher met and married in London in and returned to Brisbane in 1957 to 'meet the family'. Fridemanis, 'Contemporary Art Society', 24.
48 Ibid., 25.
49 Cooke, *A Time Remembered*, 36.
50 Melville Haysom, 'Only Few Shine at Art Show', *Telegraph*, 8 December 1959, 2. Haysom describes the show as 'generally mediocre', but notes: 'Outstanding in the abstract division are June Green's 'Sugar Cane', Roy Churcher's 'Night in the Bush' and John Dalton's 'County Stanley, Parish of Indooroopilly'.
51 CAS Catalogues of exhibitions. CAS Papers, Fryer Library, The University of Queensland, Box FGF120. Gallery Society News, Fryer Library, The University of Queensland, 61UQ_ALMA.
52 Cover, *Architecture and Arts*, July 1960.
53 Cooke, *A Time Remembered*, 74.
54 CAS 7 Catalogue Autumn Exhibition, 1965, Finney's Auditorium. Image of Tristan by J. Dalton is listed for 50 Gns.
55 Email correspondence with Paul Memmott 14 November 2021.
56 Harry Seidler, 'Painting toward Architecture', *Architecture*, 37, 122.
57 Ibid.
58 Jean Cathelin, *Jean Arp* (New York: Grove Press Inc., 1959), 10.
59 Ibid., 61.
60 Ibid., 52.
61 Ibid., 49–50.
62 Elizabeth Musgrave and Douglas Neale, 'Architectural Image and Idiom: Making Local', in Dawne McCance, ed., *Mosaic: A Journal for the Interdisciplinary Study of Literature* (Winnipeg: University of Manitoba, 2004), 255–73.
63 Gordon Cullen introduced this concept in 'Immediacy', *The Architectural Review* 113, no. 676 (April 1953): 235–9.
64 Churcher, *Molvig*, 2 and 7.
65 Betty Churcher, *Understanding Art: The Use of Space, Form and Structure* (Adelaide: Rigby, 1973). Churcher's book, initially a school text, became a best-seller and was awarded the senior award for an information book by *The Times* in 1974.
66 Fridemanis, 'Contemporary Art Society Queensland Branch', 25.

67 Churcher citing Andrew Forge, *Soutine* (1965) in *Molvig*, 8.
68 Churcher, *Molvig*, 7.
69 Andrew Wilson and John Macarthur, *Birrell: Work from the Office of James Birrell* (Melbourne Vic.: NMBW Publications, 1997), 42; *Brisbane: A Map Guide to the Architecture of the City* (RAIA Queensland Chapter 1983), paginated; 'UQ Remembers', Neville Matthews obituary accessed 24 January 2014. http://www.uq.edu.au/uqcontact/uq-remembers.
70 'The Ten Best Houses for 1959–1960', *Architecture and Arts* VII, no. 83 (September 1960): 27–36. Other winners include: House at Cronulla by Anchor, Mortlock and Murray, House at South Yarra by Robin Boyd at Grounds Romberg and Boyd, House at Frankston by Chancellor and Patrick and House at Mount Lawley by Ivan Iwanoff.
71 Mumford, 'An Address to Architectural Students in Rome', 31.
72 Ibid.
73 John Dalton, 'Queensland's Pragmatic Poetry', *Architecture and Arts* VII, no. 82 (August 1960): 32.
74 The Oxford English Dictionary 2nd. ed., 624, defines idiomatic as 'peculiar to or characteristic of a particular language; pertaining to or exhibiting the expressions, constructions or phraseology approved by the peculiar usage of a language, esp as differing from a strictly grammatical of logical use of words; vernacular; colloquial.'
75 Boyd, 'Port Phillip Idiom', 309.
76 Goad, 'Constructing Pedigree', 4–29.
77 Dalton, 'Queensland's Pragmatic Poetry', 32.
78 'Dalton's Residence, Fig Tree Pocket, Brisbane', *Architecture and Arts* VII, no. 82 (August 1960): 35.
79 Dalton, 'Queensland's Pragmatic Poetry', 32.
80 Sylvia Lavin, 'Open the Box: Richard Neutra and the Psychology of the Domestic Environment', *Assemblage* 40 (December 1999): 18, 17.
81 'The Ten Best Houses for 1959–1960', 35.
82 John Dalton, 'John Dalton Asks: "What Is Wrong with the Diploma Course?"' *AASA Symposium, The Magazine of the Australian Students' Association* (March 1961): 45.
83 Ibid., 45.
84 Richard Neutra, 'Notes to the Young Architect', *Perspecta* 4 (1957): 50–7.
85 Transcript of radio address.
86 Robert Cummings, lecture delivered at Rostrum, 1941. Unpublished manuscript, Cummings Archive, Faculty of Architecture, The University of Queensland.
87 Musgrave and Neale, 'Architectural Image and Idiom: Making Local', 257 and 272.
88 John Dalton, 'the verandah', *Architecture in Australia* 53, no. 1 (March 1964): 99.
89 Karl Langer, *Subtropical Housing* (Brisbane: The University of Queensland, 1944), 2, 6 & 8.
90 Harry Sowden ed. and photo, *Towards an Australian Architecture* (Sydney, London: Ure Smith, 1968), 76.
91 Dalton, Letter to Editor, *Architecture in Australia*, 23 December 1964.
92 Haig Beck and Jackie Cooper, 'The Contemporary Queenslander', in Miranda Wallace and Sarah Stutchbury eds., *Place Makers: Contemporary Queensland Architects* (South Brisbane, Qld.: Queensland Art Gallery, 2008), 25.
93 Conversation with Ray Hughes at The Hughes Gallery, 270 Devonshire Street, Surrey Hills, Sydney, at 15.00 on 5 December 2014.

Chapter 3

1. D. K. H. Lee, 'Physiological Principles for Tropical Housing with Especial Reference to Queensland' (1944). D. K. H. Lee, 'Assessment of Tropical Climates in Relation to Human Habitation', *Transactions of the Royal Society of Tropical Medicine and Hygiene* 33, no. 6 (1940): 613.
2. W. A. Greig, 'Climate and Design in Brisbane' (B.Arch diss., St Lucia, Qld., 1965), 3.
3. Ibid., 23.
4. Ibid., 47. In his discussion Greig suggests that the 'underheated period' which occurs in July largely between 2 am and 8.15 am can be addressed by 'the addition of clothing', the established practice to make the Queensland house bearable in Winter. Underheating can equally be addressed through the use of high heat capacity elements, but this solution was seen to be in conflict with demands of the building envelope during the overheated periods of the year when mass elements result in night-time discomfort in warmer months.
5. *Cross-Section* 153 (1 July 1965): *Cross-Section* 154 (1 August 1965).
6. *Cross-Section* 146 (1 December 1964). Dalton's archive contains an unpublished letter written to the editor of the *Architectural Forum* dated 1 September 1959 in which he references an article by Robin Boyd, 'Architectural Erotica' to further disparage style-driven design responses. In the July issue we were treated to two perfect examples of 'Cosmetic Architecture' that justify his [Boyd's] criticism. In heaven's name, if we must have poetry, let it be a pragmatic poetry which stems from the firm conviction that Architecture serves man [sic] and his needs. There is more beauty in a cubic yard of Kahn's concrete than in a square mile of Stone's screens.
7. Dalton had observed a disparity between the Student's Union Building and Trotter's claims made in *Cities in the Sun* (1963) and 'Need for Climatically Suitable Buildings … ', *Architecture and Arts* (November 1964): 44.
8. Frank Lloyd Wright in Ulrich Conrads and Michael Bullock trans., *Programs and Manifestos in Twentieth Century Architecture* (Cambridge, Mass.: MIT Press, 1970), 125; Breuer, 'Sun and Shadow', in Cranston Jones ed., *Marcel Breuer: Buildings and Projects: 1921–1961* (London: Thames and Hudson, 1962), 254; Louis I. Kahn, 'Kahn on Beaux-Arts Training', *The Architectural Review* 155, no. 928 (June 1974): 332; Harry Seidler, 'Sunlight and Architecture', *Architectural Science Review* 11, no. 1 (1959): 47–8.
9. Seidler, 'Sunlight and Architecture', 47–8.
10. William Hardy Wilson, *Old Colonial Architecture in New South Wales and Tasmania* (Sydney: Union House, 1924). Republished by Ure Smith in 1975.
11. Letter from Dalton to The Editor, *The Women's Weekly*, Sydney, dated 9 February 1966.
12. Oxford English Dictionary Online http://www.oed.com/view/Entry/177212?rskey=q XU96P&result=1#eid Accessed 19 September 2016 at 11:00.
13. For instance: Michael Brawne, 'Geometry of Shade', *The Architectural Review* 123, no. 737 (1 June 1958): 424.
14. Dalton completed houses for the following UQ academics: Dr Barrett (Classics), Dr Whitehead (Physics), Professor Hughes (Political Science), Professor Neale (History), Dr Jamieson (Zoology), Reverend Dr Strugnell (Theology) and Sir Zelman Cowen (Vice-Chancellor). The Kelly, Magee, Farbach and MacFarlane commissions were houses for jazz musicians.

15 For instance: Wilson, 'Simple Dignity in Ranch', *The Australian Home Beautiful* (June 1963), 8–11; *Sunday Mail Magazine*, 25 October 1964, 14.
16 Eric Wilson 'Queensland's Best for 1964' Wilson describes the Wilson House's distinctive 'Australian flavour'; Liz Johnston, 'Hint of Japan in a Not Too Dinky-di Home', *The Australian*, 23 December 1969, 5.
17 See technical information regarding the use of slabs as heat sinks: 'Skill: Thermal Comfort and Building Structure', *The Architectural Review* 129, no. 770 (1 April 1961): 284–5; 'Technical Section: 23 Heating and Ventilation', *The Architect's Journal* 128, no. 3325 (20 November 1958): 758–959, 761–2.
18 Interview with Noela Whippel and Jill Hammond in Toowoomba on 18 February 2016.
19 '10 Best Houses and Buildings for 1961–1962', *Architecture and Arts* (November 1962): 33. Also 'The Best', *Telegraph*, Wednesday, 23 October 1963, 55. Included in the *Telegraph* article were houses by Robin Gibson, Aubrey H. Job & Froud, Hayes & Scott and R. Martin Wilson & Son. The Leverington House was awarded a Commendation by the Queensland Chapter RAIA in 1962. The RAIA 'House of the Year' in 1962 was a house by Robin Gibson.
20 John Maxwell Freeland, *Architecture in Australia: A History* (Ringwood Victoria: Penguin, 1968), 286.
21 Undated copy in Dalton's papers.
22 Dalton's files contain correspondence from potential clients who thought brick veneer might save building costs.
23 Haig Beck and Jackie Cooper interviewed at North Stradbroke Island on 11 January 2017.
24 Ibid.
25 *Telegraph*, March 1964.
26 Eric Wilson 'Queensland's Best for 1964'.
27 Photographs in *Telegraph*, 29 August 1966; 'Boost to Living Outdoors', *Australian House and Garden*, October 1966, 31.
28 John Dalton, 'Houses in the Hot-Humid Zones', *Architecture in Australia* 52, no. 1 (March 1963): 73–80.
29 This argument was first developed in Elizabeth Musgrave and Douglas Neale, 'Architectural Image and Idiom: Making Local', in Dawne McCance ed., *Mosaic: A Journal for the Interdisciplinary Study of Literature* (Winnipeg: University of Manitoba, 2004), 255–73.
30 John Dalton, 'the verandah', *Architecture in Australia* (March 1964): 99.
31 Robert Shand, 'Report into Investigation of Designs of Houses for Commonwealth Railways', *Architecture in Australia* 52, no. 1 (March 1963): 83–98; Balwant Singh Saini, 'Housing in the Hot-Arid Tropics', *Architecture in Australia* 52, no. 1 (March 1963): 57–66.
32 Dalton, 'Architect's Comments'. Undated copy for publication in Dalton's papers.
33 Interview with Haig Beck and Jackie Cooper at North Stradbroke Island on 11 January 2017.
34 Conversation with Haig Beck. This event, which took place in the office of John Dalton and Associates, is also described in transcripts of interview with Haig Beck conducted on 11 January 2013. Digital Archive of Queensland Architecture http://qldarch.net accessed on 01 March 2016 at 17:00.

35 Philip Goad, 'Bringing It All Home: Robin Boyd and Australia's Embrace of Brutalism 1955–1971', *Fabrications* 25, no. 2 (June 2015): 189.
36 Judith O'Callaghan, 'The New Suburban Dream: The Marketing of Pettit and Sevitt Project Houses 1961–1978', *Additions to Architectural History: Proceedings of the Nineteenth Conference of SAHANZ* (October 2002): 6–7. Also Stephen Batey, 'Carlingford Homes Fair 50th Anniversary Tour', *Architecture AU: Postcards* http://architectureau.com/articles/carlingford-homes-fair-50th-annivesary-tour/ viewed 12 April 2015.
37 Ken Woolley, 'Architect's Own House, Mosman (Wilkinson Award 1962)', *Architecture Australia* 52 (December 1965): 76–79; Peter Johnson, 'Architect's Own House, Chatswood', *Architecture Australia* 52 (December 1965): 80–3.
38 *Cross-Section* 133 (November 1963).
39 *Cross-Section* 153 (July 1965).
40 Elizabeth Musgrave, 'A Golden Anniversary: 50 Years of the Split Skillion Roof in Queensland', in Ann-Marie Brennan and Philip Goad eds., *Gold: Proceedings of SAHANZ 33* (Melbourne: SAHANZ, 2016), 528–37.
41 *Cross-Section* 142 (August 1964).
42 Interview with Charles Ham, at Caloundra, on 25 September 2015.
43 Letter from Dalton to Ian McKay dated 2 February 1970 in response to a query about illustrations for his book. In this letter, Dalton refers to the Hughes House: 'Verandahs used extensively with slight cripple to roof pitch'. Also Haig Beck and Jackie Cooper, 'The Contemporary Queenslander', in Miranda Wallace and Sarah Stutchbury eds., *Place Makers: Contemporary Queensland Architects* (Brisbane: Queensland Art Gallery, 2009), 52.
44 Copy for *Architecture and Arts* contained in a letter to the editor dated 3 February 1967.
45 Boyd, 'The State of Australian Architecture', *Architecture in Australia* (June 1967): 454–6.
46 In carpentry, cripple refers to a stud or rafter cut to a shorter length. https://www.dictionary.com/browse/cripple.
47 Described by Eric Wilson as an 'aerofoil'. '"Aerofoil" takes the sting out of summer: Roof shapes uses the breeze to exhaust internal warm air', *Australian Home Beautiful* (July 1970): 20–2.
48 Johnston, 'Hint of Japan in a Not Too Dinky-di Home', 5; 'Brisbane Example for Expo Japan', *Telegraph Home Show Feature*, Thursday 12 March 1970, 18–19. Only one other Queensland work was selected for display, Union College by James Birrell.
49 'Seven Just Square', *The Architectural Review* 144, no. 858 (August 1966): 142–3.
50 'Residence of the Year', *Telegraph Home Show Feature*, Thursday 12 March 1970, 18–19.
51 Ibid.
52 *Cross-Section* 174 (1 April 1967). Dalton, Queensland's anonymous contributing editor writes: 'The need for cross section and warm air egress at roof level in Brisbane's Hot Humid Climate prompted the "section" of these two houses.'
53 This episode of *The Inventors* went to air on 5 October 1970.
54 Dalton quoted by Howard Tanner, *Australian Housing in the Seventies* (Sydney: Ure Smith, 1976), 21.
55 Tracey Avery, Peta Dennis and Paula Whitman, *Cool: The 60s Brisbane House* (Brisbane: School of Design and Built Environment, QUT, 2004), 27.

Chapter 4

1. Peter Bycroft and Paul Memmott, 'Towards an Understanding of Architecture: A student report', The University of Queensland, 1971. An completion of his undergraduate thesis in 1972, Peter Bycroft established the Environment Research and Development Group Pty Ltd. See also Glen Hill and Lee Stickells, 'Pig Architecture', Architecture Australia 101, no.2 (March 2012): 75–76.
2. Howard Tanner, *Australian Housing in the Seventies* (Sydney: Ure Smith, 1976), 21; Haig Beck, 'Detailing National Identity and a Sense of Place in Australian Architecture', *International Architect* (1984): 52.
3. Dalton owned a copy of Lawrence Halprin, *Cities* (USA: Reinhold Publishing Co., 1963). Jane Jacobs, *The Death and Life of Great American Cities* (New York: Random House, 1961). Gehl's research into the interaction between 'public space and public life' began with a funded research trip to Italy in 1965. 'Life between Buildings' was published in Danish in 1971 and was translated into English sixteen years later [http://gehlarchitects.com/ accessed 29 April 2015 at 12:25].
4. Chermayeff, 'Design as Catalyst: The March out of Chaos towards Community', The AS Hook Memorial Lecture, *The Consequences of Today: A Record of Papers Given at The Royal Australian Institute of Architects Centenary Convention May 22–28, 1971* (North Sydney NSW: RAIA Publications, 1971), 633.
5. Stephen Boyden, 'Man in a Changing Environment', *The Consequences of Today*, 655–9.
6. Brisbane's first Town Plan was finally adopted in 1964.
7. Copy of letter from Dalton to Sir Fred Schonell, Vice-Chancellor of the University of Queensland, dated 27 August 1965.
8. Copy of letter from Dalton to the Lord Mayor of Brisbane, Alderman, Clem Jones dated 16 August 1965. Reply to Dalton from E. Bullock, Private Secretary to the Lord Mayor dated 27 August 1965. Dalton's Papers courtesy of Suzanne Dalton.
9. Copy of letter from Dalton to Under Secretary, Department of Works, Sir David Longland dated 16 August 1965.
10. John Dalton, 'Redevelopment of Brisbane's Central Areas', *Queensland Master Builder* (11 August 1966): 8–12 and *Architecture in Australia* (September 1966): 143–4.
11. 'Bank Demolition Reflects Poorly on Qld', *Courier Mail*, 22 May 1967; 'Race to Save a Bank', *Courier Mail*, 9 May 1967, 9.
12. 'Action on New Art Gallery Advocated', *Courier Mail*, Friday 25 November 1966, 2. Feature article was a response to an article by Sir Leon Trout C.M. 14 November 1966.
13. 'Tramless Queen Street Could Look Like This', *Courier Mail* c.1967.
14. Letter to the editor, 'More Costly than Opera House', *Courier Mail*, 7 October 1965, 5. Follow-up letter 8 October 1965 in which Dalton explains his ethical position on structural integrity in architecture. 'The Holy Spirit Church of England Kenmore, Brisbane', *Architecture and Arts* XII, no. 11 (November 1964): 30–1 and Cover.
15. *Cross-Section* 155 (1 September 1965) Dalton cited interviews with Karl Langer, James Birrell and J. P. S. Pacinek, Reader in Town Planning in this article.
16. John Dalton, 'We Should Build to Suit the Climate', *Courier Mail*, 21 July 1965, 2. Much of the text for this article is recycled from the text of a talk given on ABC Radio Station 4QG on 5 December 1964, titled 'Sunlight, Shade and Shadow'.

17 John Macarthur, Donald Watson and Robert Riddell, 'Civic Visions for Brisbane', in John Macarthur, Deborah van der Plaat, Janina Gosseye and Andrew Wilson eds., *Hot Modernism: Queensland Architecture 1945–1975* (London: Artifice, 2015), 218, 224–7.
18 Dalton, 'Redevelopment of Brisbane's Central Areas', *Queensland Master Builder* (11 August 1966): 8–12 and *Architecture in Australia* (September 1966): 143–4.
19 Letter from Mr McConnell to John Dalton dated 3 June 1964.
20 Dalton, 'Architectural Criticism: Is it good for the profession', Transcript of speech to RAIA Queensland Convention, 1965. Dalton's papers. Courtesy Sue Dalton.
21 'Report of architecture during 1963', *Cross-Section* 135 (1 January 1964).
22 On 31 January 1964 Dalton receives a letter from Qld Chapter Council citing Article 52 of the RAIA Articles of Association and Code of Ethics. Letter from Neville Quarry dated 4 February 1964.
23 Correspondence with Neville Quarry. John Dalton's papers.
24 *Cross-Section* 161 (March 1966).
25 Donald Gazzard was RAIA national vice-president (publications) responsible for *Architecture in Australia* when Dalton was Queensland's contributing editor.
26 Dalton, 'What Is Wrong with the Diploma Course?' papers. Transcript of speech to the AASA Symposium, March 1961, Dalton's papers, Courtesy Sue Dalton.
27 Faculty of Architecture, Sub-Committee to report on proposed new faculty of Environmental Design. Dalton's papers. Undated. Courtesy Sue Dalton.
28 Richard Blythe, 'Science Enthusiasts: A Threat to Beaux-Arts Architectural Education in Australia in the 1950s', *Fabrications* 8, no. 1 (1997): 120.
29 AASA Convention Perth 1966 keynote speakers included John Voelker, Jacob Bakema, Aldo van Eyck and Buckminster Fuller. Brisbane 1967 keynote speakers included Gio Ponti, Tony Gwilliam, Gilbert Herbert, Harry Seilder and James Birrell. Hobart 1968 keynote speakers included Thomas Maldando, Cedric Price, Theo Crosby and Ralhp Erskine. Sydney 1970 keynote speakers included Buckminster Fuller, Roberto di Stefano, Denis Crompton, Tony Dugdale, John Andrews and Ian Chappel. 1971 Auckland keynote speakers included Sym van der Ryn and Serge Chermayeff.
30 Max Bannah, Symposium, 5 May 2013, Queensland State Library. 'Politics was the curriculum'.
31 Dalton was appointed Queensland correspondent for *Architecture in Australia*. Letter from Colin Brewer, editor, dated 7 February 1963. After the formalization of the Institute's policy on publications, Dalton became chair of the Queensland Chapter Publications Committee. Copy of letter from Dalton to the editor *Architecture in Australia* dated 16 December 1966.
32 'Letters: Student Representation', *Architecture in Australia* (August 1969): 2. Drawing from an address by Dennis Pryor at an RAIA convention.
33 'Letters: Student Representation', *Architecture in Australia* (August 1969): 2.
34 Paul Memmott Interview. Memmott does not recall the name of the key note speaker.
35 The 'Two Dead Chickens' incident occurred at a performance art 'happening' at the Rialto Theatre West End when students leapt onto the stage with live chickens which they proceeded to swing around in the air. Paul Memmott interview. See also Janina Gosseye and John Macarthur 'Angry Young Architecture: Counterculture and the Critique of Modernism in Brisbane 1967–1972', Macarthur et al., *Hot Modernism*, 35.
36 Dalton's files contain nine *Broadside* issues from 1966, seven issues from 1967 and six from 1968. The 1968 issues were numbered but not dated. Issues of *Broadside* were stored in plastic sleeves marked with their respective dates.
37 *Scarab* 1 (May 1965).
38 *Scarab* 3.

39 Copy of letter from Dalton to Andrew Metcalf dated 7 July 1967. Walpamur Paints and Hardboards Australia Limited were also sponsors.
40 http://oxforddictionaries.com/us/definition/american_english/broadside Accessed 5 May 2013.
41 Metrication in Australia began in 1966 with conversion to decimal currency. The conversion of measurements commenced in 1971.
42 Paul Memmott, 'Aboriginal Architecture', in Philip Goad and Julie Willis eds., *The Encyclopaedia of Australian Architecture* (Melbourne: Cambridge University Press, 2012), 1–4.
43 *Broadside*, Unnumbered issue (1966).
44 *Broadside*, Unnumbered issue (1966). The list of nominees forewarded in the handbill included Robin Boyd, Peter Kollar, William Nankivell, Paul Ritter, Balwant Singh Saini, Ross Thorne and Neville Quarry. Dalton also wrote to Kevin Borland encouraging him to apply for the position. Gareth Roberts was appointed as Professor at The University of Queensland.
45 *Broadside* unnumbered issue, (1966).
46 'Letter to an American Student', *Program: The Journal of the School of Architecture*, Columbia University 3 (Spring 1964): 72–4. The original 1964 letter was reproduced with a 'Letter to architect-teacher' dated 1 August 1981, *Journal of Architectural Education* 35 (1 October 1981): 9.
47 A.S.M. No 3. Competition sought solutions to the problem of 'High Density Housing'. Graham de Gruchy, Maurice Hirst and John Dalton were the competition assessors.
48 Jens Ivo Engels, 'Modern Environmentalism', in Frank Uekoetter eds., *The Turning Points of Environmental History* (Pittsburgh, PA: University of Pittsburgh Press, 2010), 125.
49 *diametrix* 3 (1971).
50 *diametrix* 11 (1970) and *diametrix* 1 (1971).
51 *diametrix* 3 (1971).
52 *diametrix* 4 (1971). Also included a series of quotes from key architects about how to best to respond through design to unfettered growth.
53 *diametrix* 7 (1971).
54 *Broadside* 4 (1968).
55 *diametrix* 6 (1971).
56 'Scores of Americans, abandoning the American Dream … ', *diametrix* 12 (1969). Report on Tomales Bay, fifty miles north of San Francisco, an alternative community supported by Synanon Inc.
57 Also purchasing property on the Darling Downs in the 1970s and 1980s were architects Bal Saini and architect and watercolourist Peter Cheney and artists Sam Fullbrook and Nevil Matthews.
58 Dalton, 'Updating the Colonial Tropical Image', *Architecture, Building, Engineering* (2 September 1967): 41.
59 Dalton, 'Updating the Colonial Tropical Image', 41.
60 Dalton, 'Updating the Colonial Tropical Image', 41. *Cross-Section* 161 (1 March 1966): 1.
61 'Australian Homes for Expo '67', *The Australian Women's Weekly* (21 December 1966): 2.
62 Letter from Robin Boyd to John Dalton dated 28 March 1966. Written on Romberg and Boyd letterhead; Eric Wilson 'A Brisbane House with International Appeal', *The Australian Home Beautiful* (July 1967): 22–5. Experiment Farm, comprising cottage and farm, was established at Paramatta, west of Sydney, in 1789 to test the new

colony's capacity for self-sufficiency. Experiment Farm Cottage *c*.1843 is the one of the earliest colonial residences still extant.

63 Charles Ham interview at Lethbridge Court, Caloundra on 25 September 2015.
64 Zelman Cowen, *A Public Life: The Memoirs of Zelman Cowen* (Melbourne: The Miegunyah Press, 2006), 259. Interview with Charles Ham at Caloundra, 25 September 2015. Dalton was so overwhelmed by the significance of this commission that he disappeared for a few days to his Toowong office to work undisturbed, returning only after he was happy with his solution.
65 Zelman Cowen, 'Address by His Excellency Sir Zelman Cowen AK, GCMG, KStJ, QC, Governor-General of the Commonwealth of Australia, on the occasion of the Fiftieth Anniversary of the New South Wales Chapter of the RAIA, at the Sydney Opera House, Friday 13 July 1979'. Transcript in Dalton's papers.
66 Interview with John Dalton, Monday 21 June 1999 at 38 Sylvan Road, Toowong. Elizabeth Watson Brown and Gail Pini, 'Preliminary Report, House at 55 Walcott Street St Lucia: Former Vice-Chancellor's Residence', Elizabeth Watson Brown Architects, 9 July 1999.
67 Cowen, *A Public Life*, 267–78. Cowen describes many Queenslanders as ambivalent about their University. Many members of Brisbane's establishment were suspicious of the University and considered it a source of radicalism.
68 Judith Musgrave recalls discussions with Dalton about Wolston House. Wolston House was constructed in 1852 on land between Brisbane and Ipswich and is the oldest extant residential farmhouse in Queensland. In 1963 it was acquired by the then newly formed National Trust Queensland.
69 Jennifer Taylor, 'History and Place in Recent Australian Architecture', in Leon Pariossien and Michael Griggs eds., *Old Continent, New Building: Contemporary Australian Architecture* (Sydney: David Ell Press in Association with Design Arts Committee of the Australia Council, 1983), 53.
70 'Preliminary Report House at 55 Walcott Street St Lucia', Elizabeth Watson Brown Architects, 9 July 1999.
71 Ibid.
72 Sir Zelman Cowen, 'Address by his Excellency Sir Zelman Cowen A.K. G.C.M.G., K.St.J, Q.C., Governor-General of the Commonwealth of Australia on the Occasion of the Fiftieth Anniversary of the New South Wales Chapter of The Royal Australian Institute of Architects at the Sydney Opera House Friday 13 July 1979'. Transcript in Dalton's papers.
73 John Dalton, 'Sunlight Shade and Shadow', *ABC Television Documentary*, VHS video, 1978.
74 *Broadside* (1967) cites Aldo van Eyck; *Broadside* 4 (1968) cites Jacob Bakema, van Eyck and Tony Gwilliam of Archigram.
75 Anne Leonhard, 'Cool Houses for Hot-House Climates', *Australian House and Garden* (December 1975): 75.

Chapter 5

1 Stefan Muthesius, *The Postwar University: Utopian Campus and College* (London: Yale University Press, 2000), 94.
2 Greg Logan and Eddie Clarke, *State Education in Queensland: A Brief History* (Brisbane: Policy and Information Services Branch, Department of Education, Queensland, 1984), 14.

3   Awarded a RAIA Queensland Chapter citation for meritorious architecture in 1976. 'On-campus buildings are medal winners: Firm hits top with 13th award', *Courier Mail,* Friday, 15 October 1976.
4   The HRKG was awarded a citation for meritorious architecture in 1979. In 1982 the HRKG was awarded a Queensland Chapter Civic Design Award. The Queensland Chapter Bronze medal winner was The Education Resource Centre Kelvin Grove College of Advanced Education by John Andrews International Pty Ltd. 'Top design award for college', *Courier Mail,* Friday, 19 October 1979. The HRKG was selected by the Architecture and Design Committee to represent Australian architecture in an exhibition travelling to London, Paris, New York and Los Angeles. The HRKG is the only building by Dalton to be listed on the state heritage register.
5   Bardon Professional Development Centre was recognized with a citation for meritorious architecture in 1977 and the RAIA Bronze Medal in 1978 and was demolished in 2014. In 1977 the Bronze medal was awarded to Townsville Civic Centre Stage 1, Lund Hutton Ryan Morton Pty Ltd. *Architecture Australia* (December 1977/January 1978), 29.
6   Interview Charles Ham at Lethbridge Court, Caloundra on 25 September 2015.
7   In particular Paul Ritter, *Educreation: Education for Creation, Growth and Change* (London: Pergamon Press, 1964).
8   Dalton was appointed to Faculty Board of Architecture at The University of Queensland in 1969.
9   Philip Goad, 'Open Field, Open Street, Open Choice: John Andrews and the South Residences, University of Guelph (1965-68)', in Alexandra Brown and Andrew Leach eds., *Proceedings of the Society of Architectural Historians, Australia and New Zealand: 30, Open* (Gold Coast, Qld: SAHANZ, 2013), 639-50; Susan Holden and Jared Bird, 'An Open Plan: Campus Plan, 1966-1973', in Alexandra Brown and Andrew Leach eds., *Proceedings of the Society of Architectural Historians, Australia and New Zealand: 30, Open* (Gold Coast, Qld: SAHANZ, 2013), 723-36. Philip Drew, *The Third Dimension: The Changing Meaning of Architecture* (London: Pall Mall, 1972). Hannah Lewi and David Nichols eds., *Community: Building Modern Australia* (Sydney: UNSW Press, 2010).
10 Peter Wicks, *First Decade: A Memoir of DDIAE 1972-1982* (Darling Heights, Qld.: TEC Print in conjunction with Community Books Australia, 2009), 4.
11 Ibid., 16. Director of DDIAE Lindsay Barker, although an engineer/metallurgist, had a strong commitment to the arts especially the Performing Arts. Wicks describes a backlash against an entirely science and technology based or vocational approach to education.
12 Queensland Institute of Technology (QIT) was the former Brisbane Central Technical College. Logan and Clarke, *State Education in Queensland,* 14. The Education Act 1964 led to the establishment of QIT in Brisbane in 1965 and its two satellite institutes in Toowoomba and Rockhampton in 1967. The 1970 Education Act Amendment Act introduced a new stream of post-school education throughout Australia giving institutes of advanced education autonomy. Shortly afterwards the DDIAE came under the control of its own council. DDIAE became the University of Southern Queensland in 1992.
13 Barbara Whiteman, 'Its in the bag: How a noted American film director teaches Toowoomba students to be actors', *Courier Mail* Saturday 29 September 1973. Robert Gist an American actor who starred in popular television series, would leave DDIAE after twelve months to start up the Australian School of Television and Film in Sydney.

14 John Dalton Architect and Associates, Department of Works, *Queensland Institute of Technology Darling Downs Art Crafts and Music Teaching Building: Design Report*. Undated, unpaginated. Charles Ham's wife Ruth was a ceramicist who was consulted for this project.
15 Muthesius, *The Postwar University*, 7 and 31. Muthesius describes a reaction against the 'individual, instrumentalised professional interests' of the red brick universities versus an idealized 'utopianist wholeness' of the New University programme.
16 Shadrach Woods in Michael Brawne ed., *University Planning and Design: A Symposium* (London: published for the Architectural Association by Lund, Humphries, 1967), 115.
17 Urban Study and Demonstration Mat-Building (1968–72) in Alison Smithson, 'How to Recognise and Read Mat-Building. Mainstream Architecture as it has Developed Towards the Mat-Building', *Architectural Design* (September 1974) 179–90.
18 John Dalton, *Design Report*, unpaginated.
19 Examples of courtyards created by the positioning of building blocks include Casson and Condor at Birmingham in 1957, (AJ 31-10-1957: 649); Cambridge Churchill College competition winning scheme by Sheppard, Robson and Partners 1960–64 (AJ 14-8-1959: 6–7) or St Catherine's College Oxford by Arne Jacobson 1960–64 (AR 10-1963: 279).
20 John Dalton, *Design Report*, unpaginated.
21 Ibid.
22 Professor Peter Goodall, Dean (Faculty of Arts) and Pro-Vice-Chancellor (Social Justice), 'Foreword', in Staff of the Facilities Management USQ eds., *A Block Creative Arts Building* (Toowoomba: University of Southern Queensland, c2012), 1.
23 Copy of letter from Dalton to Robert McGowan, Head, Visual Arts Program, DDIAE, School of Arts, 16 August 1979.
24 Philip Drew elaborates on the role of horizontal planes in the work of third-generation architects: 'As an extension of architecture, they assisted in relating the architectural and landscape forms.' Philip Drew, *Third Generation: The Changing Meaning of Architecture* (London: Pall Mall Press, 1972), 39. See also: Sigfried Gideon, *Space Time and Architecture* 5th edition (Cambridge, Mass.: Harvard University Press, 1967), 668.
25 Copy of letter from Dalton to Head of Visual Arts, Robert McGowan 16 August 1979 in which Dalton refers to the 'idea of the roof being a carpet of daisy's, flowers, life, health' or at least with 'ivy over the walls as [we] requested'.
26 Letter from Head, Visual Art Program, Robert McGowan to Dalton, 6 August 1979.
27 Paul Walker, 'Reassessing John Andrews' Architecture: Harvard Connections', in Alexandra Brown and Andrew Leach eds., *Proceedings of the Society of Architectural Historians, Australia and New Zealand: 30, Open* (Gold Coast, Qld: SAHANZ, 2013), 612.
28 Jennifer Taylor, *Australian Architecture since 1960* (Sydney: Law Book Company, 1986), 24.
29 Robert Riddel recollection of comment from Jon Voller. Oral History Interview. Digital Archive of Queensland Architecture. Accessed: 14 February 2015, 14:50. http://qldarch.net/beta/#/architect/interview/aHR0cDovL3FsZGFyY2gubmV0L29t ZWthL2l0ZW1zL3Nob3cvMTc3NQ==?architectId=aHR0cDovL3FsZGFyY2gubm V0L3JkZi8yMDEyLTEyL3Jlc291cmNlcy9wZW9wbGUvMTE%3D. See also Graham Bligh in Oral History Interview. *Digital Archive of Queensland Architecture*. Accessed: 14 February 2015, 14:55.

30 'On-campus buildings are medal winners', 3.
31 John Dalton, 'In Service Training Centre: Design Report', John Dalton Architect and Associates in association with Department of Works Queensland, undated, unpaginated.
32 Roger Johnson, *Griffith University Site Planning Report* (Brisbane: Griffith University Press, 1973), 55, Appendix C.
33 F. J. Willett, 'Foreword', in Roger Johnson, *Griffith University Site Planning Report*, 1. Principles underpinning the New University programme in the UK had already been implemented in Australia's newer generation of universities such as Flinders and la Trobe.
34 Johnson, *Planning Report*, 41. Also Susan Holden, Parallel Narratives of Disciplinary Disruption: The Bush Campus as Design and Pedagogical Concept, in Elke Couchez and Rajesh Heynickx eds. (Abingdon, Oxon; New York: Routledge, 2022), 170-1.
35 Ibid., 172.
36 Muthesius, *The Postwar University*, 111-13.
37 The lake never eventuated because an environmental report identified that damming the creek placed an endangered species of amphibian at risk.
38 Taylor, *Australian Architecture since 1960*, 128.
39 Ibid., 130.
40 Ibid.
41 Muthesius, *The Postwar University*, 5.
42 Dalton, 'In Service Training Centre: Design report', unpaginated.
43 'Personality Profile: John Dalton', *Queensland Chapter News*, December 1978, 7.
44 Goad, 'Open Field, Open Street, Open Choice', 639-50.
45 Dalton, 'In Service Training Centre: Design Report', unpaginated.
46 Taylor, *Australian Architecture since 1960*, 122.
47 'Where Teachers Keep Up with the Times … ', *Sunday Mail*, 6 March 1977, 18.
48 'Personality Profile: John Dalton', 7. Phil Heywood, 'A Modern Tragedy of the Commons', *Brisbane Review*, Thursday 29 July, 1993, 3.
49 Ibid.
50 'Where Teachers Keep Up with the Times … ', 18; Awarded a Bronze in 1978. 'Architects' Queensland awards: Judges praise high skills', *Courier Mail*, Friday 27 October 1978.
51 Leon Paroissien and Michael Griggs eds., *Contemporary Australian Architecture: Old Continent New Building* (Darlinghurst, NSW: David Ell Press in assoc. with Design Arts Committee of the Australia Council, 1983).
52 'Winning house exemplifies Queensland timber and tin tradition: Local Climate influenced construction', *Courier Mail*, 15 September 1982. 'Top Design Award for College', *Courier Mail*, Friday 19 October 1979, 3.
53 John Dalton, 'Kelvin Grove Hall of Residence Design Report', unpaginated.
54 Muthesius, *The Postwar University*, 50.
55 Jennifer Taylor and John Andrews, *John Andrews: Architecture a Performing Art* (Oxford: Oxford University Press, 1982), 126-9.
56 John Dalton, 'John Dalton: Hall of Residence, Brisbane Qld (1982)', *International Architect* 4 (1984): 52.
57 'Winning House Exemplifies Queensland Timber and Tin Tradition', *Courier Mail*, 15 September 1982.
58 'Kelvin Grove Hall of Residence', Dalton's papers.

59 Jury Report, Dalton's papers. 'August Village' at Kooralbyn by Harry Seidler and Associates received a commendation in 1982 but was overlooked for the Civic Design award.
60 'John Dalton Hall of Residence, Brisbane (1982)', *International Architect: Detailing, National Identity and a Sense of Place in Australian Architecture* 4 (1984): 52.
61 Muthesius, *The Postwar University*, 276.
62 Robin Boyd, 'Architecture in Australia', *RIBA Journal* 78 (January 1971): 12.
63 Ibid., 20.
64 Graham Jahn, *Contemporary Australian Architecture* (East Roseville, NSW: Gordon and Breach Arts International, 1994), 7.

Chapter 6

1 John Dalton in 'Sunlight Shade and Shadow', *ABC Television Documentary*, VHS video, 1978.
2 Ibid.
3 Lech Blaine, 'Top Blokes: The Larrikin Myth, Class and Power', *Quarterly Essay* 83 (2001): 8. Ipswich (Queensland) born Blaine traces the myth of a classless society.
4 Ibid., 24–5.
5 John Dalton, 'Design Lecturer Profile', *Proscenium* 1 (February 1983): 28. Dalton's description ignores completely the prior occupation of the continent by Aboriginal and Torres Strait Islander peoples and is emblematic of the persistence of a colonial mindset within Australian society.
6 Michael Leo interviewed by Elizabeth Musgrave on 30 September 2022.
7 Charles Jencks, *Modern Movements in Architecture* (Harmondsworth, Middlesex: Penguin Books, 1973); Charles Jencks, *Late Modern Architecture and Other Essays* (London: Academy Editions, 1980); Peter Cook, *Architecture: Action and Plan* (London: Studio Vista; New York: Reinhold Publishing Corporation, 1967).
8 For instance, Todd Gitlin 'Style for Style's Sake: Catching Up with the Elements That Make Post-modernism Popular, Plastic and Plagiaristic', *Weekend Australian* (January 1989): 21–22.
9 John Dalton, 'Point of View: Messy Magic', *Vogue Living* 4 (May 1987): 160.
10 Charles Ham conversation with Elizabeth Musgrave, February 2022.
11 Haig Beck, 'Detailing, National Identity and a Sense of Place in Australian Architecture', *International Architect* 4 (1984): 32–3, 40, 52.
12 Howard Tanner, *Australian Housing in the Seventies* (Sydney: Ure Smith, 1976), 21.
13 'Local Climate Influenced Construction', *Courier Mail*, 15 September 1982. Interview with Gabriel Poole and Lindsay Clare at West End, 2 November 2015.
14 Paul Hogben 'The Aftermath of "Pleasures": Untold Stories of Postmodern Architecture in Australia', Maryam Gusheh and Naomi Stead eds., *PROGRESS: The 20th annual conference of SAHANZ*, Sydney, 2–5 October 2003. The conference is considered a pivotal moment in the history of critical discourse in Australia.
15 *Architecture Australia* 69, 1 (Feb/March 1980): 66.
16 Andrew Metcalf, 'Fabricating Engehurst', *Architecture Australia* (April/May 1980): 40.
17 Janina Gosseye and Don Watson, 'Architects on the Verge: Distance in Proximity at "The Pleasures of Architecture"', in Victoria Jackson Wyatt, Andrew Leach and Lee

Stickells eds., *Proceedings of the Society of Architectural Historians, Australia and New Zealand 36, Distance Looks Back* (Sydney: SAHANZ, 2020), 187–91.
18 *Architecture Australia* 71, 5 (September 1982): 58–60.
19 Submissions were eventually received from academics at UQ, Peter O'Gorman, Donald Watson and Brit Andresen (calling their submission OWA) and from Daniel (Dan) Callaghan and William Spencer (Spence) Jamieson and Andris Stenders from QIT. Gosseye and Watson described the submission from OWA as an attempt to find 'alternative (non-modernist, non-post-modernist) critical approaches'. Gosseye and Watson, 'Architects on the Verge', 184, 195.
20 Andrew Metcalf, 'Fabricating Engehurst', *Architecture Australia* (April/May) 1980: whole issue.
21 John Dalton, 'Point of View: Messy Magic,' *Vogue Living* 4 (May, 1987): 160.
22 'Rem Koolhaas', *Transition* 1, no. 4 (November 1980): 14.
23 Ibid.
24 John Dalton, 'Sunlight Shade and Shadow', *ABC Television Documentary*, VHS video, 1978.
25 Dan Callaghan interview 13 January 2013.
26 RAIA Queensland Chapter, *Chapter News* (March 1983): 3. Then edited by Spence Jamison, lecturer at Q.I.T.
27 Ibid., 4.
28 Mark Thomson, 'Entrepôt: Students Taking the Initiative', *Proscenium* 1 (February 1983): 55–8. *Proscenium* 1 was edited by Mark Roehrs.
29 'Retrospective Four', *Proscenium* 1 (February 1983): 42.
30 Dalton, 'Design Lecturer Profile', 28.
31 'News Item', *Chapter News* (March 1984): 3.
32 Donald Watson, *The Queensland House: A Report into the Nature and Evolution of Significant Aspects of Domestic Architecture in Queensland* (Brisbane, Queensland: The author, 1981).; Max Bannah and Kent Chadwick, *Timber and Tin*, 16mm colour stock film, National Trust of Queensland with assistance from the Australian Government National Estate Programme: Bannah Chadwick Productions, 1976.
33 Such as Peter Bell, *Timber and Iron: Houses in North Queensland Mining Settlements, 1961–1920* (St Lucia, Qld: UQ Press, 1984).; Balwant Singh Saini, *The Australian House: Homes of the Tropical North* (Sydney, New York: Lansdowne Press, 1982).
34 City Council demolition and character housing regulations were yet to be formulated and State Heritage legislation would not come into effect until 1992.
35 Interview with Sue Dalton at Allora, 21 May 2012.
36 Interviews with Sue Dalton, 21 May 2012 and Mary-Lou O'Dwyer, 3 July 2017.
37 Paul Walker and Karen Burns, 'Constructing Australian Architecture for International Audiences: Regionalism, Postmodernism and the Design Arts Board 1980–1988', *Fabrications* 28, no. 1 (February 2018): 29–35.

Conclusion

1 Noel J. Robinson, 'Dalton Houses 1956–1975: An Exemplar for Brisbane's Domestic Architects?' (B.Arch Thesis, The University of Queensland, 1976), 54.
2 Charles Ham (interview by E. Musgrave) Caloundra, 15 September 2015.

3 Ibid.; Robinson, 'Dalton Houses 1956–1975', 10 and 42.
4 Jennifer Taylor, *Australian Architecture since 1960* (Sydney: Law Book Co., 1986), 46–7.
5 Deborah van der Plaat and Lloyd Jones, *Light Space Place: The Architecture of Robin Gibson* (Melbourne: Uro Publications, 2022), 50–3.
6 Fergus Johnston and Jane Johnston (interview by E. Musgrave), St Lucia, 25 June 2022. The Penthouses was illustrated in Ian McKay, Robin Boyd, Hugh Stretton and John Mant, *Living & Partly Living* (Melbourne: Thomas Nelson Pty Ptd, 1971), 166–9.
7 'Top Design Award for College', *Courier Mail*, Friday 19 October 1979, 3. Interview with Fergus Johnston and Jane Johnston (interview by E. Musgrave).
8 Robinson, 'Dalton Houses 1956-1975', 52.
9 Michael Grigg and Craig McGregor, *Australian Built: A Photographic Exhibition of Recent Australian Architecture* (Sydney: Design Arts Board of the Australia Council with the RAIA, 1985).
10 Ibid., 5.
11 Ibid., 66.
12 Peter Skinner, 'A Queensland School: Firmness, Commodity and Delight in Recent Award-winning Houses' in Julie Willis, Philip Goad and Andrew Hutson eds., *FIRM(ness) Commodity DE-light?: Questioning the Canons: Papers from the Fifteenth Conference of the Society of Architectural Historians of Australia and New Zealand* (Melbourne: SAHANZ, 1998), 330. Graham Jahn, *Contemporary Australian Architecture* (Roseville East NSW: Craftsman House, 1994), 53; Haig Beck and Jackie Cooper, 'The contemporary Queenslander', in Miranda Wallace and Sarah Stutchbury eds., *Place Makers: Contemporary Queensland Architects* (Brisbane: Queensland Art Gallery, 2008), 25.
13 Michael Keniger in Patrick Bingham-Hall, *Short History of Brisbane Architecture: Including Ipswich and the Sunshine Coast* (Balmain, N.S.W.: Pesaro Publishing, 2001), unpaginated; Philip Goad and Patrick Bingham-Hall, *New Directions in Australian Architecture* (Balmain, N.S.W.: Pesaro Publishing, 2001), 15.
14 Jahn, *Contemporary Australian Architecture*, 3.
15 Gabriel Poole cited in Miranda Wallace and Sarah Stutchbury eds., *Placemakers: Contemporary Queensland Architects* (South Brisbane: Queensland Art Gallery, 2008), 247.
16 Silvia Micheli and Andrew Wilson, 'International Influences in Post-War Queensland: Protagonists, Destinations and Models', in John Macarthur et al., eds., *Hot Modernism: Queensland Architecture 1945-1975* (London: Artifice, 2015), 131.
17 Skinner, 'A Queensland School', 323.
18 Rex Addison, 'AA 1904-2004 "Homegame"', *Architecture Australia* (September/October 2004): 20.
19 'Cluster Housing (1965)', *Andresen O'Gorman: Works 1965–2001: UME 22* (2011): 2–3.
20 Julie McGlone, *HEAT: Queensland's New Wave of Environmental Architects* (Brisbane: Creative Industries Unit, Department of Tourism, Regional Development and Industry, 2008), 7.
21 Jason Haigh (interview by E. Musgrave), Kenmore, Brisbane, 12 May 2022. Taylor is recalled for her ability to 'unpick ideas' and 'make them accessible to students'.
22 Jason Haigh.; Mark Thomson (interview by E. Musgrave), UQ, Brisbane, 13 September 2022.

23 *Cool: The 60s Brisbane House,* eds., Tracey Avery, Peta Dennis and Paula Whitman (Brisbane: School of Design and Built Environment, University of Queensland Technology, 2004); Peta Dennis, 'Innovative Architecture for Living: Brisbane Architect-designed Houses of the 1960s' (B.Arch Thesis, University of Queensland Technology, School of Architecture Interior and Industrial Design, 1999).
24 Jason Haigh (interview by E. Musgrave).
25 Ibid.
26 Ibid.
27 Aaron Peters, (interview by E. Musgrave).
28 Stuart Vokes and Aaron Peters (interview by E. Musgrave), Vokes + Peters, West End, 12 May 2022.
29 Stuart Vokes, (interview by E. Musgrave). The Chick House is located in Roedean Street, Fig Tree Pocket. It sits in a precinct of remarkably intact architect-designed modernist houses that have been a magnet for research, and includes houses by Conrad and Gargett, Darby Munro, Graham Bligh, Maurice Hurst and Don Woollard.
30 Stuart Vokes, (interview by E. Musgrave).
31 Esther da Costa Meyer, 'Architectural History in the Anthropocene: Towards Methodology', *The Journal of Architecture* 21, no. 8 (2016): 1217. DOI: 10.1080/13602365.2016.1254270; Daniel A Barber and Isabelle Douchet in Sophie Hochhäusl and Torsten Lange et al., 'Field Notes: Architecture and the Environment', *Architectural Histories* 6 (2018): 1–13, 20. DOI: https://doi.org/10.5334/ah.259.
32 Stuart Vokes and Aaron Peters interviewed by Elizabeth Musgrave at Vokes + Peters, West End on 12 May 2022.
33 Michael Keniger, Judy Vulker and Mark Roehrs, *Australian Architects: Rex Addison, Lindsay Clare and Russell Hall* (Manuka, ACT: Royal Australian Institute of Architects, 1990), 4–5.

GENERAL BIBLIOGRAPHY

Addison, Rex. 'AA 1904-2004: "Homegame"'. *Architecture Australia* 93, no. 5 (September/October 2004): 20-1.

Anderson, Michelle Elizabeth. 'Barjai, Miya Studio and Young Brisbane Artists of the 1940s: Towards a Radical Practice'. B.Arts Honours diss., The University of Queensland, 1987.

Apperly, Richard, Robert Irving and Peter Reynolds. *A Pictorial Guide to Identifying Australian Architecture: Styles and Terms from 1788 to the Present*. North Ryde, N.S.W.: Angus & Robertson, 1989.

Architecture and Arts. 'Two Projected Buildings by Theo Thynne & Associates, Architects'. *Architecture and Arts* (November 1956): 20-3.

Architecture and Arts. 'The Emergence of a Tradition'. *Architecture and Arts* VII, no. 75 (January 1960): 27-9.

Architecture and Arts. 'The Ten Best Houses for 1959-60'. *Architecture and Arts* VII, no. 83 (September 1960): 27-36.

Architecture and Arts. 'Post War Domestic Architecture'. *Architecture and Arts* VIII, no. 92 (June 1961): 37-51, 43.

Architecture and Arts. 'Ten Years of Architecture and Arts'. *Architecture and Arts* X, no. 1 (January 1962): 19-28.

Arnold, David. *The Problem of Nature: Environment, Culture and European Expansion*. Oxford, UK: Blackwell Publishers Inc., 1996.

Avery, Tracey, Peta Dennis and Paula Whitman, eds. *Cool: The 60s Brisbane House*. Brisbane: School of Design & Built Environment, University of Queensland Technology, 2004.

Barber, Daniel A. 'le Corbusier, the Brise-Soleil and the Socio-Climatic Project of Modern Architecture, 1929-1963'. *Thresholds* 40 (2012): 21-32.

Barber, Daniel A. *A House in the Sun: Modern Architecture and Solar Energy in the Cold War*. Oxford: Oxford University Press, 2016.

Barber, Daniel A. 'The Form and Climate Research Group or Scales of Architectural History'. In James Graham, ed., *Climates: Architecture and the Planetary Imaginary*. New York: Lars Muller Publishers Columbia Books on Architecture and the City, 2016, 303-17.

Barber, Daniel A. 'Architectural History in the Anthropocene'. *The Journal of Architecture* 21, no. 8 (2016): 1165-70, DOI: 10.1080/13602365.1258855.

Barber, Daniel A. *Modern Architecture and Climate: Design before Air Conditioning*. Princeton and Oxford: Princeton University Press, 2020.

Barber, Daniel A., Lee Stickells, Daniel J. Ryan, Maren Koehler, Andrew Leach, Philip Goad, Deborah van der Plaat, Cathy Keys, Farhan Karim and William M. Taylor. 'Architecture, Environment, History: Questions and Consequences'. *Architectural Theory Review* 22, no. 2 (2018): 249–86. https://doi.org/10.1080/13264826.2018.1482725.

Baweja, Vandana. 'Otto Koenigsberger and Modernist Historiography'. *Fabrications* 26, no. 2 (June 2016): 202–26.

Beck, Haig, ed. 'Detailing, National Identity, and a Sense of Place in Australian Architecture'. *UIA International Architect* 4 (1984): 1–58.

Beck, Haig and Jackie Cooper. 'The Contemporary Queenslander'. In Miranda Wallace and Sarah Stutchbury, eds., *Place Makers: Contemporary Queensland Architects*. Brisbane: Queensland Art Gallery, 2008.

Bentley, Ian, ed. *Responsive Environments: A Manual for Designers*. Amsterdam; Boston: Elsevier/Architectural Press, 1985.

Bingham-Hall, Patrick. *Short History of Brisbane Architecture: Including Ipswich and the Sunshine Coast*. Balmain, N.S.W.: Pesaro Publishing, 2001.

Blaine, Lech. 'Top Blokes: The Larrikin Myth, Class and Power'. *Quarterly Essay* 83 (2021): 1–116.

Blake, Peter. *Marcel Breuer: Sun and Shadow*. New York: Dodd Mead & Co., 1955.

Blythe, Richard. 'Science Enthusiasts: A Threat to Beaux-Arts Architectural Education in Australia in the 1950s'. *Fabrications* 8, no. 1 (1997): 117–28.

Boddy, Adrian. 'Photography and Architecture: 100 Years of Picturing Australian Buildings'. *Architecture Australia* 93, no. 4 (July/August 2004): 20–1.

Boesiger, W. 'Foreword'. In *Richard Neutra:1950–60: Buildings and Projects*. Zurich: Editions Girsberger, 1959.

Boyd, Robin. 'The Functional Neurosis'. *The Architectural Review* 119, no. 710 (February 1956): 86.

Boyd, Robin. 'Port Phillip Idiom: Recent Houses in the Melbourne Region'. *The Architectural Review* (November 1952): 309–10.

Boyd, Robin. *The Walls around Us: Told and Illustrated for Young Readers by Robin Boyd*. Melbourne: F.W. Cheshire, 1962.

Boyd, Robin. 'The State of Australian Architecture'. *Architecture in Australia* (June 1967): 454–65.

Boyd, Robin. *Australia's Home: Its Origins, Builders and Occupiers*. Ringwood Vic.: Penguin, 1968.

Boyd, Robin. 'Architecture in Australia'. *RIBA Journal* 78 (January 1971).

Boyd, Robin and Peter Newell. 'St Lucia: A Housing Revolution Is Taking Place in Brisbane'. *Architecture* (1950): 106–9, 114.

Boyden, Stephen. 'Man in a Changing Environment'. In Barry Davis and Colin Brewer, eds., *The Consequences of Today*. Sydney: RAIA Publications, 1971.

Bradbury, Keith and Glenn Cooke. *Thorns & Petals: 100 Years of the Royal Queensland Art Society*. Brisbane: Royal Queensland Art Society, 1988.

Brawne, Michael. 'Skill: Geometry of Shade'. *The Architectural Review* 123, no. 737 (June 1958): 424–34.

Brawne, Michael, ed. *University Planning and Design: A Symposium*. London: Published for the Architectural Association by Lund, Humphries, 1967.

Breuer, Marcel. 'Sun and Shadow'. In *Marcel Breuer: Buildings and Projects: 1921–1961*. London: Thames and Hudson, 1962.

Broadbent, Geoffrey and Anthony Ward. *Design Methods in Architecture*. London: Lund Humphries, 1969.

Browne, Kenneth and Lance Wright. 'Brisbane'. *The Architectural Review* CLXIV, no. 979 (September 1978): 185-97.

Bunning, Walter R. *Homes in the Sun: The Past, Present and Future of Australian Housing.* Sydney: Nesbit, 1945.

Bunzil, Malcolm. 'How the AILA Came into Being'. *Landscape Australia* 3 (August 1991): 202-4.

Callinan, Ian. *Belvedere Woman.* North Melbourne, Vic.: Arcadia, 2016.

Cantacuzino, Sherban. *Modern Houses of the World.* London: Studio Vista Ltd., 1964.

Carr, W.H. 'Solar Air-Conditioned House'. *Architecture in Australia* (March 1965): 123.

Carson, Rachel. *Silent Spring.* London: Hamilton, 1963.

Cathelin, Jean. *Jean Arp.* New York: Grove Press Inc., 1959.

Chang, Jiat-Hwee and Tim Winter. 'Thermal Modernity and Architecture'. *The Journal of Architecture* 20, no. 1 (February 2015): 92-121. DOI: 10.1080/13602365.2015.1010095

Chasling, Scott. 'Frank Costello: City Architect 1941-1952 City Planner 1946-1952'. B.Arch diss., The University of Queensland, 1997.

Chermayeff, Serge. 'Design as Catalyst'. In Barry Davis and Colin Brewer, eds., *The Consequences of Today.* Sydney: RAIA Publications, 1971.

Chermayeff, Serge and Christopher Alexander. *Community and Privacy: Towards a New Architecture of Humanism.* New York: Doubleday, 1963.

Churcher, Betty. *Understanding Art: The Use of Space, Form and Structure.* Adelaide: Rigby Ltd., 1973.

Churcher, Betty. *Molvig: The Last Antipodean.* Ringwood Vic.: Penguin Books Australia Ltd., 1984.

Cilento, Sir Raphael, Colin Clark, Douglas H. K. Lee, L. P. D. O'Connor, E. J. A. Weller and R. P. Cummings. 'Report on Tropical Housing 1943' (unpublished). Sir Raphael Cilento Papers, Fryer Library, The University of Queensland, UQFL44, Box 29, item 219.

Clarke, Eddie. *Technical and Further Education in Queensland: A History 1860-1990.* Brisbane Department of Education Queensland and Bureau of Employment, Vocational and Further Education and Training, Queensland, 1992.

Conrads, Ulrich, trans. Michael Bullock. *Programs and Manifestos in Twentieth Century Architecture.* Cambridge, MA: MIT Press, 1970.

Cook, Peter. *Architecture: Action and Plan.* London: Studio Vista; New York: Reinhold Publishing Corporation, 1967.

Cooke, Glenn R. *A Time Remembered: Art in Brisbane 1950 to 1975.* South Brisbane: Queensland Art Gallery, 1995.

'Cool Australian House Is a Peaceful Oasis in a Tropical Setting'. *Vogue's Guide to Living* 1, no. 4 (November 1968-January 1969): 52-5.

Couchez, Elke and Rajesh Heynickx, eds. *Architectural Education through Materiality: Pedagogies of 20th Century Design.* London: Routledge, 2022.

Cowen, Zelman. 'Address by his Excellency Sir Zelman Cowen A.K. G.C.M.G., K.St.J, Q.C., Governor-General of the Commonwealth of Australia on the Occasion of the Fiftieth Anniversary of the New South Wales Chapter of The Royal Australian Institute of Architects at the Sydney Opera House Friday 13 July 1979'. Dalton's personal papers.

Cowen, Zelman. *The Memoirs of Zelman Cowen: A Public Life.* Melbourne: The Miegunyah Press, 2006.

Cruise, Kathryn. 'An Airy Retreat Down by the Bay'. *Sunday Sun Magazine,* 23 October 1988.

Cuffley, Peter. *Australian Houses of the Forties and Fifties*. Knoxfield, Vic.: Five Mile Press, 1993.
da Costa Meyer, Esther. 'Architectural History in the Anthropocene: Towards Methodology'. *The Journal of Architecture* 21, no. 8 (2016): 1217. DOI: 10.1080/13602365.2016.1254270.
Dalton, John. 'House at Ferny Grove, Brisbane: Regional Humanism'. *Architecture and Arts* (April 1957): 20.
Dalton, John. 'Cover'. *Architecture and Arts* VII (July 1960).
Dalton, John. 'House at Fig Tree Pocket, Brisbane'. *Architecture and Arts* VII, no. 82 (July 1960): 33–5.
Dalton, John. 'Queensland's Pragmatic Poetry'. *Architecture and Arts* VII, no. 82 (August 1960): 32.
Dalton, John. 'Flats at Toowong, Brisbane'. *Architecture and Arts* VIII, no. 94 (August 1961): 46–7.
Dalton, John. 'What Is Wrong with the Diploma Course?' AASA *Symposium*. March 1961. Transcript.
Dalton, John. 'Extracts from an Address to the Queensland Architectural Students Association at University of Queensland, April 1962'. Transcript.
Dalton, John. 'Houses in the Hot Humid Zones'. *Architecture in Australia* 51, no. 1 (March 1963): 73–80.
Dalton, John. 'House at Buderim Mountain, Qld'. *Architecture and Arts* XI, no. 5 (May 1963): 40–1.
Dalton, John. 'House at Aspley, Brisbane'. *Architecture and Arts* XI, no. 5 (May 1963): 42.
Dalton, John. 'House at Moggill, Brisbane'. *Architecture and Arts* XI, no. 5 (May 1963): 43.
Dalton, John. 'the verandah'. *Architecture in Australia* 53, no. 1 (March 1964): 99.
Dalton, John. 'Holy Spirit Church, Kenmore'. *Architecture and Arts* XII, no. 11 (November 1964): Cover, 30–31.
Dalton, John. 'House at Mt Coot-tha, Brisbane'. *Architecture in Australia* 53, no. 4 (December 1964): 101–2.
Dalton, John. 'Sunlight, Shade, and Shadow'. ABC Radio 4QG. Aired 5 December 1964. Transcript.
Dalton, John. 'We Should Build to Suit the Climate'. *Courier Mail*, 21 July 1965.
Dalton, John. 'Four Queensland Homes'. *Architecture and Arts* XIII, no. 8 (August 1965): 12–5.
Dalton, John. 'How Far Should an Architect Follow His Client's Instructions?' Transcript of presentation to Qld Chapter Convention, Chevron Hotel, Surfers Paradise, 24–26 September 1965.
Dalton, John. 'More Costly than the Opera House'. *Courier Mail*, 7 October 1965.
Dalton, John. 'Architectural Criticism … Is It Good for the Profession?' Transcript of talk given at Qld Chapter Convention, 1965.
Dalton, John. 'Design in Industry'. 1965. Undated transcript of presentation.
Dalton, John. 'House for J. Smith'. *Architecture in Australia* 55, no. 4 (July 1966): 149–50.
Dalton, John. 'Redevelopment of Brisbane's Central Areas'. *The Queensland Master Builder* (August 1966): 8–12.
Dalton, John. 'Action on New Gallery Advocated'. *Courier Mail*, 25 November 1966.
Dalton, John. 'A Legacy of Gutlessness for Australia's Artistic Future!'. *The Australian*, 30 June 1967.
Dalton, John. 'Queensland Governor "Names" the F. Bruce Lucas Library at RAIA Chapter H.Q.' *Architecture, Building, Engineering* (September 1967): 1–2.

Dalton, John. 'Updating the Colonial Tropical Image'. *Architecture, Building, Engineering* (2 September 1967): 41.

Dalton, John. 'Tramless Queen Street Could Look Like This'. *Courier Mail*, 1967.

Dalton, John. '"Life Enhancing" An Occasion for Living – Plea by Architect'. *Architecture, Building, Engineering* (1 June 1970): 15–20.

Dalton, John. 'Sunlight, Shade and Shadow'. ABC Television Broadcasts to Schools: Secondary and Technical. Aired 15 March 1979.

Dalton, John. 'Messy Magic'. *Vogue Living* 4 (May 1987): 160.

Dalton, John. 'Choosing an Architect'. *Telegraph Home Show Guide*. Undated copy prepared for the RAIA Queensland Chapter.

Dalton, John. 'Talks to Students of Brisbane Girls' Secondary Schools'. Undated transcript.

Dalton, John. 'In Service Training Centre: Design Report'. John Dalton Architect and Associates in association with Department of Works Queensland, undated, unpaginated.

Dalton and Heathwood. 'Four Houses. by Dalton & Heathwood'. *Architecture and Arts* (September 1959): 58–63.

Danz, Ernst. *Architecture and the Sun: An International Survey of Sun Protection Methods*. London: Thames and Hudson, 1967.

Darling Downs Institute of Advanced Education. *Performance*. Toowoomba: DDIAE Dept. Performing Arts, 1977.

Davis, Barry and Colin Brewer, eds. *The Consequences of Today: A Record of Papers Given at the RAIA Centenary Convention*. 22–28 May 1971 [Supplement to Architecture in Australia (August 1971)].

de Gruchy, Graham. *Architecture in Brisbane*. Bowen Hills, Brisbane: Boolarong Publications with Kookaburra Books, 1988.

de Gruchy, Graham. 'Architecture in Queensland'. *Art &Australia* 6, no. 4 (March 1969): 297–302.

De la Vega de Leon, Macarena. 'A Tale of Inconsistency: The Absence and Presence of Australia in the Historiography of Modern Architecture'. *Fabrications* 28, no. 1 (2018): 47–66.

Dennis, Peta. 'Innovative Architecture for Living: Brisbane Architect-Designed Houses of the 1960s'. B.Arch diss., University of Queensland Technology, School of Architecture Interior and Industrial Design, 1999.

Dewey, John, Albert C. Barnes, et al. *Art and Education: A Collection of Essay (3rd Ed.)*. Merion, Penn.: The Barnes Foundation Press, 1954.

Dewey, John, Albert C. Barnes, et al. *Art as Experience*. New York: Capricorn Books, G.P. Putnam's Sons, 1958.

Drew, Philip. *The Third Dimension: The Changing Meaning of Architecture*. London: Pall Mall, 1972.

Drysdale, J. W. 'Climate and House Design with Reference to Australian Conditions'. *CEBS Technical Bulletin* 3 (1947).

Drysdale, J. W. *Climate and House Design: Summary of Investigations 1945–1947*, Duplicated Document 21. Sydney: Commonwealth Experimental Building Station, June 1947.

Drysdale, J. W. *Natural Ventilation, Ceiling Height and Room Size. Notes Regarding Minimum Provisions in Dwellings, with Respect to Australian Conditions*. Duplicated Document 22. Sydney: Commonwealth Experimental Building Station, 1947.

Drysdale, J. W. *The Thermal Behaviour of Dwellings*. Technical Study 34. Sydney: Commonwealth Experimental Building Station, 1950.

Drysdale, J. W. 'Tropical Housing'. In *The Australian Academy of Science Symposium on Man and Animals in the Tropics*. St Lucia, Brisbane: The University of Queensland, 1956.

Edwards, Zeny. *William Hardy Wilson: Artist, Architect Orientalist Visionary*. Sydney: Watermark Press, 2001.

Emery, Fred. 'Man as Individual', in 'The Consequences of Today: A Record of Papers given at the RAIA Centenary Convention, May 22-28, 1971'. Supplement to Architecture Australia (August 1971): 660-3

Engels, Jens Ivo. 'Modern Environmentalism'. In Uekoetter Frank, ed., *The Turning Points of Environmental History*. Penns: University of Pittsburgh Press, 2010. Accessed on-line 13 Aug 2014 01:27 GMT.

Farbach, Rick. *Cleftomania*. Montville Qld.: The Oracle Press, 1999.

Fisher, Rod and Brian Crozier. *The Queensland House: A Roof over Our Heads*. Brisbane: The Queensland Museum, 1994.

Fitzgerald, Ross. *From 1915 to the Early 1960s: A History of Queensland*. St Lucia: University of Queensland Press, 1984.

Fitzgerald, Ross. *A History of Queensland from Dreaming to 1915*, Vol. 1. St Lucia: UQ Press, 1986.

Frampton, Kenneth. *Modern Architecture: A Critical History*. London: Thames and Hudson, 1980.

Freeland, John M. *Architecture in Australia: A History*. Ringwood Victoria: Penguin, 1968.

Freestone, Robert and Darryl Low. 'Enriching the Community: The Life and Times of Frank Costello (1903-1987)'. *Australian Planner* 50, no. 1 (2013): 56.

Fridemanis, D. Helen. 'Contemporary Art Society Queensland Branch, 1961-1973: A Study of the Post-War Emergence and Dissemination of Aesthetic Modernism in Brisbane'. Master of Arts diss., The University of Queensland, 1989.

Fry, Maxwell and Jane Drew. *Tropical Architecture in the Dry and Humid Zones*. London: Batsford, 1956.

Fry, Maxwell and Jane Drew. *Tropical Architecture in the Humid Zone*. London: Batsford, 1964.

Garlick, Grace. 'Serenity ... at a Price but for All Time'. *The Sunday Mail Colour Magazine*, 20 August 1972.

Garlick, Grace. 'House of the Year: Sculptural, Streamlined and Full of Space'. *The Sunday Mail Colour Magazine*, 28 December 1975.

Garlick, Grace. 'New Life for Old Ideas'. *The Sunday Mail Colour Magazine*, 18 February 1979.

Garlick, Grace. 'White, Open and Just Right for Us'. *The Sunday Mail Colour Magazine*, 17 June 1979.

Garlick, Grace. 'Home Is a Work of Art'. *The Sunday Mail Colour Magazine*, 29 July 1979.

Garlick, Grace. 'Why Our Homes Are the Greatest: Refining the Queenslander'. *The Sunday Mail*, 1 December 1996.

GA Houses No 7. *Special Issue: Charles Moore and Company*. Tokyo: A.D.A. EDITA Tokyo Co. Ltd., 1980 Publications, 1980.

Goad, Philip and Patrick Bingham-Hall. *New Directions in Australian Architecture*. Balmain, N.S.W.: Pesaro Publishing, 2001.

Goad, Philip. 'Homes in the Sun: Climate and the Modern Australian House 1945-1965'. In *Celebration: Proceedings of the XXII Annual SAHANZ Conference*, Napier New Zealand (September 2005): 133-9.

Goad, Philip and Julie Willis, eds. *Encyclopaedia of Australian Architecture*. Melbourne, Vic.: Cambridge University Press, 2012.

Goad, Philip. 'Constructing Pedigree: Robin Boyd's "California-Victoria-New Empiricism" Axis'. *Fabrications* 22, no. 1 (July 2012): 4–29.

Goad, Philip. 'Open Field, Open Street, Open Choice: John Andrews and the South Residences, University of Guelph (1965–68)'. In Alexandra Brown and Andrew Leach, eds., *Open: Proceedings of the 30th Annual SAHANZ Conference*, Gold Coast, Queensland (July 2013): 639–50.

Goad, Philip. 'Bringing It All Home: Robin Boyd and Australia's Embrace of Brutalism 1955–1971'. *Fabrications* 25, no. 2 (June 2015): 176–213.

Goad, Philip. 'New World: Harry Seidler, Brazil and the Australian City'. *Fabrications* 31, no. 1 (2021): 54–84.

Gosseye, Janina and Don Watson. 'Architects on the Verge: Distance in Proximity at "The Pleasures of Architecture"'. In Victoria Jackson Wyatt, Andrew Leach and Lee Stickells, eds., *Distance Looks Back: Proceedings of the 36th Annual SAHANZ Conference*, Sydney, NSW (July 2019): 187–91.

Gott, Shirley. 'Houses of "To-morrow" at Show'. *Courier Mail*, 8 August 1957.

Gregory, Sydney A., ed. on behalf of Design and Innovation Group, University of Aston in Birmingham. *The Design Method*. London: Butterworths, 1966.

Greig, William (Bill) A. 'Climate and Design in Brisbane'. B.Arch diss., Department of Architecture, The University of Queensland, 1965.

Griffiths, Tom and Libby Robin, eds. *Ecology & Empire: Environmental History of Settler Societies*. Seattle: University of Washington Press, 1997.

Griggs, Michael and Craig McGregor, eds. *Australian Built: Responding to the Place*. Sydney: Design Arts Board of the Australia Council, 1985.

Grillo, Paul Jacques. *What Is Design?* Chicago, Ill.: P. Theobald, 1960.

Grove, Richard H. *Green Imperialism: Colonial Expansion, Tropical Island Edens and Origins of Environmentalism 1600-1860*. Cambridge; New York: Cambridge University Press, 1995.

Haese, Richard. *Rebels and Precursors: The Revolutionary Years of Australian Art*. Ringwood Vic.: Allen Lane, Penguin Books, 1981.

Hailey, Shan. 'Australian Homes for Expo'. *The Australian Women's Weekly* (December 1966): 1–16.

Halprin, Lawrence. *Cities*. USA: Reinhold Publishing Co., 1963.

Hampson, Alice LTM. 'The Fifties in Queensland Why Not? Why!?' B.Arch diss., Department of Architecture, The University of Queensland, 1987.

Hanna, John and Tracey Arklay. *The Ayes Have It: The history of the Queensland Parliament, 1957–1989*. Canberra: The Australian National University Press, 2010.

John, Hay. 'Ranch-Style Home with a Classic Look'. *The Sunday Mail Colour Magazine*, 13 January 1963.

John, Hay. 'A House on a Mountain Top'. *The Sunday Mail Colour Magazine*, 11 August 1963.

John, Hay. 'You Don't Need a Ranch to Go Ranch Style'. *The Sunday Mail Colour Magazine*, 26 July 1964.

John, Hay. 'Making the Best of Two Worlds'. *The Sunday Mail Colour Magazine*, 25 October 1964.

Hay, Peter. *Main Currents in Western Environmental Thought*. Sydney: UNSW Press, 2002.

Haysom, Melville. 'Only a Few Shine at Art Show'. *Telegraph*, 8 December 1959.

Heath, Tom. 'Regionalism and Its Implications'. *Architecture Australia* 75, no. 9 (Nov 1986): 19.

Heywood, Phil. 'A Modern Tragedy of the Commons'. *The Brisbane Review*, 29 July 1993.

Hill, Glenn and Lee Stickells. 'Pig Architecture: The Architecture Student Strike of 1972 at The University of Sydney Ushered in a New Era of Architectural Education'. *Architecture Australia* 101, no. 2 (March/April 2012): 75–6.

Hinton, E. *The Outsiders*. New York: Viking Press, 1976.

Hitch, John. *John Hitch: Record of a Life in Architecture*. Mt Macedon, Vic.: Self-published, 2002.

Hochhäusl, Sophie and Torsten Lange et al. 'Field Notes: Architecture and the Environment'. *Architectural Histories* 6 (2018): 20, 1–13. DOI: https://doi.org/10.5334/ah.259

Hogben, Paul. 'Maintaining an Image of Objectivity: Reflections on an Institutional Anxiety'. *Architectural Theory Review* 6, no. 1 (2001): 63–75. DOI: 10.1080/13264820109478416.

Hogben, Paul. 'The Aftermath of "Pleasures": Untold Stories of Post-Modern Architecture in Australia'. *PROGRESS: The Twentieth Annual Conference of SAHANZ*, Sydney (October 2003): 146–51.

Hogben, Paul. 'The Commercialization of Architecture Australia 1975–1980'. *Fabrications* 9, no. 1 (1999): 53–67. Published online: 06 July 2012.

Hogben, Paul. 'Architecture and Arts and the Mediation of American Architecture in Post-war Australia'. *Fabrications* 22, no. 1 (2012): 30–57. Published online: 27 July 2012.

Holden, Susan and Jared Bird. 'An Open Plan: Campus Plan, 1966–1973'. In Alexandra Brown and Andrew Leach, eds., *Open: Proceedings of the 30th Annual SAHANZ Conference*, Gold Coast, Qld. (July 2013): 723–36.

Hughes, Robert. *The Art of Australia*. Ringwood, Vic.: Penguin Books Ltd., 1970.

Irving, Robert. *The History and Design of the Australian House*. Melbourne: Oxford University Press, 1985.

Jackson, Daryl. 'From Edge to Centre: Sense and Stylism in Current Australian Architecture'. *International Architect* 4 (1984): 4–5.

Jackson, Iain. *The Architecture of Edwin Maxwell Fry and Jane Drew [electronic resource]: Twentieth Century Architecture, Pioneer Modernism and the Tropics*. Surrey, England; Burlington, VT: Ashgate, 2014.

Jahn, Graham. *Contemporary Australian Architecture*. East Roseville, NSW: Gordon and Breach Arts International, 1994.

Jencks, Charles. *Modern Movements in Architecture*. Harmondsworth, Middlesex: Penguin Books, 1980 [first published 1973].

Jencks, Charles. *Late Modern Architecture and Other Essays*. London: Academy Editions, 1980.

Jensen, Robert. 'Design and Process: Four Projects by the John Andrews Office'. *Architectural Record* 147, no. 2 (February 1970): 131–46.

Johnson, Donald Leslie. *Australian Architecture 1901–51: Sources of Modernism*. Sydney: Sydney University Press, 1980.

Johnston, Liz. 'Hint of Japan in a Not Too Dinky-di Home'. *The Australian*, 23 December 1959.

Johnson, Roger. *Griffith University Site Planning Report*. Brisbane: Griffith University, April 1973.

Johnston, Ross. 'The Johnstone Gallery and Art in Queensland: 1940s–70s'. *Art and Australia* 15, no. 4 (1978): 395–6.

Juppenlatz, Martin. 'Design Principles for "Solair" House'. *Architectural Science Review* (March 1962): 23–30.

Keniger, Michael, Judy Vulker and Mark Roehrs. *Australian Architects: Rex Addison, Lindsay Clare and Russell Hall*. Manuka, A.C.T.: Royal Australian Institute of Architects, 1990.

King, Stuart. 'A Climate of Confusion: The Significance of Climatic Adaptation in 19th Century Queensland Architecture'. In *Panorama to Paradise: Proceedings of the 24th Annual SAHANZ Conference*, Adelaide, South Australia (21–24 September 2007): 1–14.

Kite, Stephen. *Shadow-makers: A Cultural History of Shadows in Architecture*. London: New York: Bloomsbury Academic, 2017.

Koenigsberger, Otto and Robert Lynn. *Roofs in the Warm Humid Tropics*. London: Lund Humphries for the Architectural Association, 1965.

Koenigsberger, Otto et al. *Manuel of Tropical Housing and Building*. London: Longman, 1974.

Landau, Royston. *New Directions in British Architecture*. London: Studio Vista, 1968.

Landau, Royston. 'British Architecture. The Culture of Architecture: A Historiography of the Current Discourse'. *International Architect* 5 (1984): 5–9.

Langer, Karl. *Sub-Tropical Housing*. St Lucia Brisbane: University of Queensland Press, 1944.

Lavin, Sylvia 'Open the Box: Richard Neutra and the Psychology of the Domestic Environment'. *Assemblage* 40 (December 1999).

Leach, Andrew Antony Moulis and Nicole Sully, eds. *Shifting Views: Selected Essays in the Architectural History of Australia and New Zealand*. Brisbane: University of Queensland Press, 2008.

Leatherbarrow, David. *Uncommon Ground: Architecture, Technology, and Topography*. Cambridge, Mass.; London: The MIT Press, 2002.

Leatherbarrow, David. *Architecture Oriented Otherwise*. New York: Princeton Architectural Press, 2009.

Leatherbarrow, David and Richard Wesley, 'Performance and Style in the Work of Olgyay and Olgyay'. *Architectural Research Quarterly* 18, no. 2 (June 2014): 167–76. http://journals.cambridge.org/ abstract_S1358135514000475.

Lee, Douglas H. K. *Physiological Principles in Tropical Housing with Especial Reference to Queensland*. Brisbane: The University of Queensland, 1944.

Leonhard, Anne. 'Cool Houses for Hot-house Climates'. *Australian House and Garden* (December 1975): 73–7.

Lewi, Hannah and David Nichols, eds. *Community: Building Modern Australia*. Sydney: UNSW Press, 2010.

Littlemore, D.S. 'Building in the Tropics'. *Architectural Science Review* (November 1958): 31–8.

Logan, Greg and Eddie Clarke. *State Education in Queensland: A Brief History*. Brisbane: Policy and Information Services Branch, Department of Education, Queensland, 1984.

Lyndon, Donlyn, Charles Moore, Patrick J. Quinn and Sim van Der Ryn. 'Toward Making Places'. *Landscape* (Autumn 1962): 31–41.

Macarthur, John, Deborah van der Plaat and Janina Gosseye. *Digital Archive of Queensland Architecture* http://qldarch.net

Macarthur, John, Deborah van der Plaat, Janina Gosseyeand Andrew Wilson, eds., *Hot Modernism: Queensland Architecture 1945–1975*. London: Artifice, 2015.

Macarthur, John. 'Architecture, HEAT and the Government of Culture'. In Paul Hogben and Judith O'Callaghan, eds. *Architecture, Institutions and Change: Proceedings of the 32nd Annual SAHANZ Conference*, Sydney (July 2015): 366–77.

MacFarlane, W. V. 'Thermal Comfort Zones'. *Architectural Science Review* (November 1958): 1–14.
Malouf, David. *Johnno*. Ringwood, Vic.: Penguin Books Aust., 1976.
Malouf, David. *12 Edmonstone Street*. Ringwood, Vic.: Penguin Books Aust., 1985.
Martin-Chew, Louise. '"Like Topsy": The Johnstone Gallery 1950–1972'. Master of Creative Arts diss., Townsville: James Cook University, 2001.
McDougall, Ian Richard Murphy and Cathy Peake, eds. 'The Pleasures of the Architecture Conference 1980: The Interviews: Rem Koolhaas'. *Transition* 1, no. 4 (October 1980): 14–18.
McGlone, Julie. *HEAT: Queensland's New Wave of Environmental Architects*. Brisbane: Creative Industries Unit, Department of Tourism, Regional Development and Industry, 2008.
McGregor, Craig. 'The Men Who Draw Tomorrow's World: The Shapemakers: The Architects'. *The Sydney Morning Herald*, 23 November 1968.
McGregor, Craig et al. *In the Making [Australian Art and Artists in the Making]*. Melbourne: Thomas Nelson (Australia), 1969.
McKay, Ian, Robin Boyd, Hugh Stretton and John Mant. *Living and Partly Living*. Melbourne: Thomas Nelson (Aust.) Pty. Ltd., 1971.
McKew, Maxine. 'Remembering Johnno'. *Meanjin Quarterly* 76, no. 4 (Summer 2017): 4.
McNamara, Andrew and Ann Stephen, 'The Story of the Sixties …. A Pile-Up on the Freeway of Advanced Art'. In Jaynie Anderson, ed., *The Cambridge Companion to Australian Art*. Melbourne: Cambridge University Press, 2011.
McQueen, Humphrey. 'Queensland – A State of Mind'. *Meanjin* 38, no. 1 (1979).
McQueen, Humphrey. *Suburbs of the Sacred: Transforming Australian Beliefs and Values*. Ringwood, Vic.: Penguin Books Australia Ltd., 1988.
Micheli, Silvia and Andrew Wilson. 'International Influences in Post-war Queensland'. In John Macarthur, Deborah van der Plaat, Janina Gosseye and Andrew Wilson, eds., *Hot Modernism: Queensland Architecture 1945–1975*. London: Artifice, 2015, 117–33.
Mitchell, John G. and Constance L. Stallings. *Ecotatics: The Sierra Club Handbook for Environment Activists*. New York: Pocket Books, 1970.
Moulis, Antony. *Le Corbusier in the Antipodes: Art Architecture and Urbanism*. London, New York: Routledge, 2021.
Mumford, Lewis. *The Transformations of Man*. London: George Allen and Unwin Ltd., 1957.
Mumford, Lewis. 'An Address to Architectural Students in Rome'. Reprinted in *Architecture and Arts* (August 1960): 29–31.
Mumford, Lewis. *The City in History: Its Origins, Its transformations and Its Prospects*. London: Secker and Warburg, 1961.
Mumford, Lewis. *The Condition of Man*. London: Mercury Books, 1963.
Musgrave, Elizabeth and Douglas Neale. 'Architectural Image and Idiom: Making Local'. In Dawne McCance, ed., *Mosaic: A Journal for the Interdisciplinary Study of Literature* (2004): 255–73.
Musgrove, John, ed. *Sir Banister Fletcher's A History of Architecture*. 19th edition. London: Butterworth, 1987.
Muthesius, Stefan. *The Postwar University: Utopianist Campus and College*. London: Yale University Press, 2000.
Neale, Douglas. 'The "Essentials" of the Sub-Tropical House: An Exegesis of the "Modernistic" Town Planning Principles'. In *Limits: Proceedings from the 21st annual SAHANZ conference*, Melbourne, Victoria (September 2004): 346–52.

Neutra, Richard. *Mystery and Realities of the Site: Richard Neutra on Building*. Scarsdale, NY: Morgan & Morgan, 1951.
Neutra, Richard. *Survival through Design*. New York: Oxford University Press, 1954.
Neutra, Richard. 'Notes to the Young Architect'. *Perspecta* 4 (1957): 50–7.
Oakman, Harry. 'Pioneering the Profession'. *Landscape Australia* 3 (1991): 201.
O'Callaghan, Judith and Charles Pickett. *Designer Suburbs: Architects and Affordable Homes in Australia*. University of New South Wales. Sydney: New South Publishing, 2012.
Olgyay, Aladar and Victor Olgyay. *Solar Control and Shading Devices*. Princeton, N.J.: Princeton University Press, 1957.
Olgyay, Victor and Aladar Olgyay. *Design with Climate: Biometric Approach to Architectural Regionalism*. Princeton, N.J.: Princeton University Press, 1963.
Olkowski, Helga, B. Olkowski, T. Javits and the Farallones Institute staff. *The Integral Urban House: Self-Reliant Living in the City*. San Francisco: Sierra Club Books, 1979.
O'Neill, Helen. *A Singular Vision: Harry Seidler*. Sydney: HarperCollins Publishers, 2013.
Paine, Ashley. 'Institutional Polychromy: The Striped Architecture of Don Watson and Spence Jamieson'. In Paul Hogben and Judith O'Callaghan, eds., *Architecture, Institutions and Change: Proceedings of the 32nd annual SAHANZ conference*, Sydney (July 2015): 473–4.
Papanek, Victor. *Design for the Real World*. London: Thames and Hudson, 1972.
Paroissien, L. and Michael Griggs, eds. *Contemporary Australian Architecture: Old Continent New Building*. Darlinghurst NSW: David Ell Press in assoc. with Design Arts Committee of the Australia Council, 1983.
Philips, Ralph O. *Sunshine and Shade in Australasia: A Study in the Principles Involved in Finding the Extent and Direction of Sunlight and Shadows on Buildings*. Duplicated Document 23, 1st edition. Sydney: Commonwealth Experimental Building Station, 1948.
Phillips, Juanita. '"Local Character" Trend Emerges in Architects' Awards'. *Courier Mail*, 17 September 1982.
Pickett, Charles. *The Fibro-Frontier: A Different History of Australian Architecture*. Sydney: Powerhouse Museum, 1977.
Preiser, Wolfgang, ed. *Environmental Design Perspectives: Viewpoints on the Profession, Education and Research*. Virginia: College of Architecture, Virginia Polytechnic Institute and State University, 1972.
Radbourne, Jennifer, ed. *Brisbane Arts Theatre: The First Fifty Years 1936–1986*. Brisbane: Brisbane Arts Theatre, 1986.
Read, Herbert. *The Meaning of Art*. Harmondsworth, Middlesex: Penguin Books in assoc. with Faber and Faber, 1954.
Read, Herbert. *The Forms of Things Unknown: Essays towards an Aesthetic Philosophy*. London: Faber and Faber, 1960.
Read, Herbert. *Contemporary British Art*. Harmondsworth, Middlesex: Penguin Books Pty. Ltd., 1964.
'Rem Koolhaas'. *Transition* 1, no. 4 (November 1980): 14.
Richards, J.M. 'Seven Just Square'. *The Architectural Review* 144, no. 858 (August 1968): 142–5.
Ritter, Paul. *Educreation: Education for Creation, Growth and Change*. London: Pergamon Press.
Robinson, Noel J., 'Dalton Houses 1956–1975: An Exemplar for Brisbane's Domestic Architects?' B.Arch. diss., The University of Queensland, 1976.

Rudofsky, Bernard. *Architecture without Architects: A Short Introduction to Non-Pedigreed Architecture*. New York: MoMA, 1965.

Rudofsky, Bernard, Architektur Zentrum Wien ed. in association with the Getty Research Institute, Los Angeles and the Centre Canadien d'Architecture. *Lessons from Bernard Rudofsky: Life as a Voyage*. Basel; Boston: Birkhäuser, 2007.

Ryan, Daniel. 'Settling the Thermal Frontier: The Tropical House in Northern Queensland from Federation to the Second World War'. PhD diss., The University of Sydney, NSW, School of Architecture Design and Planning, 2017.

Rykwert, Joseph. 'Universities as Institutional Archetypes of Our Age'. *Zodiac* 18 (1968): 61–3.

Saini, Balwant Singh. 'Housing for the Sub-Tropics'. *Architecture in Australia* 51, no. 1 (March 1963): 57–66.

Saini, Balwant Singh. *Architecture in Tropical Australia*. Carlton Vic.: University of Melbourne Press, 1970.

Saini, Balwant Singh. *Building in Hot Dry Climates*. Chichester [Eng.]; New York: J. Wiley, 1980.

Saniga, Andrew. *Making Landscape Architecture in Australia*. Sydney: New South Publishing, 2012.

Schama, Simon. *Landscape & Memory*. New York: Vintage, 1996.

Serle, Geoffrey. *The Creative Spirit in Australia: A Cultural History*. Richmond Vic.: William Heinemann Australia, 1987.

Serle, Geoffrey. *Robin Boyd: A Life*. Carlton, Vic.: Melbourne University Press, 1995.

Seidler, Harry. 'Painting toward Architecture'. *Architecture* 37, no. 4 (October 1949): 119–24.

Seidler, Harry. 'Sunlight and Architecture'. *Architectural Science Review* 1 (1959): 48.

Shand, Robert. 'Report into Investigation of Designs of Houses for Commonwealth Railways'. *Architecture in Australia* 52, no. 1 (March 1963): 83–98.

Sheridan, N.R. and P.A. Juler. 'Engineering of the "Solair" Experimental House'. *Architectural Science Review* (March 1962): 31–8.

Sim, Jeanne, Brian Hudson, Danny O'Hare and Helen Armstrong. *Report 2: Thematic Studies of the Cultural Landscapes of Queensland*. Brisbane: University of Queensland Technology, Cultural Landscape Research Unit, 2001.

Sims, Stephen. 'Writing the Landscape: Architectural Invention and the Synthesis of Environmental and Architectural Design'. B.Arch. diss., The University of Queensland, 2000.

Sinnamon, Ian and Michael Keniger. *Queensland Architecture: Ideas into Practice 1937-1987: A Commemorative Review of the Department and Its Alumni*. St Lucia, Brisbane: Dept. Architecture University of Queensland, 1987.

Skinner, Peter. 'A Queensland School: Firmness, Commodity and Delight in Recent Award-Winning Houses'. In Julie Willis, Philip Goad and Andrew Hutson, eds., *FIRM(ness) Commodity DE-Light?: Questioning the Canons: Papers from the Fifteenth Annual SAHANZ Conference*, Melbourne (September 1998): 323–31.

Skinner, Peter and Michael Keniger. 'Recent Traditions – Architectural Evolution in Northern Australia'. In *Tradition and Modernity Conference Proceedings*. Jakarta: Mercu Buana University, December 1996, 113–36.

Smith, Bernard. *Australian Painting: 1786-1970*. Melbourne: Oxford University Press, 1971.

Smith, Bernard. *Antipodean Manifesto: Essays in Art and History*. Melbourne: Oxford University Press, 1976.

Smith, Bernard 'The Truth about the Antipodeans'. *Praxis M* 8 (1985).
Smith, Bernard. *Place, Taste and Tradition: A Study of Australian Art since 1768*. Melbourne: Oxford University Press, 1988.
Smith, Elizabeth, ed. *Blueprints for Modern Living: History and Legacy of the Case Study Houses*. Los Angeles: The Museum of Contemporary Art, 1989.
Sowden, Harry, ed. *Towards an Australian Architecture*. Sydney, London: Ure Smith, 1968.
Spooner and Malcolm Bunzli. 'How the AILA Came into being'. *Landscape Australia* 3 (1991): 202.
Stead, Naomi, Deborah van der Plaat and John Macarthur. 'A Taste for Place: The Cultivation of an Audience for Climate-Responsive Architecture in Queensland'. In Antony Moulis and Deborah van der Plaat, eds., *Audience: Proceedings of the 28th International Conference of SAHANZ*, Brisbane (July 2011).
Stephen, Ann, Andrew McNamara and Philip Goad. *Modernism & Australia: Documents on Art, Design and Architecture 1917–1967*. Carlton, Vic.: Miegunyah Press, Melbourne University Publishing, 2006.
Stephen, Ann, Andrew McNamara, Philip Goad, Philip Goad and Andrew McNamara, eds. *Modern Times: The Untold Story of Modernism in Australia*. Carlton, Vic.: Miegunyah Press; Sydney, N.S.W.: in association with Powerhouse Publishing, 2008.
Stewart, James R. 'Architecture: Building on Our History'. *Courier Mail*, 16 November 1982.
Stickles, Lee. 'Other Australian Architecture: Excavating Alternative Practices of the 1960s and 1970s'. In *Fabulation: Myth, Nature, Heritage: Proceedings of the 29th Annual Conference of SAHANZ*, Launceston, Tasmania (July 2012): 1058–105.
St John Wilson, Colin. 'Open and Closed'. *Perspecta* 7 (1961): 97–102.
St John Wilson, Colin. 'The Committed Architect'. *Journal of the Society of Architectural Historians* 24, no. 1 (March 1965): 65.
St John Wilson, Colin. 'Two Letters on the State of Architecture: 1964 and 1981'. *JAE* 35, no. 1 (Autumn 1981): 9–12.
Steedman, Neil. [University and Campus Buildings in Australia] *Architecture in Australia* 59, no. 2 (April 1970): 223–49.
Steedman, Neil. 'Student Magazines in British Architectural Schools'. *Architectural Association Quarterly* 3, no. 3 (July/September 1971): 36–40.
Sumner, Ray. *Settlers and Habitat in Tropical Queensland*. Monograph Series 6. Townsville: Department of Geography, James Cook University of Northern Queensland, 1974.
Szokolay, S.V. *Climate, Comfort and Energy: Design of Houses for Queensland Climates*. St Lucia, Qld.: Architectural Science Unit, The University of Queensland, 1991.
Tanner, Howard. *Australian Housing in the Seventies*. Sydney: Ure Smith, 1976.
Taylor, Jennifer. 'History and Place in Recent Australian Architecture'. In L. Paroissien and Michael Griggs, eds., *Contemporary Australian Architecture: Old Continent New Building*. Darlinghurst NSW: David Ell Press in assoc. with Design Arts Committee of the Australia Council, 1983.
Taylor, Jennifer. *Australian architecture since 1960*. Sydney: Law Book Co., 1986.
Taylor, Jennifer and John Andrews. *John Andrews: Architecture a Performing Art*. Oxford: Oxford University Press, 1982.
Taylor, Thomas Griffith. 'Introduction to Tropical Climatology'. In *Proceedings of The Australian Academy of Science Symposium on Man and Animals in the Tropics*. St Lucia, Brisbane: The University of Queensland, 1956.

Teymur, Necdet. *Environmental Discourse: A Critical Analysis of 'Environmentalism' in Architecture, Planning, Design, Ecology, Social Sciences and the Media.* London: Question Press, 1982.

Trotter, Stephen E. *Cities in the Sun.* Enoggera, Brisbane: Crusade Press, 1964.

Turner, Paul Venable. *Campus: An American Planning Tradition.* New York: Architectural History Foundation; Cambridge, MA: MIT Press, 1984.

Uekoetter, Frank. *The Turning Points of Environmental History.* Penns: University of Pittsburgh Press; accessed on-line. 13 Aug 2014 01:27 GMT.

Van der Plaat, Deborah and John Macarthur. 'Bringing Architecture to the People: Defining Architectural Practice and Culture in Post-War Queensland'. In John Macathur et al., eds., *Hot Modernism: Queensland Architecture 1945–1975.* London: Artifice, 2015.

Van der Plaat, Deborah, Andrew Wilson and Elizabeth Musgrave. 'Twentieth Century (Sub) Tropical Housing: Framing Climate, Culture and Civilisation in Post-War Queensland'. In John Macarthur et al., eds., *Hot Modernism: Queensland Architecture 1945–1975.* London: Artifice, 2015.

van der Ryn, Sym. 'Integral Design'. In Olkowski, Helga, B. et al., *The Integral Urban House: Self-Reliant Living in the City.* San Francisco: Sierra Club Books, 1979.

Walker, Paul. 'Kenneth Frampton and Fiction of Place'. In Andrew Leach, Antony Moulis and Nicole Sully, eds., *Shifting Views: Selected Essays in the Architectural History of Australia and New Zealand.* Brisbane: University of Queensland Press, 2008, 70–80.

Walker, Paul. 'Reassessing John Andrews' Architecture: Harvard Connections'. In Alexandra Brown and Andrew Leach, eds., *Open: Proceedings of the 30th Annual SAHANZ Conference Society of Architectural Historians, Australia and New Zealand,* Gold Coast, Qld. (July 2013): 2: 612.

Walker, Paul and Karen Burns. 'Constructing Architecture for International Audience: Regionalism, Postmodernism and the Design Arts Board 1980–1988'. *Fabrications* 28, no. 1 (February 2018): 25–46.

Wallace, Miranda and Sarah Stutchbury, eds. *Place Makers: Contemporary Queensland Architects.* South Brisbane, Qld.: Queensland Art Gallery, 2008.

Watson-Brown Architects. 'House at 55 Walcott Street St Lucia: Former Vice-Chancellor's Residence'. Unpublished report for Property and Facilities, The University of Queensland, 9 July 1999.

Watson, Donald. *The Queensland House: A Report into the Nature and Evolution of Significant Aspects of the Domestic Architecture in Queensland.* Brisbane: National Trust of Queensland, 1981.

Weller, E. J. A. *Buildings of Queensland.* Brisbane: Jacaranda Press, 1959.

Whitfield, Cynthia. 'A New Glamour for a Standard Material'. *Australian House and Garden* (January 1958): 38, 92.

Whitfield, Cynthia. 'Queensland Builds a Plywood House'. *Australian House and Garden* (March 1958): 56.

Whitfield, Cynthia. 'Low Maintenance House Has Quality Finish'. *Australian House and Garden* (December 1967): 38–9, 7.

Wicks, Peter. *First Decade: A Memoir of DDIAE 1972–1982.* Darling Heights, Qld: TEC Print in conjunction with Community Books Australia, 2009.

Wilber, Smith and Associates with Brisbane City Council and Queensland Main Roads Department. 'Brisbane Transportation Study, 1965.

Willis, Julie and Philip Goad. 'A Bigger Picture'. *Fabrications* 18, no. 1 (2012): 6–23. Published online: 01 August 2012.

Wilson, Andrew, ed. *Hayes and Scott: Post War Houses*. St Lucia, Qld.: University of Queensland Press, 2005.
Wilson, Andrew. 'California Dreaming: Civic Ambitions and Sub-Tropical Housing in Post-War Queensland'. In Miranda Wallace and Sarah Stutchbury, eds., *Place Makers: Contemporary Queensland Architects*. South Brisbane, Qld.: Queensland Art Gallery, 2008, 31–9.
Wilson, Andrew and John Macarthur. *Birrell: Work from the office of James Birrell*. Melbourne, Vic.: NMBW publications, 1997.
Wilson, Beth. *Brisbane Houses with Gardens: The Story of the People Who Built Them*. Spring Hill, Brisbane: Self-published, 2017.
Wilson, Eric. 'Breeze and Fine Styling Too'. *The Australian Home Beautiful* (September 1961): 18–21.
Wilson, Eric. 'Simple Dignity in Ranch'. *The Australian Home Beautiful* (June 1963): 8–11.
Wilson, Eric. 'Trendsetters' in Projects'. *The Australian Home Beautiful* (October 1964): 5–11.
Wilson, Eric. 'Garden View Was Northern Lure'. *The Australian Home Beautiful* (May 1966): 4–7.
Wilson, Eric. 'A Brisbane House with International Appeal'. *The Australian Home Beautiful* (July 1967): 22–5.
Wilson, Eric. 'Old and Rambling'. *The Australian Home Beautiful* (December 1968): 29–31.
Wilson, Eric. 'Brisbane's on the Move'. *The Australian Home Beautiful* (February 1969): 35–9.
Wilson, Eric. '"Aerofoil" Takes the Sting Out of Summer'. *The Australian Home Beautiful* (July 1970): 20–2.

NEWSPAPER ARTICLES (WITHOUT BYLINES)

Courier Mail. 'Plywood house may be cheaper'. *Courier Mail*, 17 April 1957.
Courier Mail. 'In best 10 for home'. *Courier Mail*, 27 November 1958.
Courier Mail. 'Our only "top ten" building'. *Courier Mail*, 7 December 1961.
Courier Mail. 'Tall Gums set off Kenmore home'. *Courier Mail*, 20 May 1965.
Courier Mail. 'Bank demolition reflects poorly on Qld'. *Courier Mail*, 22 May 1967.
Courier Mail. 'Would you believe these are UNITS'. *Courier Mail*, 24 September 1971.
Courier Mail. 'Hybrid house with plenty of features'. *Courier Mail*, 24 September 1971.
Courier Mail. 'On campus … Buildings are medal winners for two'. *Courier Mail*, October 1976.
Courier Mail. 'Where teachers keep up with the times'. *The Sunday Mail*, 6 March 1977.
Courier Mail. 'Architect's Queensland awards: Judges praise high skills'. *Courier Mail*, 27 October 1978.
Courier Mail. 'Top design award for college'. *Courier Mail*, 19 October 1979.
Courier Mail. 'City home for bush students'. *Courier Mail*, 7 November 1979.
Courier Mail. 'Winning house exemplifies Queensland tin and timber tradition: Local climate influenced construction'. *Courier Mail*, 15 September 1982.
Telegraph. 'The Best'. *Telegraph*, 23 October 1963.

Telegraph. 'Brisbane example for Expo in Japan'. *Telegraph Home Show Feature,* 12 March 1970.

MAGAZINES AND NEWSLETTERS

Magazines published by the Queensland Architecture Students Association (QASA):
Scarab Issue no. 1–3 (May 1965–May 1966)
ASM (1967–8)
MK II (1970–1)
Proscenium 1 (1983) [QIT Student Newsletter]

Pamphlets published by John Dalton Architect:

Broadside (1966–9)
diametrix (1970–2)

Other newsletters:

Cross-Section (September 1961–71) Melbourne: University of Melbourne Depart. of Architecture.
Centreline (1962–71) Brisbane: RAIA Queensland Chapter Newsletter.
Chapter News (1971–89) Brisbane: RAIA Queensland Chapter Newsletter.
Queensland Architect (1989–96) Brisbane: RAIA Queensland Chapter Newsletter.
Architecture, Building, Engineering [previously *Architectural and building journal of Queensland*].
Queensland Master Builder.
Newsletter (1967–70) Brisbane: Contemporary Art Society, Queensland Branch.
Gallery Society News (1962–73) Brisbane: Royal Queensland Art Gallery Society.

ARCHIVES MANUSCRIPTS AND EPHEMERA

'Architectural Practice in Postwar Queensland (1945–75): Building and Interpreting an Oral History Archive'. http://www.uq.edu.au/atch/architectural-practice-in-postwar-queensland
'Digital Archive of Queensland Architecture'. http://qldarch.net
Brisbane City Council Archives
Queensland Government Department of Works Drawing Archive
Griffith University Property and Facilities Drawings Archive
Fryer Library, The University of Queensland collections and papers relating to:

John Dalton
Professor P.E. Cummings *Mostly from the Diaries of R.P. Cummings*. Manuscript, 1977.
Royal Queensland Art Society: Gallery Files
Johnstone Gallery
Contemporary Art Society Queensland Branch 1960–70.
Royal Queensland Art Gallery Society. *Gallery Society News*. Brisbane. 1962–73
Brisbane Arts Theatre

INDEX

Aalto, Alvar 23, 38, 40, 80, 151, 155
    'From Doorstep to Living Room' 108
Aboriginal and Torres Strait Islander
    people 9, 35–6, 99, 184 n.5
Aboriginals Protection and Restriction of
    the Sale of Opium Act 1897 9
Adams, Philip, *The Adventures of Barry
    McKenzie* 138
Addison, Rex 30, 144, 153–7
    Homegame 156
Adelaide 44, 93, 135, 141
air-conditioning 4–5, 123–4, 126, 131,
    135, 163 n.8
Aland, John 49
Albers, Josef 11
Aldington, Peter 151–2
Allom, Richard 35
Alsop, Will 142
Ancher, Sydney 44, 105, 151
Anchor Mortloch & Woolley 134
Andrews, John 154
Anglican Church, Kenmore 92, 117
The Architectural Review journal 45, 51,
    65, 86, 116, 139
Architecture & Arts journal 25, 37, 40, 49,
    53, 55–6, 81
    'The 10 Best Houses' 40, 53, 56, 67,
    173 n.70
    'Four Houses' 37, 41–6
    'Post War Domestic Architecture' 35,
    44–5
Architecture in Australia journal 37, 50, 53,
    59–61, 78, 93, 98, 104, 140
Arp, Jean 50–1
    'The Mermaid' 51
Art and Music Building ('A' Block), DDIAE,
    Toowoomba 117–23, 135, 161

Arts and Architecture journal 28
Arts Theatre Petrie Terrace project 117
Ashes Test at Leeds (1934) 164 n.10
Assisted Passage Migration Scheme 11, 15.
    See also migration
Athfield, Ian 143
atrium 61, 72–3, 83, 108–9, 114
Australasian Architecture Students
    Association (AASA) Symposium
    57, 95, 99, 101, 117
    AASA Congress '71 103
    AASA *Educreation* Convention 99
    AASA Perth Conference 100
    Adelaide AASA Conference 96
    'City Synthesis' conference 96
*Australia Built: A Photographic Exhibition
    of Recent Australian Architecture*
    exhibition 154–5
The Australian Artist television series 137,
    139
Australian Broadcasting Commission
    (ABC) 137–9
Australian Council Design Arts Board 35
Australian Domestic Style 81
Australian Environmental Studies
    Building 124
Australian Home Beautiful magazine 37,
    46
Australian Referendum (1967) 9
authentic architecture 5, 8, 26, 89, 93, 101,
    103, 112, 115, 158
Avery, Tracey 157

Baird, George 140–1
Bakema, Jaap 127
Baldwinson, Arthur 25
Bannah, Max, *Timber and Tin* 144

Barber, Daniel 7
Bardon Professional Development Centre 6, 23, 117, 123, 127–30, 137, 161, 181 n.5
Barker, Lindsay 118, 181 n.11
Barrett House 67
Barron Falls Bridge project 22
Bauhaus 89, 100
'Bay Region Style' 54
Beck, Haig 22–4, 35, 62, 71, 78, 134, 139, 143, 175 n.34
Behrens, Peter 11
Belagoi House 67
Bentley, Ian, *Responsive Environments: A Manual for Designers* 33
Beresford, Bruce, *The Adventures of Barry McKenzie* 138
Birrell, James 122, 124
 University Executive Building by 121
 Wickham Terrace Car Park 53
Bjelke-Petersen, Johannes 33, 90, 93, 141
Blackman, Charles 47, 72
Blair Wilson and Associates 124
Bligh, Graham 21, 167 n.74
Borland, Kevin 154
Boyd, Arthur 35
Boyden, Stephen 91
Boyd, Robin 25, 29, 35, 43–4, 46, 66, 81, 86, 105, 107, 135, 155, 160
 'Architectural Erotica' 174 n.6
 Australia's Home: Its Origins, Builders, and Occupiers 29, 81
 'Cosmetic Architecture' 174 n.6
 'House of Tomorrow' 39–40
 'Mornington Peninsula' 46
 'Port Phillip Idiom: Recent Houses in the Melbourne Region' 2, 4, 45–6, 54
 'The State of Australian Architecture' 81, 167 n.84
 Victorian Modern: One Hundred and Eleven Years of Modern Architecture in Victoria, Australia 45
breeze-block screens 65
Brennan House 41, 43–4, 105
Bretnall, Athol 18, 23
Bretnall, Bligh Jessop 126
Breuer, Marcel 11, 65
 'House in the Garden' 40

Brick Manufacturer's House 67–8
Brisbane Architect's Group (BAG) 142
Brisbane City Council (BCC) 15–16, 96
Brisbane Development Association (BDA) 141
Brisbane International Airport, shield design 20
Broadside (*Broadsheet*) handbill 5, 8, 26, 95–102, 117, 178 n.36, 179 n.44
Brown, Peter 22, 26, 137
brutalism 79, 120, 123
Buchanan, Eric 16, 76–7
Buckley House 67, 79
Buckminster Fuller, Richard 34, 97–8
Bucknell House 84–5, 135
Building Owners and Managers Association (BOMA) 142
bungalow 2, 28, 156
Bunning, Walter Ralston, *Homes in the Sun* 28
Burgess, Greg 154
Burnie Board Administration Building 19–21, 171 n.24
Burnie Board House 20
Burns, Karen 35
Burrawood 25–6, 156
Bycroft, Peter 177 n.1
 'Towards an Understanding of Architectural Education: A Student Report' 90
Bythe House 144, 148

Californian Case Study House programme 151
Callaghan, Daniel 142–3, 164 n.10
Cambridge Churchill College competition 182 n.19
Cameron, Betty 48, 172 n.47
Cameron, Chisholm and Nichol 25
Cameron House 106
Cameron, Ian 16, 165 n.37
Cameron, June 16, 165 n.37
capsule syndrome 103
Carew, Topper 99
Carr, Bill 95, 156–7
Carson, Rachel, *Silent Spring* 32
Cassab, Judy 47
Casson and Condor Architect 21, 182 n.19
Central Technical College (CTC) 1, 18, 47

Chadwick, Kent, *Timber and Tin* 144
Chalk, Warren 98, 102
Chancellor, David 25, 44
Chapel Hill House (Owen, Vokes and Peters) 159
Chermayeff, Serge 98, 103
  A.S. Hook Memorial Lecture 91
Chew, Clifford 166 n.43
Chick House 83, 105, 113–15, 139, 158–9, 187 n.29
Chilton, Peter 22, 117
chimney 65, 70, 75, 104, 108, 132–3, 146
Choy, Howard 102
Churcher, Betty 47, 52
  Understanding Art: The Use of Space, Form and Structure 172 n.65
Churcher, Roy 48–9, 52, 172 n.47
Church of the Holy Trinity project, Banyo 23
Cilento, Raphael 168 n.89
Ciriani, Henri 143
Clare, Kerry 157
Clare, Lindsay 140, 157
Clarke Gazzard and Partners 152
Clayfield, the Morahan House 144
clerestory 43, 54, 72, 171 n.24
climate 3, 5, 23, 31–2, 35, 38, 45, 79, 137–40, 150, 160
  of Brisbane 63–6, 92
  climate science 28, 65, 87–8
  Dalton's opinion on design for 88–9
climate responsive design 2, 7, 10, 26–9, 37, 40, 61–6, 71, 74, 76–8, 131, 151, 158, 160
cluster housing 8, 113, 130–1, 134, 157
Codd, Edwin 142
Coughlan House, Allora 8, 147–8
Cold War 33
Collins, Peter 3
colonial architecture 28, 44–5, 66, 86, 92–3, 140
Colt ventilators 87
Commonwealth Department of Works 19–20, 166 n.48
Commonwealth Experimental Building Station (CEBS) 28, 64–5, 67
composition process 71
Conrad and Gargett Architects 94, 126
Consolidated Housing Industries (CHI) 6

Contemporary Art Society (CAS) 5, 17, 46–9, 52, 66, 90, 96, 103
Cook, Peter 139, 142
Cook, Sallie 164 n.3, 164 n.8
'Cool: the 60s Brisbane House' exhibition 157–8
Cooper, Jackie 22, 35, 62
Corrigan, Peter 140–1
Costa, Lúcio 7
Costello, Frank Gibson 15–16
Cottier, Keith 105
Couche, D. D. 104
Coughlan House 147–8
courtyards 19, 55, 65, 69, 73–4, 81, 106–15, 119–20, 128, 130–2, 134, 146, 182 n.19
Covalevich House 105, 113
Cowen, Anna 107
Cowen, Zelman 107, 111–12
  A Public Life: The Memoirs of Zelman Cowen 180 n.64
Cox, Philip 140
cripple 78, 81, 176 n.46
critical regionalism 30, 140–1, 156–7. *See also* regionalism
Crocodile Dundee film 138
Cooke, Glenn 47
Crooke, Ray 47
Cross-Section journal 26, 65, 79, 87, 93–4, 104
cross-ventilation 28, 43, 57, 64, 67, 75, 79, 105, 108, 124
Crozier House 67, 79
Cullen, Gordon 18, 139
  immediacy 51
Cullen House 171 n.24
culture/cultural identity 2–4, 6–7, 20–1, 27–8, 33–6, 63, 101, 140
Cummings, Robert 18, 59, 64, 173 n.86
Cuppaidge, Judy 49

Dalton, Arthur Harold (Harold Dalton) 12–13
Dalton, Bettie 12
Dalton detail 38, 80
Dalton & Heathwood Architects 21, 37, 38–41, 46
  'Four Houses' 37, 41–6, 62
Dalton, Helen 12–13

INDEX 207

Dalton House 4–5, 8, 25, 30, 44, 50, 53–5, 62, 66, 73, 148, 151, 154, 159, 161
　budget houses 5, 84
　crippled and split skillion roof forms 78–85
　Dalton House Fig Tree Pocket 55–7, 66, 78
　hot humid zones 76–8
　linear house 66–76
Dalton, Jane (Penelope) 18, 55
Dalton, Laura (nee Skitt) 12–13
Dalton, Sallie 12
Dalton (nee Harvey), Sheila 16–18, 24–5, 48, 50, 165 n.37
Dalton section 8, 78, 80, 85–9, 151
Dalton, Sue (Stirling, nee Crozier) 17, 24–6, 49, 103, 164 n.12, 165 n.30
Darling Downs Institute of Advanced Education (DDIAE) 22, 118, 181 n.12
　Art and Music Building ('A' Block) 117–23, 135, 161
　Resource Material Centre 122
Davey, Peter 142
Davis, Graham 144
Davis, Wayne 102
Day Residence 20, 105
Dean, Andrea Oppenheimer 142
de Gruchy, Graham 25, 49, 96
de Gruchy, Joy, Craftsman's Market 62
delight (in architecture) 3, 7, 37, 59, 62, 89, 138, 148, 150–1, 157
Dennis, Peta 157, 166 n.41, 166 n.56
Design Arts Board of the Australia Council 154
Dewey, John 3, 34, 61–2
diametrix handbill 5, 8, 26, 95, 97–9, 101–3
Dickson & Platten Architect 135
Dione McIntyre and Associates 44
Dobie House 155–6
Dods, Robin 156
Doxiadis, Constantino A. 12, 16
Drew, Jane 21, 65
Drew, Philip, *Third Generation: The Changing Meaning of Architecture* 182 n.24
Drysdale, J. W., *Climate and House Design* 64

Dudok, Willem Marinus 15
Dunlop House 83–4, 144
Dunlop, Pamela 137
Dunphy, Miles 94
Dysart, Michael 79

early life and education of Dalton 1–2, 7, 11–20
ecology/ecological 4–5, 32–3, 36, 91, 99–103, 117–18, 120, 128, 143, 150
ecosystems 4, 102, 160
Ecotactics 102
Education Amendment Act (1970) 181 n.12
Edward, Lindsay 53
Elizabeth Watson-Brown (EWB) Architects 111–12
end elevations 69, 71–2, 80
Engehurst 140
environmentalism 5, 7–8, 32–4, 101
environment/environmental approach 3–8, 10, 26–7, 30–2, 36, 59–60, 91, 100, 103, 114–15, 136, 150, 155, 157, 160–2
　environmental crisis 7, 101–2
　environmental degradation 32
　Environmental Era 32–4
　environmental movements 4–5, 32, 101
　human-environment 4, 6–7, 34
　immediate 3, 8
　in institutional projects 134–6
　urban 91, 131–2
Erskine, Ralph 143
Europe/European 11, 15–18, 21, 35, 50, 141
　European modernism 16–17, 151
　European settlement in Queensland 27
Everage, Dame Edna 138
Experiment Farm 105, 179–80 n.62
Expo'67 exhibition, Montreal, Canada 25, 35, 105
Expo'70 exhibition, Osaka, Japan 25–6, 35, 86
expressionism 52

Fairweather, Ian 47
Falmer House 124
Fanning, Michael 22

Farbach House 67
farmhouse 74–5, 84, 110, 180 n.68
F. B. Lucas Library 94
'feel height' 23
feminism 6, 9
fernery 40–1, 83
fictional landscapes of Australia 34–6
Fink, Arne 26, 73–4, 106
fireplace 70, 72, 75, 84, 133
First Nations people 5, 33, 35–6, 99, 162
flyscreens 61, 72–4, 83, 114
Frampton, Kenneth 156
Freie Universitat, Berlin 119
Fry, Maxwell 21, 65
Fullbrook, Sam 47
Fulton, Charles 18
Fulton Collin and Partners, University of Queensland Student Union Building 65
functionalism 3, 33
'Functions of Architecture' 143

Gallery One Eleven 62
Gammage, Bill 35
garden/garden setting 28, 42, 54, 57, 73–4, 76, 87, 106, 113–15, 137, 145, 152–3
Gazzard, Donald 94, 152, 178 n.25
Gazzard, Marea 94
Gehl, Jan 91
  'Life between Buildings' 177 n.3
Gehry, Frank 140
generic housing models 64
Germany 14–15, 18
Gibbs, Chris 22
Gibson, Robin 18–23, 26, 40, 53, 65, 92, 105, 123, 126, 139, 144, 151–2
Gist, Robert 118, 181 n.13
Glashen, David 31
Goad, Philip 54
  'A Bigger Picture: Reframing Australian Architectural History' 164 n.17
Goldsmith, E. R. D 98, 102
Goodsir, Bruce 144
Graham House 79–81, 83, 86
Graves, Michael 140–1, 144
Greenburg, Clement 49
Greer, Germaine 138

Greig, William 64–5
  underheated period 174 n.4
Griffiths, Tom 35
Gunn, Graeme 31, 135, 154
Gwilliam, Tony 98
  'Nova' 102

Haigh, Jason 158–9
Haines, Robert, 'Notes from the Gallery' radio programme 47
Hall of Residence, Kelvin Grove (HRKG) 117, 130–4, 137, 139, 181 n.4
  Site Model 132
Hall, Rodney 47
Hall, Russell 144, 155–6
  'Bananas and Mangoes' 142
Halprin, Lawrence 3, 91, 177 n.3
Ham, Charles 22–4, 26, 117–18, 127, 137, 139
Hammerschmidt, Carl 16
Hardboard Australia 97
Harris, Phil 157
Harry Seidler and Associates 184 n.59
Harvey, Richard Stoddard 16
Harvey, Sheila. *See* Dalton (nee Harvey), Sheila
Hawke, Bob 138
Hayes and Scott: Post-war Houses exhibition 158
Hayes, Edwin 1, 20, 76
Hayes & Scott 29, 158
Hay, John 46, 111
Haysom, Melville, 'Only Few Shine at Art Show' 48, 172 n.50
H.C. Richards and L.C. Harvey Memorial Competitions 48
Head House 30, 43, 45, 75
Heath, Tom 142
Heathwood, Peter 7, 21–2, 25, 30, 38–9, 41, 43, 53, 76, 105, 166 n.56, 171 n.28
Heating Ventilation Air Conditioning (HVAC) system 116, 120
HEAT: Queensland's new wave of environmental architects initiative 32
Hendry House 144, 148
Heywood, Phil 130
Hillier, Bill 142

Hills, Noela 35
Hill, Timothy 159
Hitch, John 18
Hitch, Lilly 18
Hogan, Paul 138
homestead 8, 35, 46, 67, 74–5, 106, 146
Hughes House 80–2, 106, 176 n.43
Hughes, Ray 62
Hughes, Robert 138
Humphries, Barry 138
Hunt, John Horbury 107
Hurst, Maurice 65, 79, 151
Hutton, Beatrice 156
hybrid architecture 116, 120, 126, 158

Ibbotson House 106
idiom/idiomatic form 2–5, 7, 35, 54, 62, 69, 77, 86, 131, 134, 140, 149–51, 173 n.74
indigenous response architecture 5, 99, 111, 144, 160
Indooroopilly House (Vokes and Peters) 159
industrialised building technique 37, 41, 62
interdisciplinary 4, 6, 33, 117
International Architect: Detailing, National Identity and a sense of Place in Australian Architecture 35, 134
International House 158
The Inventors television series 87

Jackson, Daryl 35, 140–1
Jacobi House 29–30
Jacobs, Jane 91
Jacobsohn, Heinz 16
Jacobson, Arne 38
Jagera people 9
Jahn, Graham 135–6
    Contemporary Australian Architecture 31
    on proto-environmental architects 32
Jain, Uttman 143
James, Clive 138
James, Colin 94
James Cubit & Partners 21
Jamieson, William Spencer (Spence) 143
jazz 17, 66, 165 n.37, 166 n.40
JD Storey Administration building 107, 111

Jencks, Charles, *Modern Movements in Architecture* 139
Job Book 23
John Andrews and Associates (Benjamin Offices) 122
John Andrews International 122, 124, 131
John Dalton Architect & Associates 5, 7–8, 22–3, 25, 30, 44, 46, 53, 62–3, 104, 107, 116, 118, 124, 130, 161
    university campus buildings by 116–17 (*see also specific buildings*)
Johnson, Donald Leslie 167 n.84
Johnson, Peter 154
Johnson, Roger 123–4
Johnstone Gallery 47, 62
Johnstone, Marjorie 47
Johnston, Fergus 152–3
Joint Board of Architectural Education 95
Jokusch, Peter 135
Jones, Clem 92
Josephson, Helen 144
Just, Verlie 47

Kahn, Louis 65, 174 n.6
Kangaroo Point Pedestrian Footbridge project 22
Keane and Dauth brothers 66
Kelly, Betty 16–17, 24, 165 n.37, 166 n.40
Kelly, Brian 16–17, 24, 165 n.37, 166 n.40
Kelly House 67
Kelly, Ned 138
Kelvin Grove College of Advanced Education (CAE) 117
Kempsey Farmhouse 156
Keniger, Michael 142, 144
    Australian Architects: Rex Addison, Lindsay Clare and Russell Hall 31
Kevin Roach John Dinkaloo and Associates 122
Kidd, Hedley 22, 26, 117
King House 79
Konstantinidis, Aris 7
Koolhaas, Rem 140–1
Korab House 67, 79
Kupfer, John 22

Lambtail Cottage, Allora 8, 26, 103, 145
lanai (atrium) 73, 83, 114–15

Landau, Royston, *New Directions in British Architecture* 7
Landscape Architects 26, 74, 92
landscapes 3, 6–8, 16, 34–6
    bushy 61, 69, 72–4, 76, 87, 101, 104, 123–7, 159, 161
    fictional 34–6
    gardenesque (*see* garden/garden setting)
Langer, Gertrude 11, 47, 61
Langer, Karl 11, 16, 18, 28, 42
    Subtropical Housing 28, 64
Larrikinism 86, 138, 140
Lausanne Fair exhibition, Switzerland 25
Lawson, Henry 138
Leary, Timothy 4
Leatherbarrow, David, *Uncommon Ground: Architecture, Technology, and Topography* 7
Le Corbusier 7, 23, 29
Lee, Douglas 64–5
'Leisure in the Age of Technology' 141
Leitch House 78–9, 152
Leonhard, Anne, 'Cool Houses for Hot-House Climates' 113
Leplastrier, Rick 158
Leverington, Barbara 16
Leverington, Don 16
Leverington House 46, 65, 106, 175 n.19
    breezeway 67–8
'Living with the Land' 155
Llewellyn-Davies, Richard 33
Lockhead House 105
Lockwood System 84
Longland, Sir David 92
Los Nidos Resort, Noosa 84, 104, 152
Louis House 106
Lucas, Bill 94
Lucas, Bruce 18, 64, 94

Mabo Case (1992) 9, 35
MacFarlane House 106
MacFarlane, W. V. 65
Machell, Robin 15
Macrossan, Tim 22, 117
Magee House 67, 69–70
Maki, Fumihiko 91
Mansfield, Alan 107
Marie Short House 156
Marodian Gallery 172 n.45
Marshall, Don 170 n.11
Marshall, Patricia 170 n.11
masonry 4, 65, 69–70, 75, 104, 123, 148, 151, 153, 158–9
Masters House 67, 79, 94
mat-building 8, 113, 119–20, 123, 130, 157
mateship 22, 138
Matthew, Robert 91
Matthews, Neville 53
McCaughey, Charissa 158
McConnell & Partners Architects 93
McDonald, Kenneth 25, 41
McDougall, Peter 23
McGowan, Robert 121–2
McGuckan House 105, 113, 139
McHarg, Ian 91
    'Man and Environment' seminar 33
McIntyre, Peter 25
McIntyre, Stuart 44
McKay, Ian 154
McKay, W. B., *Building Construction* Volumes 1–3 23
McLuhan, Marshall 98
McNamara, Andrew 22
McNeill, Barry 94
Meanjin 9. *See also* First Nations people
Melbourne, Victoria 2, 4, 15–16, 27, 54, 93, 154–5
    Mornington Peninsula 54
Meldrum, James 53
Memmott, Paul 25, 49, 96
    'Towards an Understanding of Architectural Education: A Student Report' 90
Metcalf, Andrew 96
'Methods of Tendering for the Redevelopment of Central Areas' guide 93
metrication 97, 179 n.41
micro-climate 5, 63, 69, 83
Miesian approach 22, 155
migration 1–2, 7, 9, 11–12, 15, 138
Mills, John 143
Mitchell, Ian 140
Mocatta House 65
Mockridge, John 25
Modern Architectural Research Society 28
Moholy-Nagy, Sibyl 3

INDEX   211

Molvig, Jon 47–9, 52, 72, 87
Monier Qld 97
Moore, Charles 131, 139–40, 144, 146
Morahan House 144
Moreton Bay Penal Settlement 9
Moriarty, Mervyn 47
Moroney, Patrick 31, 65, 79, 155
Morris, Ingrid 142
Mt Coot-tha, Toowong 45, 63, 71–2, 76, 80, 123, 127
Mt Gravatt CAE campus buildings 122–3
Muller House 105
Muller, Peter 25
Mumford, Lewis 2, 41, 62, 171 n.18
    'An Address to Students of Architecture in Rome' 41–2, 53
    Culture of Cities 34
    Technics and Civilization 34
Munro, Colin 49
Murcutt, Glenn 23, 154, 156–7
Murray Report 116
Murray & Woolley 105
Musgrave House 106, 180 n.68
Muthesius, Stefan 135, 182 n.15

Nadar, Ralph 98
Nairn, Ian 139
Nankivell, W. H., 'Organic Fallacy' 61
National Art Gallery 48, 166 n.38
National Diploma in Building Transcript of Studies 165 n.13
national romantic movements 6
National Trust of Queensland 144, 180 n.68, 185 n.32
natural disasters 27, 36
Neale House 46, 67, 69, 71
Neimeyer, Oscar 11
Netsch, Walter 122
Neutra, Richard 2, 7, 42–3, 55–6, 62, 116
    Mystery and Realities of the Site: Richard Neutra on Building 42
    'The New and the Old in Architecture' 42
    'Notes to the Young Architect' 59
    'Plywood Model Demonstration House' 40
    Richard Neutra: 1950-60: Buildings and Projects (1959) 42
    Survival Through Design 34, 42

Neville, Richard 138
Newell, Peter 29, 44
    'St Lucia: A Housing Revolution in Taking Place in Brisbane' 43–4
New Empiricism 45, 54
Newmarket House (Owen, Vokes and Peters) 159
Nicholson, Harold 98
Noémi, Antonin 7
North America 21, 123
Nussey, Eldorene Joyce (Rene) 16

O'Dywer Homestead, 'Mt Manning' 8, 146–7
O'Gorman, Andresen 156–7
O'Gorman, Peter 25, 65, 155–7
'Old Continent New Buildings' Exhibition 25
Olgyay brothers (Aladar and Victor) 64–5
Olley, Margaret 47–8
O'Reilly, Bernard, *Green Mountains* 170 n.126
Oribin, Eddie 156
O'Rorke-Graham House 156

Packer, Kerry 138
Paddington Society 94
Palm Beach House 105
Papi, Morag (Morag Leslie) 22
passive design techniques 116
Patterson, Banjo 138
Patterson, Greville 49
Patterson, Les 138
The Paul Hogan Show television series 138
pedagogy 8, 117, 119–20, 124, 135
Peden Residence 85, 106, 110–13, 115
Penfold House 152
Penthouses apartments, Darling Point 153
Perkins, Rachel 36
Peters, Aaron 158–9
Pettit and Sevitt company 23, 79
Pie, Geoffrey 151
The Plywood Exhibition House 21, 38–41, 43, 83
polemics/polemical texts 2, 5, 38, 53–4, 59, 61–2, 76, 101
Poole, Gabriel 20, 30–2, 41, 65, 144, 154–7
Populate or Perish policy 11
'Portrait of an Architect' 48

postmodernism/postmodernist 7–8, 26, 33, 134, 136, 139–41, 143, 161
Powell, Lange 166 n.44
Pratley, Helen 164 n.3, 164 n.7
protection and assimilation policies 9
protests on rights and education 9, 33, 90, 99, 107
proto-environmentalism 104–5
Pryor, Dennis 95
Prystupa, Peter 117
pyramid roof 28, 147–8

Qantas Exhibition of Australian Architecture, London 25
Qld Chapter Council 94
Quality Danish Furniture 72
Quarry, Neville 94
Queen Elizabeth II 20, 36
Queensland 1–3, 6, 8–9, 54, 59, 62, 93, 95, 112, 117, 141, 154–5, 162
   Allora 8, 16, 26, 103, 145–6
   Brisbane 1, 3, 6, 9, 12, 15, 17, 20, 22, 24, 26–9, 32, 36, 40, 43, 45–50, 52–3, 59, 62–3, 72, 74, 89–93, 97, 128, 134, 141–4, 149, 152, 158–9, 161
   Brisbane River 64, 84, 111, 114
   Brookfield 25, 82, 104–6
   Chapel Hill 66–7, 76, 87–8, 152
   climate conditions in (*see* climate)
   cultural cringe 2
   D'Aguilar Ranges 17, 64
   Darling Downs 16, 26, 46, 74, 103, 118, 120–1, 144–5, 179 n.57
   Department of Education 118, 127, 130
   Department of Public Works 22, 104, 116–17, 122–3, 130
   European settlement in 27
   Ipswich 29
   Kenmore 66, 68, 79, 92, 117
   Moreton Bay 64, 144
   postcolonial 32
   St Lucia (*see* St Lucia)
   Toowoomba 16, 118–19
Queensland Architecture Students Association (QASA) 5, 95, 117
Queensland Art Gallery 166 n.38
Queensland Art Gallery Act 1959 166 n.38
Queensland Centenary Eisteddfod Art Competition 48–50
Queensland Chapter of the Institute 143
Queensland Heritage Register 134
Queensland house/Queenslander 1–2, 8, 28–9, 37, 40–1, 53, 76–7, 86, 104–5, 148, 155–6, 174 n.4, 180 n.67
Queensland Institute of Technology (QIT) 26, 33, 96, 99, 118, 141–3, 151, 181 n.12
Queensland Master Builder journal 93
Queensland Master Builders Federation (QMBF) 142
Queensland Plywood Board Corporation 39–40
'Queensland's Culture of Flimsiness' symposium 144
Queensland Tropical House Committee (QTHC) 28, 168 n.89
Queensland University of Technology (QUT) 134, 142, 151, 157

Rabaa House 79, 83, 86–8
Railton, John 65, 79
Railton's House and Studio 79
ranch-style house 46, 67
Ray Hughes Galleries and furnishings 62
Raymond, Antonin 7
Read, Herbert 2, 61–2
regionalism 4, 10, 27, 45, 144, 155. *See also* critical regionalism
Reynolds, Henry 35
Rickardt, Bruce 23
Riddel, Robert 35, 96, 111, 142
Rigby, John 48
Ritter, Paul 98–100
Robbins Report 116
Roberts, Gareth E. 25, 167 n.77, 169 n.115
Roberts House 66–7, 75
Robertson & Hindmarsh 25
Robin Gibson and Associates Architect 152
Robin Gibson and Partners 122–3
Robin, Libby 35
Roggenkamp, Joy 47–8
Roggenkamp, Kenneth 48
Romberg, Grounds 44
Romney, Hervin 143
roof forms 43, 78–85, 104, 113, 148, 151, 153, 156. *See also* split skillion roof forms

Rose Seidler House 51
Rossi, Aldo 139
Ross Thorne Architect 105
Royal Australian Institute of Architects
    (RAIA) 135, 138, 143, 150
    Buildings of Queensland 29–30
    'The Consequences of Today' 91, 103
    Life Fellow of the RAIA 26
    'Pleasures of Architecture' 140, 144
    Queensland Chapter Council 26, 29–30,
        90, 93–5, 122, 140, 156–7, 181 n.3
Royal Institute of British Architects
    (RIBA) 93, 138, 150
Royal Institute of Chartered Surveyors 93
Royal Melbourne Institute of Technology
    (RMIT) 141
Royal Queensland Art Society (RQAS) 47
Rudofsky, Bernard 3
Ryan, Daniel 168 n.89

Saini, Balwant Singh 78, 98, 113, 142
Salter House 5, 84
Santa Monica House 140
Scandinavian architecture 23, 45
Scarab 96, 99
Schaffer, Bernard 172 n.40
Scholarship in Art 51
Schubert House 30–1, 41, 155–6
Scott, Campbell 1, 18, 20, 28, 38, 41, 76
Sea Ranch 139
Seidler, Harry 11, 25, 44, 65, 78, 105, 131,
    140
    Grecian Cycladic (Kooralbyn) project
        131, 134
    'Painting toward Architecture' 51, 53
Semi-Rural House 41, 43–6
sensory in architecture 8, 37, 43, 52–4, 59,
    61–2, 91, 101
settler culture 34–5, 101
Shand, Robert 78
Sharp, Martin 138
Shulman, Julius 55
Sibley, Andrew 47–9
Sierra Club 102
Simpson, John 122
Skitt, John 12
Smith, G. E. Kidder 3
Smith House 104–5
Smith, McConnel 122

Smith, Paul 22
Smith, Peter 142
Smithson, Alison 119, 142
Smithson, Peter 119, 142
Smith, Wilbur 92
Smout, Ruth (nee Cilento) 47
social responsibility 23, 31, 37, 41, 136
Sowden, Harry 66, 87–8
    Towards an Australian Architecture
        61, 73
Speare House 29–30, 41, 43, 171 n.24
Spence, Basil 124
Spencer, Donald 151
Spinks House 41, 43, 45–6, 75
split skillion roof forms 31, 78–85, 109–10,
    113, 123, 131, 147, 151, 153, 158
Spork, Frank 142
Spring, Martin 22
Stirling, Christopher (Kit) 24–5
Stirling, Fiona 24
Stirling, Sue. *See* Dalton, Sue (Stirling, nee
    Crozier)
St Lucia 29, 109–10, 112, 153
    Four houses in Ironside Street 153
Stoneham House 46, 67, 69, 79, 152
Stramit Industries 97
Stringer, Richard 66
Strugnell House 5, 84–5
Strugnell, John and Maureen 84
Student Project work by Dalton 19
subtropical climate 1–2, 5, 8, 12, 27–8,
    62–4, 69, 150–4, 160–2. *See also*
    tropical climate
Sullivan, Louis 144
'sunlight, shade and shadow', motto of
    Dalton 1, 8, 25, 37, 43, 53–62, 65–6,
    88–9, 104, 138, 150–2, 154–7, 160
sun/sunlight 3, 5, 7, 28, 37, 54, 57, 61, 105,
    114, 128
Sydney 11, 17, 24–5, 27–8, 47, 140, 152
    Paramatta 179 n.62
    Sydney Opera House 112, 140
    Sydney School of architecture 154
Szokolay, Steven Vajk 142

Taringa House (Rex Addison) 30, 156, 159
Taylor, Jennifer 122, 157–8, 186 n.21
    *An Australian Identity: Houses for
        Sydney 1953–63* 157

Australian Architecture Since 1960 30
Old Continent: New Building 111
Ten Pound Poms 11. *See also* Assisted Passage Migration Scheme
termites 6, 112, 158, 161
terra nullius 9, 35
Theo Thynne & Associates 20–1, 40–1, 105, 171 n.24
Thurlow blinds 40, 43
topography 28, 35, 64, 79, 106, 144, 153–4
touchstone 59, 76, 151
town and city planning 28, 91, 96, 100
Tremont Flats, Toowong 56–8, 65
'Trevenna' 107
tropical climate 2, 27, 44, 64–5, 74. *See also* subtropical climate
Trotter, Steven 151, 158
   Cities in the Sun 21
Turnbull, William 131
Turner (nee Dalton), Amanda 18, 55, 165 n.35
Turrbal people 9
'Two Dead Chickens' incident 96, 178 n.35

underheated period 174 n.4
'Under the Sun' 155
The United States 12, 28, 139, 141
University House, Griffith University 117, 123–7
   Community Services Building 124–5
   Humanities, Library and Administration Building 126
University of Queensland (UQ) 18–19, 90, 142, 150, 174 n.14
   Faculty of Architecture 25, 34, 90, 117
   Faculty of Environmental Design 34
   School of Creative Arts 135
urbanism 33, 89, 91–3, 116, 138–9
urban renewal programme 32, 99

Vadasz, Christine 154
Van den Broek, Barbara 49, 76, 124
Van der Ryn, Sim 103
Van Eyck, Aldo 98–100, 127
ventilation 41, 43, 54–5, 69, 79, 87, 114, 120, 160
Venturi, Robert 141, 156
verandah (Dalton's spelling) 2–3, 28–30, 40–1, 43–4, 46, 51, 60–1, 76–8, 81, 83, 86, 108, 110, 114, 126, 132, 140, 145–7, 160, 170 n.13, 176 n.43
Verge, John 140
vernacular architecture 1, 3, 28–30, 43, 45–6, 59, 61, 76, 87, 89, 122, 130, 137, 156
Vice-Chancellor's Residence 6, 22, 106–10, 115, 137
Victorian Type architecture 45
Vokes, Stuart 158–9, 187 n.29
von Schiller, Johann Christoph Friedrich 14

Walker House 45
Walker, Paul 35, 122
Walpamur Paints 97
Walsh, Richard 138
Warana-Caltex Art Prize 48–9
Wareham House 67
Watson, Donald 153
   'Architecture is a Community Art' 142
Welke, Adrian 158
West Coast American architecture 28
Whitehead, Alfred North 101
Whitehead House 67, 69
White Residence 140
Whitlam, Gough 98
Whitman, Paula 157
Wicks, Peter 181 n.11
Willett, F. J. 124
Williamson (Igloo) House 51
Willis, Julie, 'A Bigger Picture: Reframing Australian Architectural History' 164 n.17
Wilson, Andrew 158
Wilson, Beth 106
Wilson, Brian 111
Wilson, Colin St John 98, 100–1, 139
Wilson, Eric
   'Queensland's Best for 1964' 175 n.16
   'Simple Dignity in Ranch: New Ideas Enhance the Ranch' 46
Wilson House 6, 60–1, 69, 71–5, 78–80, 83, 106, 114
Wilson, Pam 71–2, 74
Wilson, Patrick 71–2
Wilson, William Hardy 66

Winsen, Don 20
Wippell Homestead, 'Morocco' 46, 67, 74–6, 83, 106, 146
Wippell, Noela 46, 74–6
Wippell, Stan 46
Witchell, Stanley 22
Wolston House 111, 180 n.68
women, Dalton's attitude towards 9
Woolley, Ancher Mortlock 153
Woolley, Ken 31, 79, 105, 134, 140, 154
works of Dalton
    'County Stanley, Parish of Indooroopilly' 48
    'Four Houses' 37, 41–6
    'Houses in the Hot Humid Zones' 76–7
    'Immediacy at Fingal' 48, 50–2
    'John Brown and Dalton Straw' 154
    'John Dalton: Sunlight Shade and Shadow' 137
    'Queensland's Pragmatic Poetry' 53, 101
    'sea-nymph and a sailor' 50–1
    'South Queensland Landscape – Gympie' 49
    'Sun + Life + Useful Form = Architectural Magic' 1, 53–62, 140
    'Talks to students of Brisbane Girls' Secondary School' 164 n.18
    'Thoughts on Architectural Education' 95
    'verandah series' 50–3, 59, 71, 76, 145
World Expo 88 141
Wright, Frank Lloyd 34, 65, 116

Yeates, Bronwyn 48

Zunz, Jack 142

www.ingramcontent.com/pod-product-compliance
Lightning Source LLC
Chambersburg PA
CBHW071827300426
44116CB00009B/1464